Fast on the Sand

Fast on the Sand

*The Daytona Beach Land Speed
Record Runs of 1928*

ALDO ZANA

McFarland & Company, Inc., Publishers
Jefferson, North Carolina

All photographs from the author's collection unless otherwise indicated.

ISBN (print) 978-1-4766-8087-3 ♾
ISBN (ebook) 978-1-4766-4359-5

Library of Congress and British Library cataloguing data are available

© 2022 Aldo Zana. All rights reserved

No part of this book may be reproduced or transmitted in any form or by any means, electronic or mechanical, including photocopying or recording, or by any information storage and retrieval system, without permission in writing from the publisher.

Cover image: 1928 Blue Bird published as a supplement of the February 7, 1928 issue of *The Motor*, British magazine.

Printed in the United States of America

*McFarland & Company, Inc., Publishers
Box 611, Jefferson, North Carolina 28640
www.mcfarlandpub.com*

Table of Contents

Preface   1

1. Prelude   3
2. Act One—February   6
3. Intermission—March   78
4. Act Two—April   87
5. Epilogue—May   115
6. Aftermath—1929–1935   125

Appendix 1: The Aerodynamics of the 1928 Vehicles   147
Appendix 2: Campbell's 1928 Blue Bird   160
Appendix 3: Stutz Blackhawk Special   164
Appendix 4: The Engines   171
Final Word: The Lockhart Saga—A Review   176
Chapter Notes   179
Bibliography   195
Index   197

"Time crumbles and scatters away the truth
and what is left behind transforms into legend, myth."
—*Nuto Revelli (Italy, 1948)*

"The smallest initial deviation from the truth
goes multiplied by one thousand while time flies."
—*Aristotle (Greece, 4th century* BCE*)*

Preface

The 1928 Speed Trials on the sands of Daytona Beach have never been described in so much detail before. They are a fascinating story of men and cars, drivers and designers, high-tech and do-it-yourself, applied science and arrogant ignorance. They also represent an unprecedented chapter in the history of land speed records: 32 years had to pass before another direct confrontation for the land speed record took the stage of the Bonneville Salt Flats.

The 1928 Speed Trials were the first land speed records fully sanctioned by the U.S. national and international regulatory bodies. As a show starring contenders from both sides of the Atlantic, open to the public like an ordinary sporting event, it was expected to offer a unique mix of technology, emotions, thrills, and drama. And, first and foremost, it would showcase the highest speed on land in the history of the world.

This book relives those days before they permanently fade in the gray clouds of a forgotten past. It presents the truth of the tragedy that marred the event: the death of Frank Lockhart, the young hero of U.S. racing. It also adds a chapter on the land speed record runs on the Florida beach from 1929 until 1935, when Daytona Beach was *the* place for the ultimate speed on land.

The reader will find the true facts narrated with a level of detail never before presented, based strictly on period sources thoroughly crosschecked.

Research initiated some 40 years ago in the U.S. and UK brought back to the surface photos and some either unpublished or forgotten documents, including a detailed factual report on Frank Lockhart's fatal accident on the beach. The truth about the accident and the aftermath of the young driver's death told in these pages amends the load of incorrect news and indecent theorizing aired immediately after the event and duplicated by too many authors without checking any period source.

The author in the early 1970s had the rare opportunity to meet in person a few surviving witnesses of the 1928 Speed Trials and to share documents, images, and know-how with other experts on Frank Lockhart's short life and racing career.

Special thanks go to Tom Kinney, Indianapolis, who gathered and provided local documents; to Kim Dolce, Port Orange Regional Library, Volusia County, Florida, who provided the microfilms of the local daily; and to Norman Hawkes, who reviewed the text in British English.

1

Prelude

From the marketing and promotional side, the 1928 revival on the sands of Florida's Daytona Beach of an event dating back 25 years wasn't a premium concept. The event was promoted as the "Twenty-fifth Anniversary Speed Trials." Financed and organized by the municipality and the local chamber of commerce, it was expected to relaunch Daytona Beach as the place to be for any human aiming to become the fastest on land.

From 1903 until 1910, a group of local enterprising citizens organized meetings of daring and conveniently wealthy souls who wanted to break speed barriers along the stretch of sand bordered by the Atlantic Ocean and the Halifax River.

In these seven years the highest recorded speed nearly doubled from 68.966 mph to 131.723 mph.

The beach provided an outstanding backdrop for high-speed automobile runs, at that time the newest and most exciting invention.

At a time when most of the roads across America still featured rough surfaces littered with stones, dirt, mud, and ruts, often unsuitable for speeds higher than those of a horse-drawn cart, the Florida shoreline at Daytona Beach offered 23 miles of flat, hard sand cured by the waves of the ocean. It became the world's best-known site for high speeds, surrounded by developed and civilized environs offering hotels and many amenities, well connected by road, rail, and water.

The surging American enthusiasm for speed found here its most thrilling stage. The best of the American and European automobile industry selected Daytona Beach as the place to be for top speeds, before the first racetracks in the U.S. and Europe.

Almost ironically, we don't know for sure how those runs were timed, despite some of them appearing in the land speed record logs. We can only assume they entailed a single run with the wind, measured by manual chronometers, precise yet subject to human reaction times. Speeds were quite modest, and the recorded times to the fifth of a second were accurate enough to compute the actual speed to a hundredth of a mile per hour.

All American races, including the records, were denied recognition by the Paris-based AIACR (Association Internationale des Automobile Clubs Reconnus), which claimed to be the sole regulatory body of the new world of the automobile. Regardless, some records achieved prior to 1918 in Daytona Beach found their way onto the list, despite being unsanctioned by the AIACR.

After the Great War the Americans bowed to French power, and the flying mile records sanctioned by the AAA (American Automobile Association) gained worldwide validity once homologated by the AIACR. Eight official world land speed records were recorded by the AAA in Daytona Beach from 1927 to 1935.

The AAA had to abide by the French rulebook: electrical timing, RM gear on the vehicles, speed recorded as the average of two runs in opposite directions to compensate for the effect of the wind. The return run had to be completed within half an hour of the conclusion of the first one. The interval was later doubled to a full hour, as it stands today.

The huge crowd attracted by the record runs of the Briton Henry Segrave in 1927 triggered the organization of the 1928 event for land speed and class records in Daytona Beach. As the national AIACR representative, the AAA sanctioned these records and made them eligible for homologation and worldwide acknowledgment.

The protagonists of the land speed record runs in February 1928 in Daytona Beach. From left: Malcolm Campbell, 43; Frank Lockhart, 25; and Ray Keech, 27. They are posing together for a photo op to please the media. Whilst Lockhart is wearing racing attire ready to test run his Blackhawk, the other two contenders are in civilian clothing: those were the days of jacket and tie any time, any place.

1. Prelude

The 1928 event was a first in having three contenders for the land speed record, like a Grand Prix of speed and thrill at the highest levels. The laurels were to be bestowed upon the driver exceeding 200 mph by the highest margin (the record to be beaten was actually 203.792 mph). Such a high bar conveyed the fascinating sense of a leap into the unknown, reserved for a kind of almost superhuman beings at the wheel of vehicles of inconceivable sophistication, unthinkable performance, and unreachable cost.

For the first time, two of the contenders were racing drivers, Frank Lockhart and Ray Keech, both Americans. A third, a record specialist with a significant racing career, was Malcolm Campbell, a Briton.

For the first time, then, a direct confrontation was staged between two continents: British expertise and success in aero engines versus American technical creativity and industrial might in the formative years of global automotive production leadership.

The American love for showmanship transformed the sands of Daytona Beach into an exciting stage for the few days of Speed Trials in the late winter and early spring of 1928. Crowds lined the dunes along the beach in the tens of thousands, just like at a baseball game.

Drama unfolded, always at high speed. One driver was killed: Frank Lockhart, the youngest contender at 25 and a bright star of American track racing. Two new land speed records entered the books: Malcolm Campbell in February and Ray Keech in April.

2

Act One—February

1

"I'm strictly an amateur and I'm just a beginner in palm reading. I see some nasty things in your palm. Can you take it?"

"Yes, tell me all."

"You can't possibly live more than two or three years!"

"Can't you be more specific than that?"

"I wouldn't even attempt to forecast the exact date of your death, but it could happen any time from now to June 15, 1930."

In mid–February 1928, Wilbur Shaw was not yet 26, and the forecast of his death before turning 28 made him laugh. He was a professional racing driver, a job where death was the riding mechanic, even in single-seaters. He had raced at Indianapolis (fourth as a rookie in 1927), he raced the shaky planks of board tracks at full throttle, he used the back of his hand to wipe his face covered with soot from the exhaust and mud on dirt tracks.

Mrs. Arthur Means, a self-proclaimed amateur palm reader, could have missed the point completely. She was in Daytona Beach accompanying her husband, head of the AAA officials commissioned there for the Speed Trials.

Wilbur Shaw was in the parlor of the Clarendon Hotel, Daytona Beach, with his friend Frank. Both came from Indianapolis. His friend, Frank Lockhart, was a better-known racing driver: he was the first rookie to win the Indianapolis 500, on May 30, 1926.

They got bored in the cold, windy, and rainy February days in Daytona Beach waiting for the beach to be suitable for what they were both there to do.

Whoever said that Florida enjoyed perennial summer weather? A cold wind was blowing from the wrong quarter. The sand on the beach was crisscrossed by ridges and fragments of shells pushed ashore by the ocean waves, ready to burst the tires of any car that ventured onto the sand.

No way to go down there and run.

They were both in Daytona Beach in the wintertime to star in the "Twenty-fifth Anniversary Auto Beach Races," a.k.a. "Speed Trials," a prime promotional program of the city of Daytona Beach on its wonderful strip of sand 23 miles long. The program aimed at a wider circle than the northeastern super wealthy gentlemen and tycoons who chose the Florida city as their winter retreat.

The most famous winter resident was John D. Rockefeller, 88 years old and still going strong.

The winter climate in Daytona Beach was usually fine. Not so the ocean, cold and rough. Yet down the eons it had laid a wide strip of smooth, hard sand on which it was possible to stage motor races at low tide. Like in 1903, exactly 25 years earlier.

The municipality of Daytona Beach and its chamber of commerce had organized the 1928 event at their best. From February 15 to 23 the beach would be reserved as the stage for the fastest cars in America and the world: from production (stock) cars sold at less than $1,000 to the special vehicles designed and built for the land speed record, i.e., the highest speed on land. The AAA gave their official sanction; appointed officials, judges, and timekeepers; and supplied the electric timing system.

The record to beat was 203.792 mph, established there in 1927 by the British driver Henry O'Neal de Hane Segrave in the "Mystery S" (American media nickname), the special Sunbeam 1000 HP, the first vehicle to travel at over 200 mph.

Wilbur Shaw was there to win the American four-cylinder car record, established back in 1912 by Bob Burman, an American driver in a German Blitzen Benz racer: 144.10 mph.

Frank Lockhart was there for a record, too. He aimed higher—at the top. His aim was to bring the land speed record back to America driving the Blackhawk, a car designed and built to reach this goal.

Malcolm Campbell (left) in plus fours—as a British gentleman should be in a sporting environment—staring with a puzzled expression at the Blackhawk of Frank Lockhart (right). He warned Lockhart that the car, despite being magnificently designed and built, was too small and light to withstand the stresses of record runs on the beach.

In early 1928 Charles Raymond "Ray" Keech (born in Coatesville, Pennsylvania, USA, May 1, 1900; died at the Altoona board track, Pennsylvania, June 15, 1929) was a rising star of board track racing whilst not yet a surefire winner: in six years of racing on board tracks his total purse amounted to $9,169, quite a small figure compared to stars like Jimmy Murphy ($123,160) and Tommy Milton ($134,185). Lockhart's total purse on board tracks was $40,900 in less than three seasons. At Daytona Beach Keech was hired by Jim White to tame and drive the Triplex (in the background, the windscreen), a job he performed with courage and skill, achieving the new land speed record on April 22, 1929. The peak of his career was victory in the 1929 Indianapolis 500-Mile Race at the wheel of the second Miller 91, modified by Frank Lockhart.

Two other contenders for the land speed record were in Daytona Beach on those same days: Malcolm Campbell, the British driver carrying with him an already long and glorious list of speed records and Brooklands circuit wins, and Jim White, a rich industrialist and amateur driver of fast cars from

Jim White, industrialist from Philadelphia. Fond of cars, he ordered and started the construction of the Triplex, a vehicle aiming for the land speed record, a no-nonsense car built around the principle that speed had to be achieved through brute power (three war-surplus Liberty L-12 engines claimed to produce 500 HP each) and good tire adhesion, irrespective of aerodynamics. He is wearing racing cap, goggles, and overalls, yet no record has been found of him ever taking the wheel of either a racing or a record car.

Philadelphia, who appointed Ray Keech, already a promising professional, as the driver of his Triplex record car.

They provided the direct competition to Lockhart, as he was in his usual environment: tracks and speedways all across America. But here it was every man for himself as the runs on the beach were reserved for one racer at a time.

Yet the trials provided the flavor of direct competition for the first time in the history of the land speed record. Three drivers shared the same goal of reaching a speed higher than had ever been achieved by any other man in a car.

The winter evenings were getting longer.

Frank agreed to have his palm read.

Mrs. Means studied it for a while and warned (without disclosing her inexperience): "You might just as well pack up and go home right now. You will not succeed in breaking the land speed record at this time. And it would not be wise for you to make any further attempt."[1]

2

Another beach. The other coast of the ocean. Malcolm Campbell, a wealthy and top-tier British amateur racing driver with the land speed record his key objective, had established the 174.883 mph record on February 4, 1927, on the soft and wet sand of the six-mile beach at Pendine Sands, Wales, UK. Only a month later, Segrave went faster at Daytona Beach and took the record away from him.

Malcolm Campbell's 1928 Blue Bird was the second model in the series of five land speed record cars powered by the Napier Lion aero engine, shown here in its Series VIIB "Sprint" version with power output increased to 950 HP. Built in the UK using all British components, as was the basic rule for the owner-driver, the vehicle is seen during a demo run on the Brooklands circuit, England. The rounded nose was made possible by moving the radiators to the side of the tail. Though good for reducing drag, this layout didn't work since the radiators proved ineffective being located in a low-pressure area.

Campbell accepted the invitation to Daytona Beach to try for the record again in the winter of 1928. It is quite easy to guess that he was lured there by the generous expense account offered by the organizers and by the fame and fortune that would follow if he were to set the new record.

Leo Villa, who spent the years 1923–1948 with Malcolm and then 1949–1964 with his son, Donald, sketched a portrait of his employer like this:

> I initially found Malcolm Campbell a very difficult man to get along with.
>
> With a fiery Scottish temperament, he gave no quarter and expected none.
>
> He was exacting in the extreme and could consider nothing impossible. His great wealth allowed him to indulge in a very strict form of independence. He often commented: "Don't believe in trash." In some quarters he was considered mean. His point of view, quoted at me many a time, was: "Villa, money doesn't grow on trees."
>
> He expected total loyalty above all from me during our joint endeavours. "Loyalty you cannot buy," he often said. Although extremely possessive, his great characteristics were guts and determination. Superstitious by nature, having named all his vehicles Blue Bird on the advice of a mythical Belgian playwright, once he confessed to me: "There is more attached to the stars than we shall ever know about."[2]

Dorothy Lady Campbell *née* Whittal (1884–1981), his second wife, authored a better-phrased portrait: "Money was no object where motor-cars or boats were concerned, especially if the expenditure meant an attempt to add a few miles an hour to any speed record he held or if he had set his heart on winning some particular race at Brooklands or on the road. He was a master of racing tactics, whether on road or track and succeeded by an extraordinary gift of ice-cold concentration on the job in hand, combined with the most meticulous care in preparing his car and himself for everything he undertook in racing."[3]

Furthermore:

> He really did love danger for its own sake, or was it, as I sometimes suspected, that he was attracted by what is known as the ecstasy of fear, that curious state of mind in the face of danger which possesses some, but which I have never heard explained satisfactorily. He would never have admitted it, but I have often thought that he really was possessed that way, because whenever he embarked upon one of his record-breaking exploits he was for weeks beforehand in a state of acute nervous tension.
>
> There is no doubt—there never was in my mind—he was afraid and really enjoyed the sensation. But that was all antecedent to the time when his plans had to be carried out. Then there was a complete transformation. No more tension, no more manifestation of nerves—the man was simply ice-cold in concentration on the job that had to be done. He had calculated and knew all the risks to be incurred and simply ceased to fear them.[4]

Such an approach to races and record runs was well known within the motor racing fraternity. David McDonald, a.k.a. "Dunlop Mac" (he was the racing and record tire specialist of the factory), described him as follows: "Speed became a mania with him as his reputation grew. He simply couldn't stand anyone going faster than he did. It became almost an obsession. He spent a fortune on his beloved Blue Birds, but he got his money's worth."[5]

On his return from Daytona Beach in 1928, Campbell, the great storyteller and promoter of his own public image, gave one of many interviews to *The Motor*

Malcolm Campbell in Daytona Beach together with his second wife, Dorothy Emily Evelyn, *née* Whittal (1884–1981), whom he married in 1920. They divorced in 1940 following the births of their son, Donald, in 1921 and daughter, Jane, in 1923. Donald was destined to continue in his father's footsteps, setting world speed records on both land and water: in 1964 he held both, having driven the Bluebird CN7 to 403.10 mph on land and taken the helm of the Bluebird K7 to 276.33 mph on water. Donald died trying to raise the water record on February 4, 1967, on Coniston Water, Westmorland, England.

magazine. Under the headline "Malcolm Campbell on the Surprises of Speed," his own words were:

> A great deal has been written about the necessity of being mentally equipped for record breaking, of the pluck required, etc. Believe me, it is more or less bunkum. The mental strain exists to a far greater extent before than during an attempt on the record. The preparation of the car is worrying, the "stand by" period when you are absolutely ready but the conditions are not ripe is anguish. The job itself is nothing but a sheer delight, because it represents Omega to the whole alphabet of the quest. My most vivid impression is that of the muscular or physical strain which is entailed by high-speed driving. This so dominates things that the mental side does not exist.[6]

We have to rate as more sincere the words of Lady Campbell: "Many, many times I have wished I were a psychologist, that I might have come to some settled conclusion on this side of his character, but it always eluded me. He was just one of those who are apart from their fellows and who simply baffle understanding."[7]

If Lady Campbell would have better been a psychologist to wholly understand Malcolm Campbell, her granddaughter Gina, born 1949, i.e., about one year after the death of Sir Malcolm, was quite harsh in presenting him: "He was an arrogant, self-opinionated man who would have merited the term male chauvinistic pig had it been in fashion when he was alive. The only place for women, in his view, was in bed. In fairness to Grandfather, I have to say that in anyone who has the guts to push out the boundaries of human experience the sod factor has to be high."[8]

Gina Campbell wrote those words in 1988, a completely different age. She added: "Malcolm was one of the world's greatest individualists and had only reluctantly accepted the idea of making a record attempt with other drivers competing at Daytona [Beach] at the same time."[9] This is, of course, a subjective statement: readers of this book may evaluate the facts for themselves and also guess what really crossed the minds of the three drivers seeking the land speed record in 1928.

3

A complex and difficult man as well as a determined and skilled driver was Malcolm Campbell.

Beyond the words of the wife who spent 20 years with him and the axe-strokes lowered by his only granddaughter, a better portrait of the man would come out of the biography.

Malcolm Campbell (Chislehurst, Kent, UK, March 11, 1885–Reigate, Surrey, UK, December 31, 1948) was of Scottish ancestry: his family moved from the Scottish Highlands to London on the eve of the nineteenth century, establishing a profitable diamond and jewelry business.

Malcolm's father, William, left a quarter of a million pounds when he died in 1920. The inheritance and the success Malcolm achieved in his business of libel insurance at Lloyd's were the cornerstones of the wealth that allowed him to buy the fastest racing cars and to partially fund his land speed record vehicles.

After an early infatuation with motorbikes, he soon switched to cars, the most powerful and fastest of the time. He bought two obsolete Darracq racers and entered them at Brooklands in 1911, driving the second one, a 46 HP model he named "Flapper." This was the usual name of his cars before he changed to Blue Bird in 1912.

Opposite top: **Malcolm Campbell was an incorrigible womanizer, always enjoying the company of girls. In this candid photograph, he wears an unusual bandana over his regular jacket and tie, being helped by happy servants. Here is proof that there was some fun in Daytona Beach even on the long days spent waiting for the sky to clear, the wind to blow from the right quarter, and the beach to become smooth.** *Opposite bottom:* **Another candid image of Sir Malcolm Campbell wearing racing overalls on the beach before a run on the Daytona Beach sands in 1932. His underwear was definitely not fireproof. Watching him in foreground are (left) his manager, William "Bill" Sturm, with a camera in his hand and (center) Leo Villa, chief mechanic, in white overalls.**

2. Act One—February

He then became a regular in the circle of amateur racers who drove the Brooklands circuit, buying and driving powerful but, alas, not equally reliable vehicles: Peugeot and Sunbeam, at that time at the very pinnacle of auto racing technique and performance.

His first marriage to Marjorie Dagmar Knott in 1913 ended in divorce after two years due to her blatant adultery whilst he was away fighting in the war.

After the Great War, honorably discharged with the rank of captain of the Royal Flying Corps, he returned to the Brooklands inner circle, driving good cars and recording significant victories.

He started to look at faster cars, and his attention focused on the 350 HP Sunbeam driven by Kenelm Lee Guinness to a new land speed record of 133.75 mph at the Brooklands circuit on May 17, 1922. He bought the car, renamed it Blue Bird, and hired Leo Villa as chief mechanic of his racing stable in 1923.

On September 25, 1924, at Pendine Sands, he took the record from Ernest Eldridge: at the wheel of the 350 HP Blue Bird he reached 146.16 mph. It was the first of his nine land speed records, an achievement never equaled by anybody else and one that will, for sure, never be beaten.

A formal portrait of Sir Malcolm Campbell (Chislehurst, Kent, UK, March 11, 1885–Reigate, Surrey, UK, December 31, 1948). He was granted a knighthood in 1931 by King George V after the 245.736 mph record in Daytona Beach. Called "The Skipper" by the staff, he was known by everyone else as "Captain," the rank he achieved in the Royal Flying Corps during the Great War. After 1931 he was "Sir Malcolm" to everybody. He was the only one to win the land speed record nine times, from 1924 to 1935, a feat that is sure to remain forever unbeaten.

On July 21, 1925, at Pendine Sands, driving the faithful former-Sunbeam 350 HP Blue Bird, he was the first man to go faster than 150 mph: the land speed record was raised to 150.76 mph. It was about the best he could get from the car.

Like everyone (except Henry Segrave) in the British racing drivers circle, he seldom ventured to the Continent: twice (in 1927 and 1928) he won the minor Grand Prix de Boulogne, on the French Channel coast directly opposite Kent.

In 1920 he married Dorothy Emily Evelyn Whittal. The marriage lasted until 1940, when she asked for a divorce. He was a serial womanizer, and after 20 years it became too much for his wife to bear.

Their first son, Donald, was born in 1921 and was destined to continue his father's achievements on land and water. Donald was followed by Jane, born in 1923.

In 1926 he was appointed sales agent for Bugatti and opened a showroom in central London. As a side benefit he was given some assistance from the factory when racing his own Typ-35 and Typ-37A cars.

After that, he cut down on his racing appearances, even though in 1928 he bought and drove Robert Benoist's Delage 1.5, the very best of period racing machinery. He also drove, on a couple of occasions, the 7.1-litre SS Mercedes, joining Rudolf Caracciola and Lord Howe in the works team.

Following the death of Parry-Thomas, he went back to Pendine Sands to attempt to regain the land speed record, and won it on February 4, 1927, when he drove at 174.883 mph: that was the limit at Pendine, so he started the long, sometimes troubled, yet ever-rewarding in terms of performance and money, relationship with Daytona Beach, which was due to last until March 7, 1935, when he raised the record to 276.816 mph.

Disillusioned at having missed the coveted 300 mph record, he went to the Bonneville Salt Flats in Utah, where he at last achieved his lifelong goal, reaching 301.129 mph on September 3, 1935.

Having given up car racing and records, he then became addicted to the world water speed record: once again he was motivated by rivalry with the Americans and wanted Britain to rule on land, water, and air. He had his K3 hydroplane built by Saunders-Roe.

Being a professional, he accepted the Swiss invitation to win the rich prize for setting his first water speed record on Lake Maggiore, off Locarno, where Leo Villa knew the city mayor: 126.32 mph on September 1, 1937. The boat—named Blue Bird, of course—was of the stepped-hydroplane type, powered by the well-proven Rolls-Royce R-Type engine.

On August 18, 1938, he raised the limit to 130.86 mph on Lake Hallwil, Argau, Switzerland. A new boat, K4, was designed by Reid Railton on the three-point principle. It was launched at Coniston, in the English Lake District, and on August 19, 1939, he pushed the record to 141.74 mph, far beyond the reach of the Americans. Then the war brought a halt to any more record-seeking activity on both land and water.

In 1945 he married again, to Betty Nicory.

After the war, during which the K4 boat was preserved in the family garage at Headley Grove, he commissioned Vospers to reconstruct it around the new de Havilland Goblin jet engine. He struggled with all the problems such a novel propulsion system entailed.

He didn't manage to fix them all as his health worsened after a series of strokes. He died at home on New Year's Eve, 1949.

The boat was refitted by Donald Campbell, who dumped the jet engine. He bought one of the three Rolls-Royce R–Type engines formerly owned by his father back from an American scrapyard and started his career as water speed record seeker. In the name of his father. And beyond.

4

Frank Stallworth Lockhart was barely 23 when he boarded the train in Los Angeles for the long journey to Indianapolis. In 1926 it was the first time he and his wife, Ella, 28, *née* Corsen, had been east of the Mississippi River, though he was already a shining star in Californian motor racing. Creative local pressmen had given him the imaginative nickname "Boy Wonder."

Lockhart was a young driver graced with a heavy right foot, a flashing eye, a perfect feel for racing, an exceptional knowledge of mechanics, and a great respect for the performance and limits of the cars he drove to wins on board and dirt tracks. And he was open-minded, friendly, smiling, and fair with competitors on the track and with everyone else.

Board track statistics list eight overall wins and a money purse worth $40,900.[10]

Born on March 8, 1903, in Dayton, Ohio, Frank Lockhart entered motor racing in 1923 at the age of 20. The following year he became a winner, driving a car

Frank Lockhart, 22, at the wheel of his second Miller 183/122, driven to victories whilst climbing the stairway to celebrity in California. The price tag of a new Miller was already around $5,000, but of course a used one was cheaper. In 1926 the AAA formula for the championship was changed to 91 cubic inch single-seaters: as a consequence, the older, larger-engined racers, still good for minor events, became cheaper to buy (original by Ella Lockhart; from Tom Kinney collection).

assembled from obsolete Ford parts in his garage at home. For once in his life he took a break from racing and car preparation on October 29, 1924, to marry Ella, a Californian switchboard operator of a Los Angeles telephone company. Three days later he was racing again at Ascot.

In 1925 he graduated to a 183 Miller, at that time the car to have to win races in the United States. He won, beating the big league of drivers: Ralph DePalma, Peter de Paolo, Tommy Milton, and Leon Duray.

He became a sort of resident driver-mechanic in Harry Miller's Los Angeles workshop. There he became acquainted with John Weisel, then an engineering student at Caltech. He later appointed John as one of the two graduate brother designers of his record car, the Blackhawk.

Harry Miller hired him as works team leader on the dirt tracks and as reserve driver for Bennet "Benny" Hill, works driver at Indianapolis in 1926. The agreement was that after Indianapolis Lockhart would tour the Midwest dirt track circuits at the wheel of a works Miller 122/183.

Frank reached Indianapolis on May 23, 1926, without any firm arrangement to enter the 500-Mile Race. He grabbed the offer to drive the No. 16 Miller entered for Benny Hill. In an open trial he lapped at 108.83 mph, faster than Hill's 106.75 mph. He later drove the No. 15 Miller of Peter Kreis and put in an

Official Indianapolis photograph of Frank Lockhart, winner of the 1926 race. He was the first rookie to win, and it was the first race that had to be stopped at the 400-mile mark due to heavy rain. He was driving the No. 15 Miller entered for Peter Kreis, who fell ill with severe flu and had to be taken to the hospital on May 25, five days before the race on Decoration (Memorial) Day. Lockhart qualified on May 29 at the conservative pace of 95.782 mph, good for the 20th spot on the grid of 28 cars (Indianapolis Motor Speedway photo archive).

unofficial track record time: 112.22 mph. Nobody had ever seen such a speed at the Brickyard.

Kreis was out of the game when he fell ill with a severe attack of flu that forced him to go to hospital on May 25. Harry Miller didn't hesitate in entering Lockhart in the No. 15 car after signing an agreement with Kreis to give him a new front-drive Miller for delivery in September 1926.

Lockhart took part in three practice sessions on May 27, when his fastest lap was timed at 115.488 mph, the highest single-lap speed in the history of Indy. On May 29, the eve of the race, Lockhart qualified for the grid, lapping at quite a conservative pace: 95.782 mph, good enough for the 20th spot out of 28 starters. Pole position went to Earl Cooper, No. 5 Miller Front Drive: 111.735 mph. Nobody dared bet on Lockhart to win.

Lockhart smiles happily and sips a Coke (no milk, yet) after his surprise victory in the 1926 Indianapolis 500. His winning average was 95.885 mph, fast enough to finish two laps ahead of Harry Hartz in another Miller 91. His total purse, after leading for most of the laps, amounted to $35,600. Two British cars, designed, built and branded by Ernest Eldridge started the race: one driven by Ernest Eldridge himself, and another driven by William Douglas Hawkes. Another foreign driver, Englishman John Duff, one of the Le Mans Bentley Boys, drove a Miller. The last place was taken by Frenchman Albert Guyot driving a Schmidt powered by an Argyle engine. He first entered Indianapolis in 1913 driving a Sunbeam (original by Ella Lockhart; from Tom Kinney collection).

Three laps after the start Lockhart was already in fifth place. On lap 20 he was running second, dicing for the lead with Dave Lewis (No. 1 Miller Front Drive). When Lewis pitted on lap 50 Lockhart romped into the lead until lap 71, when the race was suspended due to heavy rain.

After nearly an hour the race was restarted when the track had dried up and the sun shone through the clouds again.

Lockhart fought against Harry Hartz (No. 3 Miller) and ceded the lead to him for six laps when he had to pit for fuel. He soon got back to the front and increased his lead to two full laps by lap 140. Then the rain started again, and the track became too wet, slippery, and dangerous. The chief steward made the decision to stop the race on lap 160, 400 miles.

Frank Lockhart, the unknown rookie from California, was the winner: he was leading Harry Hartz by two laps. The 140,000 spectators cheered him as the first rookie ever to win the Indy 500, beating the best U.S. drivers. It was a magic race: first victory for a rookie, first race suspended and stopped for rain before the 500-mile traditional distance. Lockhart's purse amounted to $35,600.[11] Soaked and greasy, Frank entered Victory Lane. Still seated in the car, he hugged and kissed Ella. The photographers asked them to re-enact the scene: "Where the hell are we? Hollywood?" whispered Ella to her husband.

5

"The kid's a genius. He feels confident that his car is going to make an awful high speed. He's all tired out today, though. He has been doing too much night work on the car. For weeks he had mechanics working nights and days on it."[12] Simple words said by John Burgamy, brother of Carrie, Frank Lockhart's mother, when alighting from the train in Daytona Beach.

He was there ahead of Frank and his wife, Ella, who arrived at the local depot of the Florida East Railway on Saturday, February 14 from Indianapolis. William "Bill" Sturm, manager and PR man, was with them, along with his wife, Teressa.

The nonstop work by Lockhart and his team became a basic element of the myth: 11 years later, in 1939, George Eyston, the British record holder and author, mentioned it in his book, one of the first to focus on the history of the land speed record: "Much of it [the Blackhawk] he had built himself, working late into the night machining parts on his own lathe. Lockhart's workshops were a miracle of cleanliness, and it is said that there was never a speck of dust to be seen."[13]

John Burgamy, the owner of a company selling spare auto parts in Cincinnati, Ohio, was naturally versed in the art of pleasing the audience. He went on praising the beach and proclaimed that Frank, too, would have rated it as the best of the known record venues.

Frank must have been really tired when he reached Daytona Beach in the early morning. And not because of the long trip from Indianapolis. Not a single word from him was published in the local daily, quite unusual given that he was the best-known contender in the Speed Trials.

Top: In the "secret" workshop at the Stutz factory in Indianapolis, around the end of 1927, Frank Lockhart and Bill Sturm ponder the engine and transmission of the Blackhawk, whose components are perfectly laid out on the tables in the foreground. In the background Myron Stevens, holding a hammer, and Floyd Dreyer are working at shaping the rear section of the body. The workshop became a sort of myth due to always being so clean and tidy (original by Jim Weisel; from Tom Kinney collection). *Bottom:* Bill Sturm (left) and Frank Lockhart seated on the rear axle reflecting on the Blackhawk's transmission, laid on the floor of the workshop at the Stutz factory in Indianapolis. Note Lockhart's attire of white shirt and tie: that day he was not working with a machine tool, as he usually was. Note also the strong construction of the rear wheel, forged in steel (original by Jim Weisel; from Tom Kinney collection).

Frank soon went to Haig's Garage, selected by the Stutz Company to host the Blackhawk and the stock cars brought to race on the beach. He did a quick check of the Blackhawk and went to rest at the Clarendon Hotel. He had about a week to fine-tune the Blackhawk prior to going for the record on Sunday, February 19. The bad weather allowed ample time to do it.

A well-known image of Frank Lockhart checking the crankcase model of the engine over which the two eight-cylinder rows of the Miller 91 had to be fitted. Only for the photographer's benefit is Lockhart using a bricklayer's gauge to measure the length of the model (Tom Kinney collection).

With the Clarendon Hotel in the background, the Blackhawk is being readied for a photo op on the Daytona Beach sands. The two people in white T-shirts and caps are Jimmy Lee (left) and Jean Marcenac. Bill Sturm, as always, takes center stage in the photograph. Ray Splinder, smiling in his white overalls, is on the right. Frank Lockhart's dedication to Myron Stevens shows his very basic handwriting skills (original from Myron Stevens).

A huge crowd was expected to fill the dunes on the inner edge of the beach and the makeshift grandstand facing the measured mile. A 50-cent entry ticket was decided upon for the day: it was the first and only event in the history of the land speed record when people had to pay to watch the runs. It was the first and only time when the quest for the record descended into a show.

6

Managing a racing driver was an unknown job in Europe, yet not in America in the 1920s, where people were already ravenous for images, stories, legends, and heroes.

Frank Lockhart, when he decided to focus on the land speed record, hired mechanics, panel beaters, designers, engineers, aerodynamics experts, and William F. "Bill" Sturm as communications manager.

Sturm was a journalist who specialized in subjects dealing with the automotive world. He was a skilled PR professional promoting the image of racing drivers.

He invented the job in 1915 when he was hired by Erwin George "Cannon

Proudly posing behind the engine block in the Stutz Indianapolis workshop are, from left, Myron Stevens, Floyd Dreyer, Bill Sturm, Ray Splinder, and Jean Marcenac. From the small team of builders of the Blackhawk only Jimmy Lee and Bud Miller are missing (original by Jim Weisel; from Tom Kinney collection).

Ball" Baker (1882–1960), who crossed the Continent together with him as passenger. He was so good at the job that Cannon Ball Baker became an icon the early automobile era in the United States.

When he joined Frank Lockhart he was faced with a new professional challenge dealing with a fine driver and person.

Their working relationship soon developed into a more personal involvement, even though he had to deal with funerary issues more often than success stories. His contribution to the enterprise was effective in introducing the young Californian driver, then only a boy elevated to national prominence by his 1926 Indianapolis 500 win, into the highly competitive and tricky Indy automotive inner circle.

Sturm knew Indianapolis well. He was born into a family of nine brothers and sisters in Columbus, Indiana, on August 25, 1883, to Alsatian immigrant parents. He found an early job as proofreader at *The Indianapolis News*. The proofreading job gave him the opportunity to understand the writing styles of others and to improve his own.

He did a lot of moonlighting, writing stories about motor racing and selling them to national magazines. Thanks to in-depth knowledge of the racing world and his authoritative writing, he was selected as a member of the AAA contest board to promote the development and spread of the automobile.

Nothing would have pleased him more than seeing the day when America could challenge European supremacy in motor racing and speed records. It was a logical consequence that he did so well along with Lockhart in his quest for the land speed record.

Being well known for his skill, he was later appointed PR manager by Henry Segrave when he went to Daytona Beach in 1929. The following year he travelled to the UK to handle PR for Segrave's water speed record attempt, which ended in tragedy.

An American handling communications for a British baronet seeking the fastest possible speed on an English lake was seen as an insult to the country: as such, period British media ignored him, despite his presence and job making him very visible.

He supervised communications at the unlucky record attempt of Kaye Don's Silver Bullet at Daytona Beach in 1930 and banished any suspicions of being a jinx (two deaths and a failure) when he managed Malcolm Campbell from 1931 to 1935, glorifying his four records at Daytona Beach and the final one on the Bonneville Salt Flats.

In April 1905 he had married Teressa Hess in Noblesville, close to Indianapolis, where he spent his life and where he died on August 26, 1937.[14]

7

Frank Lockhart was a shy, unassuming boy. He avoided, whenever possible, the image-building rites that were already the cornerstone of success in America in the 1920s. William "Bill" Sturm soon took charge of fueling the Daytona Beach dailies and citizens with stories and interviews aimed at building the expectation of Lockhart's record.

Sturm raised the most sensitive issue for the average American citizen, dollars: "Lockhart's car could not be bought over the counter for a cent less than $75,000. Perhaps $100,000 would be a nearer figure. The finest of everything has gone into the diminutive racer."[15]

To prove his knowledge of the subject and his professional skill at staying in tune with the public, he added: "Frank's car has a power plant of 181 cubic inches, three litres or something like three quarts. One of Bob Burman's Blitzen Benz cylinders was of greater capacity than Lockhart's whole car, yet he did but 142 miles an hour while Lockhart plans on doing almost a hundred miles more an hour. His clever engineering has put approximately 400 horsepower into a motor no larger than a Ford power plant."

Not wanting to be too technical, Sturm also said that one piston had the diameter of a silver dollar, i.e., 1.5 inches (the correct figure for the bore was 2.188 inches). He returned to the technicalities, voicing Lockhart's idea: "He believes that a car to be successful in making a world record must have at least three cardinal principles: correct design, power and ability to stand terrific strains. His Stutz Blackhawk Special was designed by himself from nose to tail. There isn't a nut or a bolt, a single piece on the car that hasn't had Lockhart's personal inspection."

The words were PR stuff. The editor of the daily played it cool when he had to edit and complete those fanciful statements picked up by the reporter. In *The Daytona Beach News-Journal* on Monday, February 16, he opted for the easy headline: "High Power Not Vital For Top Speed, Says Lockhart."

8

On his arrival in Daytona Beach on Sunday, February 12, Jim White released an understated statement, sort of asking for mercy: "This is a purely sporting proposition. We have built the car but have never driven it. We don't even know whether or not it will run, but as a sporting proposition this speed trial for us is $20,000 worth of fun. It all depends on what we find it can do in preliminary trials."[16]

Jim White, a rich Philadelphian wire industrialist born and raised in Florida, was a fan of motor racing and made the land speed record his prime goal. He had his own ideas about what was really needed to beat wind resistance and go faster than any other human being: power, as much power as one could integrate on a single frame and transfer to the wheels. He added: "We do not have time to design and build against wind resistance. We have 1,500 HP and they will be enough for the record."

The 1,500 HP was a rounded figure for gullible people. It was one of the many bombastic statements he issued during his and Triplex's days in Daytona Beach

The White Triplex towed to the beach on a rainy morning in February 1928. The Daytona Beach streets were already tarmacked. The additional set of rear wheels was installed to provide a reverse-motion system as required by the AAA. The additional wheels were positioned lower and ahead of the rear wheels geared directly to the engines. When required to demonstrate the reverse-motion ability they were pushed to the rear to be moved by friction against the geared rear wheels.

in February 1928. And in April 1928. And before the last and tragic run on March 13, 1929.

The Triplex was a no-nonsense vehicle, a logical and rational product of the basic idea that power and torque are everything needed to reach the highest speeds. Then, tires should be able to transfer power and torque on a smooth regular surface, as the Daytona Beach sand was.

The size and weight of the vehicle invariably provoked adjectives like *monstrous*, *gigantic*, *primitive*, and *wild*. British cognoscenti and media, speaking from the platform of being the self-proclaimed masters of the land speed record, opened the flow of the fiercest and most gratuitous critical comments of it.

The car was built from a mixture of automobile parts. The frame was said to come from an old truck, while British sources[17] wrote of two pieces of low-grade steel beams usually used in construction building. The front axle was from an old Lincoln, turned upside down. The rear axle was a plain piece of bar steel three inches in diameter, to which three sets of uncovered gears were attached for the three engines. No differential and, apparently, no clutch either.

Gossip spread about baling wire being used to fix some minor parts: that Jim White was the boss of a wire manufacturing company in Philadelphia added credibility to the story.

When on the beach, the existence of a reverse-motion system on the White Triplex is confirmed by the traces of sand in the treads. When pushing both pairs of rear wheels in contact the team probably had to lower the resistance offered by the two rear engines by either removing the spark plugs or forcing one of the valves in each cylinder open. The front engine was the only one with a clutch. The AAA did not accept the system.

The Triplex had a 175.5-inch wheelbase, 63-inch track, and 8,000-pound heft, figures showing a vehicle a long way from being a leviathan. In comparison, the 1927 Sunbeam 1000 HP driven by Henry Segrave had a 141-inch wheelbase and about the same weight: 8,000–8,500 pounds. The tires were 36 × 6.5 on the Triplex and 36 × 6.75 on the Sunbeam. As for aerodynamic drag, the Triplex was probably superior.

If the drag was not so bad, the longitudinal balance was tragically wrong: the center of gravity was well back towards the rear due to the two engines behind the driver. At least the weight of the two Liberty engines provided a good load on the rear wheels. The smooth side surfaces of the body to shape the chisel nose acted as sails on the beach where the wind was blowing from the ocean: the result was the center of pressure awfully ahead of the center of gravity, making the vehicle totally unstable. A small deviation from the straight line would have been magnified by the intrinsic instability of the car. The driver had to wrestle hard to keep the car in a straight line.

It has to be said that in 1928 the study of vehicle dynamics was still in its infancy and aerodynamic optimization focused solely on achieving the lowest possible drag in a straight line.

If we take for granted the power outputs of the 1928 engines—940 HP on the Blue Bird, according to Napier, and 1,500 HP on the Triplex, as stated by White—we would have ratios of 0.37 HP/kg for the former and 0.42 HP/kg for the three Liberty engines on the Triplex. If we take the more realistic figure of 1,200 HP for the Triplex, the ratio would change to 0.33 HP/kg. Both figures compare rather closely to the Blue Bird.

Jim White summarized his theories and ideas in a long article published in the U.S. magazine *Motor Age* on July 5, 1928. The literary style may be shaky, but the basic principles are clear-cut:

> The principal reason for building the Triplex was that I could never be reconciled to the streamline theory. My idea of piercing the air is simply that the maximum size to open the air is your obstacle. The wind offers a resistance increased with speed, to overcome which the vehicle must have power and weight sufficient fully to utilize the power, and the surface to run over at high speed must be extremely smooth to ensure contact.
>
> There can be nothing done by man to overcome this [i.e., the wind resistance] in any shape or form. I was told I could never hope to accomplish the job of breaking the world's record unless the car was first tried out in a tunnel [i.e., a wind tunnel], such as provided for testing planes to determine wind resistance etc. I would not have taken advantage of such a tunnel had there been one in Philadelphia and had an invitation to use it been accorded me gratis.[18]

On Sunday, April 22, 1928, in Daytona Beach, Ray Keech in the Triplex brought the land speed record back to America, reaching 207.552 mph, beating Campbell. Jim White jumped on the success to bury everyone who criticized him: "The Triplex eventually demonstrated to my satisfaction that my idea of piercing air is correct."

9

Fate likes to recreate the past, to mix lives, to link destinies, and to complete unfinished stories. It did it with Charles Raymond "Ray" Keech, the first American to set the world land speed record on April 22, 1928, in Daytona Beach. He took the laurels away from Malcolm Campbell.

He was the winner of the 1929 Indianapolis 500-Mile Race, driving one of the Millers modified and tuned by Lockhart. He died on June 15, 1929, on the Altoona, Pennsylvania, board track at the wheel of the same racer. He met his end a few miles away from Coatesville, where he was born on May 1, 1900, on the family farm.

Burly and fearless, Ray found a way out of a dull life in agriculture by racing cars. His career was business as usual: his early races were on local dirt tracks, and then he graduated to board tracks.

The Altoona 1.25-mile board track, close to home, opened in 1923 and soon acquired the reputation of being a very fast yet deadly dangerous track. On its inaugural day, September 4, Howdy Wilcox met his death, impaled on the upper rail of a turn banked up to 32 degrees.

Ray Keech in the narrow cockpit of the Triplex in Daytona Beach. The windscreen is a metal sheet with a small piece of flat glass inserted to allow forward vision. The rear engines are immediately behind the driver's back without any protection. The driving position is quite cramped, as it usually was on period racing cars. Keech was hired by Jim White as he was, like him, a Philadelphian.

Keech was a resident of Philadelphia like Jim White. Thanks to a generous retainer, he agreed to drive the brutal, powerful, and functional vehicle.

When Lockhart's speedway racing cars went on sale, the second 91 Miller was acquired for him by Maude and Edward Yagle of Philadelphia. The car was the best available for sale in America. Keech was a rookie in the 1928 Indianapolis race: 10th on the grid, 113.421 mph, and fourth past the checkered flag, average speed 93.320 mph.

On June 15, 1928, Keech was the winner of an AAA National Championship race in Detroit.

In the 1929 Indianapolis 500, the only change to his racer was the number 2, the same number already used by Lockhart.[19] He qualified sixth with 114.905 mph. He raced conservatively until lap 160, when he came around in the lead. He remained there until the end of the race, winning a $31,950 purse.[20]

Instead of his victory, the media chose to glorify the skill of the late Frank Lockhart, who had modified the car, still a winner after two seasons.

Keech came back to Pennsylvania for a race on the Altoona board track on June 15, 1929, the anniversary of his maiden victory in the same car. Despite starting fifth, he overtook all the competitors and took the lead on lap 17. He opened up a bigger gap circling the ill-fated and dangerous track at 120 mph.

An official Indianapolis photograph of Ray Keech, winner of the 1929 500-Mile Sweepstake on Decoration (Memorial) Day, May 30. He is at the wheel of the second Miller-Lockhart, bought for him by Ed and Maude Yagle from Philadelphia: they paid $14,800 to Lockhart's estate, i.e., the regular market price of a Miller 91 plus a bonus to cover the improvements made by Lockhart. The racer was the very best available at that time (Indianapolis Motor Speedway photo archive).

On lap 121 out of 160 he was lapping Bob Robertson, who suddenly lost control and skidded to crash on the upper rail. Sixty feet of metal sheet torn off by the impact flew across the whole track.

Keech could neither brake nor avoid the obstacle and crashed into it. His car went into a vicious skid and somersaulted many times before coming to rest at the top of the banked turn at the very same spot where Joe Boyer had met his end in 1924. The car, upside down and on fire, slid slowly to the bottom edge of the track, but Keech had already been thrown out.

The race was stopped, and he was declared winner—the sole known case of a dead winner. He was rushed by ambulance to the nearby hospital, where they could do nothing other than declare him dead.

10

In 1926 Daytona Beach claimed to be the seventh largest city in Florida. Not much of a claim to fame, surely, in a state whose positive features were already widely known: mild winters, lush nature, wide open spaces, organized and well-administered towns, the roaring Atlantic on the eastern shore and the warm, quiet Gulf of Mexico on the western side. Devastating hurricanes were deliberately forgotten.

In that year Daytona Beach was officially incorporated through the merging of two adjacent communities, Seabreeze and Daytona.

Six years earlier, the "small" Daytona Beach hosted 6,000 residents, squeezed on to a narrow strip of sand between the Atlantic Ocean and the Halifax River, one section of the Florida Internal Waterways, open to small vessels all year round from Miami to Jacksonville, thanks to the quiet waters.

The number of residents had reached 25,000 in 1926 when the "big" Daytona Beach was incorporated. Yet the most impressive figure was 125,000 winter residents. The town was already well known among the richest inhabitants of northeastern and northern states of the Union as a pleasant winter retreat.

Houses and mansions had sprouted, and the tourism framework, hotels, and restaurants, were going through rapid development.[21]

The automobile races held on the beach from 1903 to 1910 had provided a nationwide boost to the fame of the town. The sand of the 23-mile beach offered a smooth and compact surface for motor vehicles. Nothing similar existed anywhere else across the U.S.: country roads were sloughs of dirt and mud, and only the few roads close to big cities were smooth and well maintained. In Florida, too, the ways across the state were cart tracks scratched by endless wheel ruts.

In the early years of the century the quest for speed records on the beach was an idea of the Florida East Coast Automobile Association of Ormond Beach (the most northerly section of Daytona Beach), when automobiles were still a novel proposal. The record attempts were sanctioned by the AAA.[22]

Every pioneer in the U.S. automobile industry converged on Daytona Beach for the trials in January or March. Such was the appeal of the events that the Europeans came too: Mors, Darracq, and Renault from France; Napier from the UK; Fiat from Italy. The most powerful German Mercedes and Benz models were already there, owned and driven by wealthy, brave American drivers.

No record established in those events should enter the historical list of land speed records as they were timed manually, in one direction only, and the AAA was not a member of the Paris-based AIACR. Nevertheless, some still stand as records despite the AIACR denying official recognition. Daytona Beach promoters and the American public didn't care about that.

The 100-mph speed over the measured mile was reached in 1905, and some period advertisements claimed a possible speed of two miles a minute, i.e., 120 mph, the stuff of sci-fi at the time!

The land speed record contenders confronted each other in match races, speeding together on the beach. Maybe the idea of the 1928 triangular challenge came from that.

The width of the beach, about 300 to 600 feet at low tide, permitted long-distance racing for 50 miles. A post in the sand was the turning point at both ends of the parallel stretches. The harshest competitor in the longer races was the tide, which was going to come in irrespective of any human will: it would have transformed the slowest cars into motor boats.

"Willie K" Vanderbilt won the first 50-mile race on January 30, 1904, driving his 90 HP Mercedes at 73.475 mph. His time was 40 minutes 49.4 seconds. The news of the day reported that he managed to win and get out of the car without getting his feet wet. The result was, of course, claimed as a new world speed record over that distance.[23] In the 1920s the Daytona Beach Chamber of Commerce lured automobile fanatics advertising miles of paved streets in the town, nice to travel on in the shadow of lush palm trees.

On March 16, 1936, the beach staged half of an oval track, whose main stretch was Atlantic Avenue, the paved road alongside the dunes. The races were open to automobiles and motorcycles.

The success of the experiment pushed a clever and far-sighted local garage owner, William Henry Getty "Bill" France, to promote races—first for bikes and later for cars—over a 4.1-mile circuit, half sand and half paved road. In the two turns linking the road and beach sections the sand soon became so rough that cars overturned and skidded, providing a thrilling and exciting show.

William Kissam II "Willie K" Vanderbilt (New York, March 2, 1878–New York, January 8, 1944), driving his 1905 Mercedes 90 HP. He was one of the key protagonists of the early Speed Trials, initiated in 1903 at Ormond Beach and relaunched in 1928 by Daytona Beach. Disappointed by the poor management of the event, he never returned after 1905. On February 27, 1904, driving an earlier model of the Mercedes 90 HP on the beach, he set the unofficial land speed record, covering the mile at 92.85 mph. In the same year he promoted and financed the Vanderbilt Cup, a major event in the early years of motor racing in America that lasted until 1916 and was briefly resurrected in 1936–1937 (original from Museum of Speed, Ormond Beach).

In 1947 the races were restricted to stock cars: it was the eve of NASCAR (National Association for Stock Car Auto Racing), the category of racing that still attracts the greatest attendance and offers the best show value in the United States.

On February 22, 1959, the death knell rang for motor races and land speed record attempts on the beach (for the latter, the last hurrah had already happened in 1935). Bill France opened the Daytona International Speedway, the 2.5-mile tri-oval circuit that became the site of the world's number-one NASCAR event: the Daytona 500.[24] No more sand and tides. Tarmac and mainland instead.[25]

11

There was a great-to-be racing driver in Daytona Beach that February 1928, Wilbur Shaw: "My part in the proposed series of record attempts at Daytona Beach was comparatively small." He was seeking the record for four-cylinder cars, a record invented by marketing wizards at Willys-Overland, a minor U.S. automobile manufacturer producing far fewer vehicles than the Detroit Big Three.

Shaw and his friend, engineer and manager Floyd Smith, were endlessly chasing good contracts from anyone who trusted them and offered the money they needed. They were professionals making a living out of racing. They owned a good Miller 91 single-seater chassis and a well-tuned four-cylinder Frontenac engine. Combining them, they had raced successfully on dirt tracks in the 1927 season.

When Willys-Overland agreed to sign them, they were of course happy to name their racer Whippet Four, the brand name used by Willys-Overland on their compact cars. The company wished to gain publicity from the new record.

Shaw and the Whippet Four reached Daytona Beach by mid–February and had to wait until Saturday, February 18 to get on the beach for preliminary trials. The goal was to beat the 144.10 mph "record" achieved by Bob Burman in his Blitzen Benz in 1912.

The managers of the company, supported by the city sales manager William Tuttle, did a good job in creating expectations and interest in the least exciting record in the February Speed Trials.

The Daytona Beach News-Journal reserved prime space for all runs of the Whippet Four, even on February 20 when it didn't go any faster than 106.53 mph with the wind, quite a modest result.[26]

Two days later the whole front page was about him: "Shaw Drives Into Water In Flames."[27] A backfire from the engine had threatened to set both car and driver afire. He gave a simple explanation in the autobiography: "The ocean was the handiest fire extinguisher I've ever used and I ran into the water deliberately to avoid being painfully burned."[28] The daily built a front-page drama, reporting that the event had happened at precisely 1:19 p.m. and the Whippet Four would be on the beach again later in the afternoon, before high tide.

Shaw knew the facts better and wrote that a good engine had been damaged

Wilbur Shaw (Shelbyville, Indiana, USA, October 31, 1902—Decatur, Indiana, October 30, 1954) at the wheel of the Whippet Four, a "special" built by him and Floyd Smith on a Miller frame, equipped with a well-tuned Frontenac engine and financed by Willys-Overland. The company asked for the car to be named as their new entry-level production car: Whippet. The "Four" was added because the car was aimed at setting the speed record for four-cylinder cars, a goal invented by clever company marketers without any link to officially recognized records. Shaw and the car never managed to improve on the existing record, set in 1912 in Ormond Beach by Bob Burman in a Blitzen Benz 200 HP at 144.10 mph. Shaw was the first three-time winner of the Indianapolis 500 and played a prominent role in rescuing the track and the whole facility after World War II. In 1945 he was appointed president and general manager of the Speedway until his death in a plane crash in 1954.

beyond repair and would have been impossible to fix before the closure of the event, set for the day after.

The space devoted to this minor event, spectacular yet of no real consequence, seems strange when viewed today because on the same day, February 22, at 4 p.m., Frank Lockhart suffered a terrible accident: speeding at 225 mph, he hit the water, damaging the Blackhawk and almost suffering death by drowning.

Shaw returned to Indianapolis, strong and fit yet disillusioned, a few days before Lockhart. He resolved to go back to Daytona Beach in April, sharing the sand with Lockhart and White. He got the AAA's sanction. The fees for the timing system and AAA officials would be split among the three of them.

The Whippet Four went back to Daytona Beach on April 16 and was on the course on Monday, April 20. Without official AAA timing it reached 141 and 153 mph, the higher figure being a calculation from the rev-counter reading. It was promptly given to the local reporter to enhance publicity.

The dark feelings across Daytona Beach after April 25 could have been cleared by Wilbur Shaw and the Whippet Four as the only contenders for a record still in the city. Shaw tried again on Thursday April 26, encouraged by the wishes of Mayor Armstrong, duly acknowledged by a large photo on the front page of the local daily.

The engine was in worse condition than expected after the work to repair it following its immersion in the salt water: it forced Shaw to abort the return run when he was on the measured mile after a 138.83 mph earlier run. He felt another piston was about to blow.[29]

At the end of the afternoon the car was back in the garage for an in-depth check-over. Mr. N.H. Pearson, the Willys-Overland manager supervising the runs, announced new trials for Sunday, April 29, hoping for a good crowd to fill the dunes.

The beach was perfect on Sunday: there was just a mild breeze and visibility was free of obstacles. Yet the car didn't go any faster than 129 mph, still a long way from Burman's record. On Monday, April 30, the southbound 134.03 mph and northbound 135.61 mph runs made everyone agree that the 134.82 mph average was the new official world record for a four-cylinder car because Burman's speed was manually timed, only one way, and never internationally acknowledged.[30]

The next day Shaw and the team decided to go back to the Midwest, and AAA officials and timekeepers went back to base in Washington.

The local daily gave the farewell to the driver with a large front-page photo and a shouty headline: "Faster Than Any Four-cylinder Car."

Shaw played it more quietly in his autobiography: "Thoroughly disgusted, I packed up the same day and headed for home with the spectre of bad luck still casting its shadow over me."[31]

12

Wilbur Shaw was an archetypal man from Indiana. He was born in Shelbyville, a small town in the suburbs of Indianapolis, on October 31, 1902. He lived, raced, became a manager, and met his death in Indiana. He was always focused on the Indianapolis Speedway.

At 16 he attempted to enter his maiden race at the Hoosier Motor Speedway, a dirt track close to Indianapolis. His entry was declined, but he persisted and raced regularly in local dirt track events, building up enough skill to be eligible to enter the Indianapolis 500, his boyhood dream. In 1927 he qualified 19th and finished an astonishing fourth in a rather old Miller, repainted gold and entered by Fred Clemons. The purse amounted to $3,500,[32] making him a rich man.

Fully aware of his capabilities, he wrote in his autobiography: "I was sure anyone who could finish fourth in a car whose top speed was ten or twelve miles an hour under that of most other entries, could win with a good automobile."[33]

Not in 1928, when he retired after 42 laps, 25th out of 29 starters. Before the Indianapolis race, he got a contract with Willys-Overland to drive his four-cylinder racer under the name of Whippet Four in the Daytona Beach Speed Trials.

Alongside his driving skill in races he began to show an inclination to manage his career and finances, being appointed as a paid driver by entrants with top-tier cars. He drove as works driver for Duesenberg, yet accepted other wheels when the bag of money was good.

In 1932 he was again at the start of the Indianapolis 500 in a Miller, but with no luck: he finished 17th, out on lap 157 due to rear axle failure. Another disappointment came in 1933 when he was forced to retire on lap 15 after qualifying in the middle of the front row.

Results began to improve: he was second in 1935 and seventh in 1936, the year of the embarrassing crash on the first turn of the opening lap of the Vanderbilt Cup in Long Island, New York.

In 1937 he scored his first victory at Indianapolis, driving a Shaw-Gilmore two-seater he entered himself: those were the years of the "Junk Formula." He won by a handful of seconds, ahead of Ralph Hepburn, whose foot was badly scalded by hot oil pouring from the engine.

He was now firmly amongst the top racing drivers and proved it by finishing second in the 1938 Indianapolis 500. The following year he drove the new Maserati 8CTF, bought for him by Mike Boyle, a Chicago mafia boss of sorts, who used racing cars and the sale of auto accessories to launder dirty money.[34] He won well ahead of every other competitor at an average speed of 115.035 mph.

The big win was repeated in 1940, when he became the first man to win the Indianapolis 500 three times. In 1941 a bad accident on lap 107 prevented his third win in a row in the same Maserati. He was forced to retire from racing for good after 13 starts at Indianapolis and began a management career at Firestone.

He then played a leading role in arranging the post-war sale of the Speedway to Tony Hulman, who refurbished and re-launched it with increasing success.

The new owner appointed him as president and general manager of the Speedway. He kept both posts from 1945 until his untimely death on October 30, 1954, in a plane crash when he was flying home to Indianapolis from Michigan.

13

The Blue Bird crate was too large to go through the hatches of the *Berengaria*. It crossed the Atlantic on the open deck chained to the bridge: it had been a wise act of foresight that the London shippers, the LEP Transport, had made the crate waterproof.

Four crates of spare parts, two gas starters for the engine, one spare engine sealed in its container, and 10 crates of Rudge-Whitworth wheels and Dunlop special tires were stowed in the hold. The wheels and tires were handled directly by Dunlop, relieving Leo Villa of the task.[35]

Malcolm and Dorothy Campbell boarded in first class whilst the team members were relegated to third class, an arrangement more suited to poor emigrants. Leo Villa, Joe Coe (mechanic), David McDonald (Dunlop tire specialist), his brother Steve, and George Miller (full-time employee of Campbell) raised strong protests about the uncomfortable arrangements and were given bigger, better, and more expensive cabins.

On the second day at sea the *Berengaria* was hit by a storm so severe that the ship's superstructure was damaged. Everyone in the team suffered from seasickness, and Leo Villa remembered in his memoirs that he felt so bad that he lost all interest in traveling to America to work on the Blue Bird.[36] Campbell, a true gentleman, never mentioned such a dull subject at all.

Berengaria moored in New York on Wednesday, February 8, shrouded by thick fog. The men of the team took charge of the customs work and the transfer of the Blue Bird crate onto the *Seminole Coaster* heading for Jacksonville, Florida. From there the car would be loaded on to a truck for transport to Daytona Beach.

The men boarded the *Dixie Flyer* train and enjoyed a pleasant and comfortable trip, accompanied by good tasty food.[37]

Malcolm Campbell stayed briefly in New York with receptions to attend and speeches to be given, arranged by Girard Hammond, who had been hired as local manager. Early on Sunday morning, February 12, he joined the team and the Blue Bird in Daytona Beach.[38]

The weather was awful; the wind was blowing from the wrong quarter, the ocean was rough, and the beach was full of ridges and waterlogged by deep puddles.

Blue Bird had not yet run for a single yard under its own power, and Campbell became anxious to start trials as soon as possible, to learn how to handle the car and to gain additional time for the tune-up and record runs.

The weather and the tide shortened the window of time available for the runs. Campbell wrote, mistakenly, that only a few minutes were left to go for the runs in between clearing and patrolling the beach, installing the flagpoles, and the timing and telephone systems before the tide rolled in again. His feelings about Daytona Beach had deteriorated since the Blue Bird had been readied on Tuesday afternoon, February 14. But it was locked away in the garage of the Ridgewood Hotel, where the British party was waiting for the right day.

He knew well that the record runs were scheduled to start on Friday, February 17, yet the disappointment due to those days wasted waiting for suitable beach conditions made him think about finding a better site, less vulnerable to the winds, far away from ocean tides in the middle of a Continent. He found just such a site in Verneuk Pan, in the middle of nowhere in South Africa, and went there in 1929 in the hope of winning the land speed record back. It was a failure that convinced him to return to Daytona Beach to achieve four new records from 1931 to 1935.

Campbell aired a different opinion of the beach when he spoke at the reunion of Daytona Beach VIPs and managers of the chamber of commerce, which had financed the Speed Trials and paid his expenses. He was the guest speaker at the dinner organized by the city Kiwanis Club on Tuesday, February 14.[39]

After standing to attention at the door whilst the band in the room struck up the British national anthem, "God Save the King," he spoke about the many niceties he had received since his arrival in town. He gave his assurance that he would take home positive impressions of the beach as the best available site for the land speed record.

Mr. Hammond, a wise PR man, had briefed him on the right things to say.

Later on, after the third return from Daytona Beach, the third record, and the third pot of gold received from the municipality and the local organizing bodies, Malcolm Campbell became a champion of American sportsmanship at home.

Addressing a British audience in 1932 he was brave enough to declare: "No nation in the world had been as grossly misunderstood by the ordinary man in the street in England as had America. They believed that Americans were not good sportsmen, and were prone to boasting, but those who have visited in America have found that no finer people existed. A spirit of sportsmanship second to none in the world exists in America."

He concluded his speech urging "a country-wide attempt to foster friendship between the two countries by dispersal of the misunderstandings such as those he had discovered and by conversion of the British press to a more favorable attitude toward American life."[40]

One is left wondering how surprising it was that Malcolm Campbell was not appointed honorary citizen or goodwill ambassador of the United States.

14

The land speed record was a matter of British national pride. A Briton holding the record affirmed the superior technology and engineering of a country that, despite being the nineteenth-century birthplace of the Industrial Revolution, was now slowly sliding behind in the circle of top industrial economies.

Britain still had the largest and most far-reaching empire, had won the Great War, and was the leader in many sports apart from motor racing. British cars were poor competition against French and Italian cars: they were distant followers in Grand Prix racing (the one exception being Segrave winning the 1923 Grand Prix de l'ACF in a Sunbeam) and had Le Mans as the key option to win endurance races. Minor races limited to club or domestic racing were staged at Brooklands. The land speed record was the main source of global glory and visibility.

Malcolm Campbell and Henry Segrave were the heroes of motoring, examples for kids and models for adults who saw the automobile as an aspirational, expensive, and hard-to-get objective.

Henry Segrave was the first man to exceed the 200 mph speed "barrier" in 1927 at Daytona Beach. The performance so impressed Sir Charles Wakefield, a wealthy British industrialist, that he established an award for the record holder. He was the founder and owner of Castrol, then and still today the leading producer of lubricants for motors.

In tune with the times, the Wakefield Trophy was a gold-plated sculpture of the Goddess of Speed. According to period sources it was worth about 1,000 guineas (i.e., 1,000 pounds and 1,000 shillings), a highly significant figure. The challenge trophy was to be given to the National Automobile Club of the record holder's country. It was complemented by a sum of £1,000 to be awarded to the record holder each year until 1930.

No mention of the cash award has been found after 1930. The Wakefield Trophy remained in the UK from 1929 until 1963: the land speed record was a British-only business. The trophy was auctioned by Christie's in London on December 3, 2002, and sold for £39,950.

We might assume that Malcolm Campbell and Henry Segrave were the sole recipients of the cash prize. Their autobiographies and period media didn't mention the subject, perhaps considering it too vulgar in a time of highly controlled communication.

Instead the U.S. media were freer and more open to all facets of the news business, including the harsh ones. In early February 1928 an Associated Press dispatch from Indianapolis was published in Daytona Beach on the eve of the Speed Trials where Malcolm Campbell would have been one of the contenders for the land speed record. Bill Sturm, Frank Lockhart's manager and PR man, attacked the rules of the Wakefield Trophy as unfair as it was awarded only to the first driver to win the record.

He explained that, as a courtesy to the foreign guest, Campbell would be the first to run on the beach during the Speed Trials. Should he take the record he would have won the trophy and the cash awards even though Lockhart had beaten him a few minutes later. He closed his remarks: "In all fairness the prizes should go to the man making the fastest record-breaking time during the event."[41]

15

Campbell was too bored, feeling like a prisoner in the Ridgewood Hotel whilst rain was pouring down and a westerly wind blew on the wet sand. It was worse than at Pendine. Furthermore, the surface was roughened by ridges and covered by sharp fragments of shells.

Blue Bird was ready to run.

Campbell had come to Florida biased by British prejudices and unfriendly stories about the natives on the other side of the Atlantic. The words he had spoken the night before at the Kiwanis Club were just a display of public relations skill.

Someone in London had warned him about possible sabotage of Blue Bird to give an unfair advantage to domestic competitors. Rumors, nonsense perhaps, yet Campbell decided that every night two team members had to sleep in the garage to guard Blue Bird. It was an accommodation worse than the one readied for them on their arrival in Daytona Beach: in Leo Villa's memoirs he wrote that it was a cubicle above the garage—small, dirty, and full of flies and other pests.[42]

The forced inactivity led Campbell to forget his image of a British gentleman who was a welcomed (and handsomely paid) guest of Daytona Beach. He aired his contempt for the site and the beach: "They told me that it was much better than that."

On Thursday, February 16, AAA officials warned him that the beach was in awful condition, yet if he waited a few days it would have improved a lot. It was the eve of the official opening of the Speed Trials, and the weather was clearing, despite a short downpour at dawn.

Campbell brought the car to the beach. He was eager to drive it for the first trial run. He told the AAA officials to have the timing system checked and ready even though he didn't want to go for the record. He wanted to know the real performance and to get additional data to check against the instrument readings.[43]

The city police had cleared the beach, deploying their usual efficiency. A large crowd was watching from the dunes: they were looking for an adrenalin-fueled show by the British speed champ.

Police officers, riding their powerful motorcycles, exchanged a few words with Campbell whilst he was waiting for the signal to go and Blue Bird was readied without its tailfin and the discs over the front wheels. Under chief Guy Hurd, policemen said something more than the usual dull words of goodwill. They pointed to their common origins. As Campbell wrote, many spoke about ancestors coming from Birmingham, Liverpool, London, and the whole of Ireland.[44]

Campbell, encouraged by the reminders of home and ignoring warnings of the danger of running on such a rough beach, climbed into the cockpit of Blue Bird and, whilst waiting for the engine to warm up, exchanged the ritual

The Blue Bird reached Daytona Beach on February 11 after crossing the ocean in a waterproof crate chained to the deck of the liner *Berengaria*: it was too large to fit through the hatches. It was carried to Florida by boat and truck. The weather in Daytona Beach was awful, yet a few photo ops were possible to please the crowd and the media, who were pressing to watch the new British wonder car. Here it is in one of its possible trims: without discs over the front wire wheels, made by Rudge-Whitworth, and without the tailfin.

propitious words with Leo Villa and Joe Coe. Then he set off southwards with the wind now blowing from the northeast, the right quarter to smooth and dry the sand in a few hours. But the sand was still rough and wet.

Blue Bird immediately displayed troublesome directional stability. Campbell wrote that he had to wrestle with the car to keep on a straight course: "As the speed mounted, Blue Bird seems to become alive and terribly strong. I had to fight against a tendency to snake from side to side, clinging to the steering wheel with all my strength."[45]

David McDonald confirmed: "It was snaking alarmingly."[46] The steering felt much heavier than in the 1927 car: Campbell later identified the source of the problem as a depression behind the front wheels due to the small fairings building up pressure on the top of the tires and increasing the load. In today's terminology, he discovered the downforce by the top of the front wheels when air is pushed upwards.

The gear lever was very difficult to move, and he had to use both hands to shift into top gear—a highly dangerous move. Such problems were to be expected on the maiden run of a new car: they would be easily fixed by the usual fine-tuning.

The roughness of the sand was to be expected, too, despite Campbell trying to ignore it. When running at about 210 mph (according to the rev-counter; the actual speed was estimated to be 180 mph), Blue Bird hit three very close bumps. The car lost adherence, and all four wheels jumped for about 30 feet over the sand, as it was measured shortly after. When it came down again on the sand it started to skid. Campbell managed to correct it and got the car back onto the right course, carrying on until its regular stop.

The police chief was on the beach close to the scene of the jump and skid and was reported as saying: "That Englishman performed a miracle by keeping the car under control. Can't imagine how a fellow can have the presence of mind under such startling conditions."[47]

The story in *The Daytona Beach News-Journal* added a few words from Campbell himself: "When a torrent of sand rushed up from the cockpit almost completely smothering me, I knew that the Blue Bird had been disabled."

When the car touched the sand again the transmission shaft was pushed upwards, hitting the driver's seat above it and delivering a severe blow to the driver's spine. Shock absorbers were broken, and the rear springs were so badly damaged that the rear of the body was touching the ground, having lost its five inches of ground clearance. Sand entered the cockpit due to the floorpan being ripped off, torn away, and crushed by the rear wheels. Leo Villa and other team members were in a car following Blue Bird at a distance and rescued the wreck.

Campbell suffered a seriously hurt spine and was limping badly when he got out of the car. His faith in the Daytona Beach sand strip suffered another, heavier blow. It wasn't the proper day for the maiden run, which had nearly ended in disaster.

The car was towed back to the garage, and the team immediately started to fix everything, asking local mechanics and panel beaters to lend a helping hand.

The rear end of Blue Bird after it landed on the sand following the skid and jump into the air on the February 16 run. The tail is touching the ground due to broken suspension. A section of the displaced floorpan is visible under the body. Note the side radiators built by Fairey Aviation Company at a cost of £450. Having been proved useless, they were later sold for scrap for £5.

A big job was awaiting them in the coming days to get the car ready again for the weekend.

If weather and sand would allow a new run.

16

Arthur Means, head of the AAA officials and assistant secretary of the contest board, wanted the rules to be strictly observed prior to any new record being set and results forwarded to the AIACR for worldwide acknowledgment. One rule in the book dealt with a reversing mechanism being fitted to every vehicle entered in the sanctioned races and events like the Daytona Beach Speed Trials—a stupid rule (when was a speed record ever set in reverse gear?), but a rule written to be complied with worldwide.

Jim White had ignored it since the early design of the Triplex, which had no gearshift. When he presented the car in Daytona Beach it was firmly rejected by Arthur Means: no reverse mechanism, no timed record.

White replied in his signature bullish way that he had not one but three reverse systems ready. In the meantime he asked for official timing. Immediately after the run, during the high tide period, he would install the reverse motion system. In less than three hours.

The dispute surfaced in the local daily under the promising headline: "White And A.A.A. Agree On Device Triplex To Race." Like most words written about the Triplex, these were much too optimistic.[48]

Jim White declared that he was in Daytona Beach at the invitation of the chamber of commerce and the municipality to run for the record without ever having asked for AAA sanction. He repeated his position in the *Motor Age* feature article. It is therefore a distortion by the British media, reprinted later by many authors, that the Triplex was "disqualified" in the February trials.[49] The truth is that the AAA and White ignored each other when the Triplex ran on the beach.

Two out of the three reverse mechanism systems didn't work. They were based on auxiliary electric motors acting directly on the rear axle. Neither

The Triplex on the beach to demonstrate the working of the reverse-motion system to AAA officials. Once again, the impression of sand in the tire treads shows that motion was achieved by friction of the engine-driven rear wheels on the lower-mounted free wheels. Only half of the tread of the former shows any sign of sand, i.e., friction: the demo was very short indeed. The extra wheels had to be removed prior to starting a run.

reached the compression of the three engines despite very high final drive ratios and a huge powerful battery pack in the empty space on the driver's side: the Triplex didn't move backwards at all.

The third and last attempt was quite crude and beyond any reasonable interpretation of the rules: two free-moving wheels were temporarily mounted on the frame rails just in front of the rear wheels. When they grazed the slightly higher rear ones, by friction through the tires they managed to move the vehicle backwards for a few inches. No additional engine was needed.

Photos of the car show the solution, yet without either official statements by White or detailed descriptions of the features of the car, period newsmen and later authors mixed up the devices and wrote about the use of an electric motor acting on the additional pair of wheels, something mechanically impossible.

White strongly believed that the device complied with the rules. Just after the demonstration to the AAA officials he intended to remove the extra pair of wheels before starting a record run.

The controversy carried on until Wednesday, February 22, awaiting the final answer by Joe Dawson, head of the AAA technical board (and the winner of the 1912 Indianapolis 500). He signed the statement that the device did not fulfill the AAA requirement for a "motor-driven reversing mechanism."[50]

White shot back that the Triplex was now fully compliant with the rules and that it would be officially timed by the AAA on the runs on the beach as soon as the weather and sand allowed.

The AAA judges denied official timing of whatever runs the Triplex made on the beach.

17

Now it was his turn.

He didn't care about the ill-fated date of Friday, February 17. Frank Lockhart was ready to test the theories applied in designing and building the Blackhawk for the beach runs. The long-awaited moment arrived at the end of five months of breathless work and the 10-lap shakedown on the Indianapolis Speedway on Sunday, January 12.

Frank Lockhart had managed to share his adventure with many parts and component suppliers, financers, and, first and foremost, Fred Moskovics, boss of the Stutz Company, who took care of the financial side as head of the Lockhart Syndicate, established to fund and manage the Blackhawk program. Frank made the best of his fame, his long list of wins, and his friendly, no-nonsense, open approach to interpersonal interaction.

Moskovics offered Lockhart the Indianapolis facilities of the Stutz Company, including a secluded workshop, to build, assemble, and finish the Blackhawk. He took care to ensure that nobody and nothing from the outside world could hamper the work of the small team. In return he asked that the beach car be named after the company's top model: Blackhawk.

The Blackhawk had a 10-lap shakedown on the Indianapolis Speedway on January 12, 1928. Frank Lockhart poses at the wheel. Bill Sturm, at center next to Lockhart wearing a cap, stands among the many onlookers on the cold and humid winter day in Indiana. Ray Splinder is just beyond him, sporting his distinctive bow tie on the white personalized overalls, here covered by an elegant coat (Indianapolis Motor Speedway photo archive).

John and Zenas Weisel, both young graduate engineers, developed into detailed drawings the ideas and solutions sketched by Lockhart, who was a mechanical genius yet lacked the technical education to transfer his ideas and solutions into manufacturing proposals.[51]

William "Bill" Sturm, appointed as program manager, dealt with the PR and communications job. Thanks to his great professionalism, he obtained excellent results in terms of visibility. In 1920s America an effective PR and communications program was already an essential tool for the success of any project, brand, or enterprise.

The beach car was the synthesis of the whole life and career of Frank Lockhart. For it he put aside track racing, despite the wins that had provided the money needed to partially finance the program. He was forced to break his friendly partnership with Ernie Olson, Jimmy Murphy's riding mechanic in his historic win in the 1921 Grand Prix de l'ACF, who had been acting as his manager. The racing program drafted by Olson also included entry in the 1927 Italian Grand Prix, a sort of European show to gain additional fame and money.

In December 1927 Eugene Pulliam, editor-in-chief of the *Daytona Beach News-Journal*, the city daily, went to Indianapolis on behalf of the Daytona Beach

Stutz provided Lockhart with full assistance to build the beach car at their Indianapolis plant and also gave him a Blackhawk Speedster tourer as a personal vehicle. Lockhart is seated at the wheel, having combed his rebellious hair for the promotional photograph. Fred Moskovics is standing alongside the car. The Mason name appears on the side of the front tire: they were suppliers to factory-built production cars (courtesy of the National Automotive History Collection, Detroit Public Library).

Chamber of Commerce to check the progress of work on the beach car and to certify Moskovics's and Lockhart's commitment to getting the Blackhawk ready to go to Florida by early February 1928. Lockhart was the star of the Speed Trials: without him the entire organizational effort and huge expense of running the event would have been for naught.[52]

With the assistance of Bill Sturm in the background, Moskovics spoke to the *Indianapolis News*:

> We have been aiding Lockhart in every way possible. We became interested in his proposition about the time of the Indianapolis 500-mile race and we believe that if anyone can bring this record back to America he can. Our interest was attracted primarily—aside from Lockhart's well-known mechanical and driving ability—because he proposed to make his record attempt with a car void of all freakish features and one which mechanically is built like a standard automobile. He expects to accomplish the great speed necessary with a small car scientifically designed and almost perfectly streamlined.
>
> Lockhart's calculations, reinforced by those of airplane wind tunnel experts from the Army aircraft service and civilian aircraft authorities, indicated that with this little car he can easily exceed the speed made by the 2,760 cubic inch, 1,000 horse-power Sunbeam, which then held the record.[53]

Beyond the closed doors of the Stutz workshop, Jean Marcenac, Myron Stevens, Floyd Dreyer, Ray Splinder, Jimmy Lee, and Bud Miller were working with

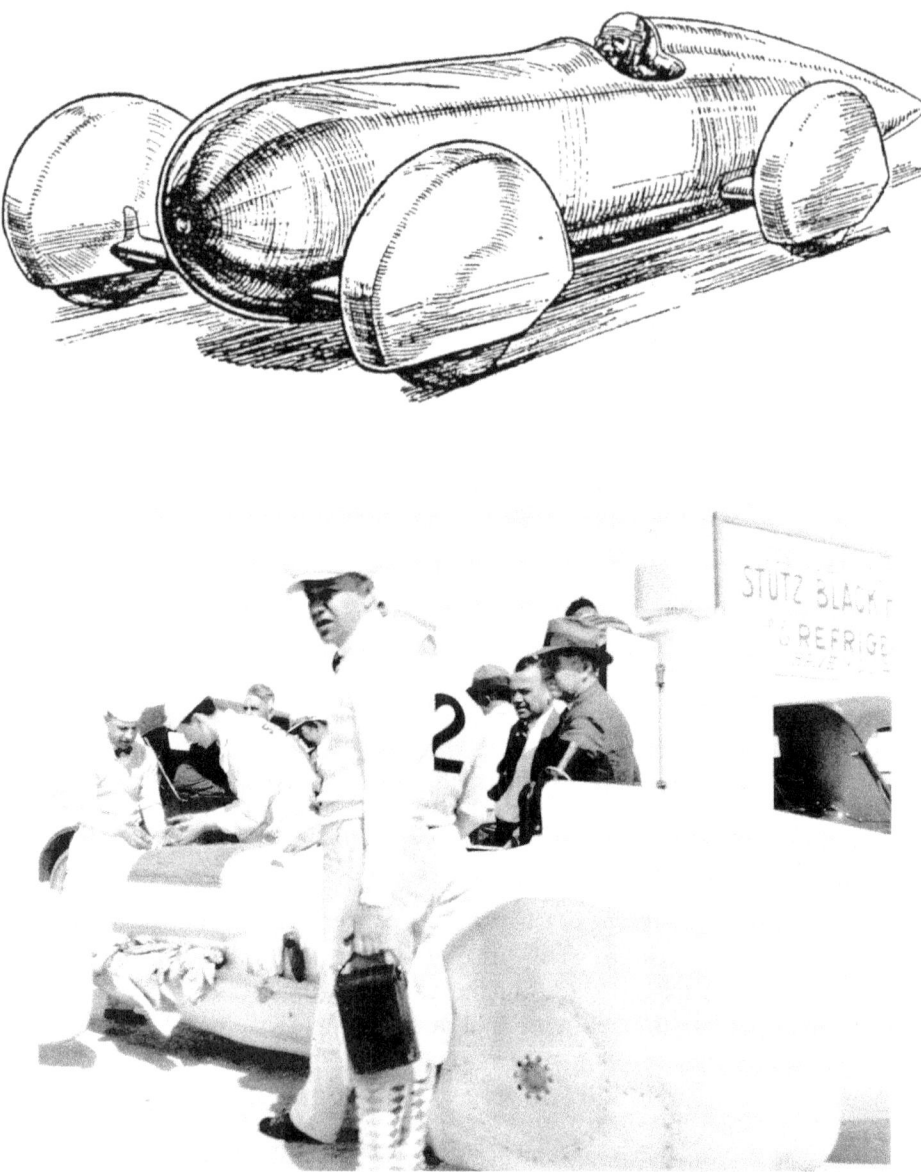

Top: A quite precise advance sketch of the Blackhawk was published in London by *The Autocar* in the January 13, 1928 issue—only by sheer coincidence on the day after the official presentation and shakedown of the beach car at the Indianapolis Speedway. The caption mentioned the "torpedo-shaped" body and was grossly wrong in claiming that it was "fabric-covered" (*The Autocar* magazine). *Bottom:* Readying the Blackhawk prior to a run on the beach, Bill Sturm, as always, takes center stage in the photograph, wearing his preferred plus fours and checkered socks. He partially obscures Frank Lockhart in one of the very few known images of him from the back. We don't know whether the number 2 on his T-shirt was his racing number in the AAA championship races or the logo of the Daytona Beach company that provided ice cubes with which to fill the cooling tank. Certainly, the company didn't miss any opportunity to promote itself and its GE-made refrigerators. A guy from the company helps one of the mechanics (Jimmy Lee, perhaps) to fill the tank. Note the shrouds to protect the air intake and exhaust ports from blowing sand.

Lockhart around the clock. Bill Sturm had the right of free access to find new and intriguing stories for the media. In the press releases, the cost of the vehicle grew: the Blackhawk cost $75,000, then $100,000, and soon it was billed as "the most expensive automobile ever built."[54]

Lee and Marcenac went to Florida in February together with the draughtsman Splinder. The minimal team was completed by Bill Sturm and his wife, Teressa.

The days spent waiting for good weather and a smooth beach gave a well-deserved respite to Lockhart and the small team after the hard work of the previous months. Yet nobody was in Florida for a winter retreat to relax.

They became impatient waiting to enter the beach. In a regular track event Lockhart could have taken advantage of his competitors' problems: Campbell with the Blue Bird in distress, standing in the garage to have the damage fixed, White out of the competition due to the AAA's ban.

The beach was very rough, and a westerly wind blew on the morning of February 17 when mechanics topped up the fuel tank with 40 gallons, then put 75 pounds of ice into the front tank and warmed up the engine.

Lockhart told the AAA judges and timekeepers, many of whom he knew well from his Indianapolis 500 days, that he was only going to have a trial run with no timing. He started southwards with the wind. The chronicle reported a 102.318 mph speed, yet we don't know if that was timed electrically or manually.

Image from dead front shows the reduced cross section of the Blackhawk, narrower at the bottom, and also the limited height of the body. Even the front axle fairings are airfoil-shaped to avoid lift. The two steering arms, without any cross bracing, have a streamlined front edge. On a cold day Lockhart reckoned it was better to wear a sweater, the same one he wore in a photograph taken when he congratulated Malcolm Campbell after the record run. The photograph could therefore have been taken on February 19, 1928.

Lockhart drove back to the north end of the course and stopped in front of the timing stand. He was engulfed by a swarm of journalists, photographers, and cameramen pressing him loudly to issue a statement, any statement.

They just gave him enough time to jump out of the cockpit and say that he had only wound the engine up to 3,000 rpm, less than half the maximum allowed, 7,000/7,500 rpm. He would go faster when the sand was smoother.

The hacks invented the story that he kept the car running "under cover" to hide its true performance.

The Blackhawk received an odd nickname with a maritime flavor: "Sand crab," a small crustacean zipping around the beaches.

18

The show was suffering. The big mid–February 1928 Speed Trials were appealing to fewer people than the previous year when Henry O'Neal de Hane Segrave, the British driver unknown to the Americans, had crossed the ocean to become the first man in the world to go faster than 200 mph.

Segrave was alone on the beach during that week in March 1927. His car only ran three times, and in the final run, on Tuesday, March 29, at around 9:30 a.m., he reached the new land speed record: 203.792 mph over the flying mile.

On Thursday, March 24, 1927, the day of Segrave's first run in the Sunbeam, about 10,000 people crowded the dunes to witness an exceptional event, duly pumped up by the media. And it was simply an untimed trial run very early in the morning, at 6:30 a.m. On Tuesday, March 29, the day of the record, *The Daytona Beach News-Journal* reported that there were some 15,000 people along the nine miles of the course on the southern section of the beach.

Cyril Posthumus, who wasn't in Daytona Beach, doubled the attendance in his biography of Segrave.[55]

Henry O'Neal de Hane Segrave (Baltimore, Maryland, September 22, 1896–Lake Windermere, UK, June 13, 1930) ranks amongst the top British racing drivers of the 1920s. He had the distinction of being the first British driver to win a major international Grand Prix, the GP de l'ACF in France, driving a British Sunbeam car, in 1923. He rivaled Malcolm Campbell for the land speed record, which he won three times, raising the record from 152 mph to 231 mph between 1926 and 1929. Receiving a knighthood in 1929, he switched to the water speed record, which he won at 98.76 mph. Alas, the final record was achieved on the day he died.

A journalist who was on the spot, Paul Ellis, wrote a long story for the local daily three years later.[56] He opened by remembering the firefighting depot siren on the mainland sounding the agreed signal, meaning that the land speed record day, March 29, 1927, had dawned.

Police officers cleared the beach, checking that neither car nor person hit the timing devices at the edges of the measured mile. They wanted to avoid a replay of what had happened on the March 24 trial runs, when the timing system recorded speeds from 166 to 280 mph due to the mix of signals from the wires hit by careless people and cars just before and after Segrave's run.

The AAA officials couldn't separate the correct signal so, to be on the safe side, they told Segrave the lowest recorded speed. The driver had seen a figure on the rev-counter corresponding to 180 mph, much faster than the 166 mph approved and released by the timekeepers. He feared that wheelspin was so severe that the engines over-revved and that, as a consequence, the available power was not transmitted to the wheels. He then decided to lower the final drive ratio. Such an erroneous decision lowered the maximum performance well below the design speed.[57]

Again to Tuesday, March 29, 1927. Police closed the coastal avenue, which was already clogged with thousands of cars. Paul Ellis described the scene in light, vivid, and modern prose:

> They came in big cars and little ones, old ones and new. They came on bicycles and on foot. A few rode horses. They streamed across the bridges and along the streets leading to the beach.
>
> Women trudged, their skirts flapping in the smart wind, pushing perambulators. Boys came running and whooping, forgetful of the school hour not far off.
>
> Within an hour a motley crowd peopled the dunes. From near the pier, along the length of the beach clear to the inlet they stood or sat. Thousands of men, women and children, quiet, intent, waiting. America's worship of speed was having the day.
>
> Then came Segrave with his Sunbeam shining red in the brilliant sunlight.[58]

They witnessed a leap forward in the history of speed: they watched the first man—and the first vehicle—to exceed 200 mph on land.

In February 1928 it was a different story. People were less interested and eager to share despite the higher media pressure and the much-publicized presence of three contenders for the land speed record, two of them Americans. The event had been designed and scheduled with a crescendo of side runs in a full week of speed, show, and pumping adrenaline.

The record trials for stock cars on the opening days, February 15 and 16, failed to meet people's expectations. The stock cars were split into three classes according to sale price: less than $1,000, between $1,000 and $2,000, and over $2,000. Incidentally an icy reaction had to be expected from the people: one could see such cars every day on America's open roads. Why would someone rush to the Daytona Beach dunes to watch them chasing a self-proclaimed record speed?

Even less exciting was the race for gentleman drivers in their own cars, scheduled for Thursday, February 15. The presence of Edward Armstrong, Daytona Beach mayor, amongst the entrants was not enough even for the local daily to publish the results.

Henry Segrave in Daytona Beach with the 1927 Sunbeam 1000 HP land speed record vehicle, the first one to exceed 200 mph. The car, designed by Louis Coatalen, was powered by two Sunbeam Matabele engines used by airships during the Great War. The body was the first to fully enclose the wheels, yet that resulted in added weight, hotter tires, greater sensitivity to side winds, and "breathing" difficulties for the engines, one in front of and the other behind the driver.

The organizers agreed on the proposal by Mr. James T. Nelson, city manager, to sell entry tickets to the dunes on Sunday, February 19 for 50 cents. The decision aimed to boost attendance on a day when, with places of work and the shops closed, every Daytona Beach resident could watch the record runs together with the thousands of people coming from outside the city.

It was an easy task to place ticket counters on the seaward side of the bridges from the mainland and the connections to Atlantic Avenue. For the first and only time in the history of land speed records, the trials became like a closed-circuit race, with a selected group of entries and an entry ticket.[59]

19

Nothing significant was happening after the test trial by Campbell on Thursday, February 16, 1928. The runs of the stock cars on the rough beach were far from providing exciting news stories. The weather was bad, yet the weekend promised a soothing northeast wind. The key act of the Speed Trials could, at last, take the stage: the direct challenge of the three contenders for the land speed record.

The Daytona Beach News-Journal printed huge headlines on the front pages, a few short news items, and impressively large photos to keep public interest in the event warm and lively. In the February 16 issue, the story of the ruinous run by Malcolm Campbell was accompanied by a large photo of the Blackhawk with Lockhart at the wheel, the caption saying that the car was ready to go for the record. It was reported to have been built "at an immense cost of money and pain."

Once again, the local daily adhered to the old journalistic rule that every bit of domestic news deserves more coverage than a story about foreign lands, people, or cars. Or records.

Another—smaller—headline was cunningly tuned to the unexpressed feelings of the average American reader about their distant cousins over the water: "Son of English Lord Pulls for Campbell to Win." The son mentioned in the headline was Ernest Lewis, Campbell's partner in the car sales business in South Kensington, London. He was portrayed as the son of Sir Edward Lewis, said to be a member of the House of Lords (wrong: the nomination was only available to those who possessed earldoms) and also the wealthy president of the Bermuda Steamship Line. Neither of those descriptions was actually true, but they succeeded in impressing the Daytoner man-in-the-street.

Mr. Lewis reportedly wanted Campbell to win the new record and was quoted repeating British visitors' praise of Daytona Beach's hospitality and oceanfront real estate as "the best in the world."[60]

Nothing new was happening.

It became increasingly difficult to build the expectation of something great and exciting. On February 17, the local daily in its regular afternoon edition launched as front page news of the day the already old story of the day before: "Campbell Speeds 193 M.P.H. Today." It was a strange story dealing with an obsolete event—and containing a big error: the speed recorded by Campbell was 180 mph, not 193 mph. This error was quite unusual, because the daily's past reporting on the Speed Trials always displayed clean and precise professionalism and respect for the true facts.

On the morning of February 17, Malcolm Campbell was confined to the garage of the Ridgewood Hotel to supervise the repairs on Blue Bird, damaged in the run the day before. The daily wrongly postponed the run to the day after, February 17, and deemed it "a success." Maybe the unknown editor thought of it as the introduction to the astonishing (!?!) news that Campbell, as soon as he returned to the hotel after the run, had received a phone call from Henry Segrave in the offices of the *London Daily News*.

Those were the big stories of the day. A trans-oceanic phone call deserved a front-page story in 1928. It was a difficult and costly exercise due to the limited bandwidth of the undersea cables and the vagaries of radio links.

The dialogue, as reported by the daily, was short and superficial. Segrave started the call by giving his greetings to Campbell and his own American friends. He asked, "What do you think of Americans?" Campbell answered with equally commonplace words: "The best sportsmen I have ever met." Such words buried forever any suspicions of the dreaded American sabotage of Blue Bird.

The final question was focused on Frank Lockhart, who was seen in the UK as the prime contender. Campbell: "He is a brilliant engineer. And his car is beyond comprehension."[61]

A few days were left to pass before the actual run, which would prove whether the words were truly praise or whether there was hidden doubt about the car's layout.

The front page would soon show the answer.

20

Malcolm Campbell, the protagonist, didn't get the story quite right. He wrote in his autobiography that Blue Bird was ready to go on the beach again on Saturday, February 18, prevented only by bad weather in the form of rain and wind from the wrong direction. He added that he personally made the decision to go for the new run early on Saturday morning, as soon as the rain clouds had blown away.[62]

Such a narrative is coherent with the man as depicted by many people who were close to him. The autobiography was published in 1935, seven years after the events took place.

David McDonald, who was present at the records, wrote about him: "He was often in an impatient mood, sometimes irritable, rushing always to start anything."

Paul Ellis, the newsman who met him in Daytona Beach, noted: "He had an indomitable will to do things his own way."[63]

Campbell wrote that it was his own decision to ask the AAA officials for picketing the sand, measuring of the course, and installing the timing devices on Sunday, February 19. He added: "There was no suggestion of making an attempt upon the record, but I told the mechanics that I would put my foot hard down if there was the least chance of reaching record speed."[64] These ambiguous words, far from the truth, can only be explained by referring to the character of the man as sketched in the above statements by third parties.

Sunday, February 19 was the key day of the Speed Trials. As said, popular fees (50 cents) had been established to access the dunes: more than 10,000 people took advantage of the discounted price and crowded on the dunes.[65]

The beach had been busy since first light, when at low tide the team of electricians, headed by George Van Deusen of the Gee Vee Electric Company based in Daytona Beach, rushed to install the timing wires, linking them to the timekeepers' stand, and to lay phone lines to the checkpoints located at every mile of the course. Other workers had thrust pickets into the sand on the sea side and positioned poles carrying large banners at the start and finish lines of the measured mile.

The whole morning was dedicated to stock cars. Tom Rooney drove his Stutz Blackhawk at 97.750 mph, a new record for the class.

The organizers had summoned the three contenders to the beach: Campbell, Lockhart, and Ray Keech in his Triplex. They knew that the Triplex hadn't been accepted by the AAA and therefore that none of its runs would be timed. They relied on the appeal of having two American contenders for the land speed record irrespective of the AAA decision.

Before Sunday the three contenders had agreed, with confirmation from the organizers, on how to split the afternoon time, bearing in mind the tide and amount of daylight in the winter: Campbell—the foreign guest—first, Lockhart second, and Keech last.

As it happened only Campbell did a record run.[66] Lockhart's Blackhawk was still slowed down by carburation problems: the engine misfired due to the inadequate flow of air through the two holes mistakenly opened flush with the engine cover, just behind the turbulence generated by the intercooler fins.

The Daytona Beach daily didn't record Lockhart runs that day. *The Indianapolis Star* published an AP wire from Daytona Beach on February 20, reporting on Campbell and adding that Lockhart did two trial runs at 181 mph average. The driver was reported as saying he wouldn't try for the record before the next day.[67]

The two dailies were unanimous about the Triplex: the car didn't move at all because, when its turn came, the light was fading and the tide rolling in to flood the course.

The words above show how, after many years, the cross-referencing of available sources reveals the true facts, which the protagonists told either differently or deliberately untruthfully.

Campbell was true to the facts when he wrote:

> The knowledge that thousands of people were on the scene made it very hard to wait quietly for ideal conditions, because I now felt that everything was right with the car [this is untrue, as we'll see]. When we set out for the beach there were heavy clouds and a strong cross-wind was blowing from the north; this would be behind me during the first run and would help the car, but it would be against Blue Bird on the return journey. I received the word that I could start as soon as I liked. Villa and the other mechanics looked around the car for the last time, then I sent the machine away. When I left the men behind I had no idea that I was about to face the worst experience of my life.[68]

21

Blue Bird was readied with the smaller tailfin and the discs over the front wheels. They hoped to improve the longitudinal stability, building on the experience of February 16.

It wasn't enough against the northeasterly side wind. Campbell wrote in *The Motor* article: "When Blue Bird took me over the measured mile she was a live, strong and powerful adversary. I literally had to fight for control. I am no physical weakling and it required all my power to keep Blue Bird to an even course. The wheel had to be gripped."[69]

Let us recall the words of the protagonists and spectators.

Malcolm Campbell: "One of the difficulties with Blue Bird, and which I had discovered during the first test run, was in changing gear, because it was impossible to completely free the clutch. When I shifted into top gear, at about 150 mph, it was as much as I could do to ram the gear home; the top gear dogs kept kicking against one another and the gear lever had to be forced in by sheer strength. The

Blue Bird in the record runs on Sunday, February 19, 1928, the key date of the Speed Trials, watched by tens of thousands of spectators, lured by the low price (50 cents) for entry tickets to the dunes and the show promised by the fastest vehicles in the world. Blue Bird was set up with discs covering the front wheels and a small tailfin, covered by the side radiators. The northeasterly wind upset the runs, and Malcolm Campbell had to wrestle with the steering wheel to keep the car on a straight course.

car went away well and I changed into top safely, then devoted myself to handling the machine and that was not easy."[70]

David McDonald: "Blue Bird was snaking in an alarming way."[71]

Paul Ellis: "His unhappy experience on February 16 on the beach had made him wary of the water edge and soft sand. So he drove high up on the beach, almost too high."[72] The lateral component of the tailwind pushed the vehicle far away from the water's edge. The snaking, impossible to damp, put Blue Bird off the optimum course.

Malcolm Campbell: "I had to wrestle with the car to maintain a straight course, fighting against a tendency to snake from side to side, clinging to the steering wheel with all my strength. Struggling to control the enormous power of the car, I had to concentrate everything upon physical effort. There was no time, no thought for anything, except to use all the strength that I had in fighting the machine. As I neared the start of the mile, I glanced at the revolution counter. It was showing 210 mph and, with my foot hard down on the throttle pedal, I went into the measured mile."[73]

Paul Ellis: "On the final trip south the right rear wheel hit a bump. We heard the crash, saw Campbell's head pop out of the cockpit, saw him duck back in, swipe his goggles back in place and straighten out the bounding Blue Bird, all in a split second."[74]

Malcolm Campbell: "The impact shot me upwards out of my seat and into the truly tremendous airstream which rushed past the cockpit. The air felt solid. It tore my goggles from my eyes and forced them down on my face. I was exposed only for the fraction of a second, but the wind seems [sic] as it would lift me from the car. I believe I should have gone, but for the tenacious grip that I had on the rim of the steering wheel. I dropped on the seat again, but my foot had lost pressure on the throttle pedal. The engine, which had been pulling at the moment we hit the bump, now exerted a braking effect (because the throttle has been partially closed) and the machine pitched into a skid, shooting into a great stretch of soft sand. I imagined that my end had come."[75]

The Autocar: "The sudden change from full to closed throttle is in any case enough to make a car extremely unsteady at high speed. In all Campbell's racing experience no moment was fraught with greater possibilities than this, and it looked almost as though the car had got itself out of the trouble by a miracle."[76]

David McDonald: "Experienced road ace that he was, he did not try to correct the skid quickly, which would surely have turned the car over. Instead he was able, by superb driving ability, to bring the car under control after a mile or so."[77]

Dorothy Campbell, 24 years later: "I was sitting in the official's stand with the Mayor of Daytona Beach, Edward Armstrong, and a party of friends when Blue Bird came through the measured mile at well over 200 miles an hour. She seems to be going magnificently and we were beginning to congratulate ourselves on what looked like the certainty of a new record, when we saw the car leap into the air, Malcolm thrown high out of the driving seat, and the car plunge into a terrific skid which took it into soft sand bordering the actual course. We could see the car, almost obscured by a flying cloud of sand, skidding wildly while Malcolm could be dimly seen struggling to regain control of the car which still seemed to be travelling at a terrific pace. It seemed as certain as anything can be that here was the end of all things. That he could come out of it alive seemed to me impossible."[78]

(Note that Lady Campbell uses "she" when mentioning the Blue Bird.)

The Daytona Beach News-Journal in the news of the day: "Mrs. Campbell watching the epochal run from the grandstand covered her face with her hands not to remove them until friends told her the run was completed safely."[79]

The Indianapolis Star from the AP correspondent's wire: "Mrs. Campbell witnessing the epochal run from the grandstand, gasped audibly when she saw her husband's car strike the bump, and she covered her face with her hands. Fearing that a serious accident had happened, Mrs. Campbell did not look up until friends told her that her husband had completed his run safely."[80]

We understand that a wife can see even with closed eyes.

We also understand that Malcolm Campbell was brave, too brave, well beyond the boundaries of his claimed attention to detail, maybe to be rated more a reckless than a careful driver. He knew well that the gearshift (designed by Joseph Maina) had some intrinsic faults preventing its smooth operation, he had no real-life experience of the car's aerodynamics and stability, and he didn't know the effects of the wind and the coefficient of adhesion of the sand. The soft sand just above the course, opposite the water's edge, was an obvious fact to be dealt with.

He had driven Blue Bird only once, at low speed and with a disastrous outcome, yet he pushed hard on the throttle to fulfill the expectations of the crowd lining the beach.

He learned that the land speed record business is not show business.

22

Campbell reached the southern end of the course. As David McDonald told it: "He was exhausted. It was clear to us that he was not relishing the return run over the same course. He looked tired and strained and in no condition for a major effort."[81]

McDonald, the Dunlop man, was at the southern end ready to change wheels/tires prior to the return run. What he wrote about Campbell is fiction, a product of a later rethink: he was standing on the sand, and Campbell was shadowed by the high sides of the cockpit. It is impossible not only that they spoke but also that McDonald could have examined Campbell so carefully. We have to note that McDonald's book was written 26 years after Campbell's autobiography and 33 years after the event.

Malcolm Campbell: "The muscles in my arms were wrenched and my whole body felt strained and I was tired. According to the programme I should have halted to change wheels as a safety measure, but I decided not to do this. I knew that if I stopped and got out of the car I should never step into the machine again. Near the waiting mechanics I began to turn, then waved to them and started straight back again."[82]

Dunlop guaranteed a useful life of three minutes for the tires, yet there was an additional margin of possible use with some safety delaying the destruction of the tiny tread, only one millimeter thick.

Campbell took a dangerous risk when he decided to avoid the tire change: by the end of the return run he would have exceeded the three-minute limit.

He wrote in his autobiography:

> I put my foot down and Blue Bird gathered speed once more. It was only when I came to change into top gear that I discovered just how much that first run had sapped my strength. I could not get the gear in and, travelling at 150 mph, I had to take both hands from the wheel, using the last of my remaining strength to force the gear-lever home. It went in and I snatched at the wheel, my foot going down on the throttle pedal. The wind was against the car now and this, as the pace rose, tended to make the machine even less tractable than it had been before. I had to fight every yard and it was when I sighted the entrance to the measured mile that I remembered the bump and the soft sand that lay near. This was now just in front of what was now the start of the measured distance. If I hit the bump and if there was another skid I knew that I should not have enough strength to hold Blue Bird, while the skid would send the car towards the sand dunes, the spectators and the cars parked in front of them.

Campbell was running on a lower course than on the first run. He didn't hit the bump again. His words: "I held my breath as the car pitched towards the mile. There was an instant of suspense, then the machine was over the tape, clear of the bump and racing on with everything rushing past me. I now seemed detached. I could hear only the rush of the wind and saw nothing clearly except the far end of the mile."83

Everything went well. Exiting the mile, Campbell gently eased his foot off the throttle and, after some two miles, applied the brakes to bring the car to a stop at the starting place, close to the big pier crossing the beach.

"He was helped out [of the Blue Bird]," as David McDonald told it, "weak and helpless as a child."84

Leo Villa: "When he got out of the cockpit Campbell was badly shaken. He told me that no money in the world would make him attempt another run with the sand in that condition, and what he had to say about the gear change is quite unprintable."85

Campbell: "I felt weak and they helped me out, then came news which was like a tonic. Leaning against the side of the car, finding it hard to stand, I realised that we had accomplished all that we had hoped."86

The timekeepers had reached him, reporting on the official data of the two runs: first run 16.76 seconds, 214.687 mph; return run 18.03 seconds, 199.677 mph; average, 206.956 mph. A new record, 3.16 mph—4.5 percent—faster than Segrave's.

Then came all the cheering, congratulations, handshakes, celebratory photos, and interviews. Frank Lockhart was the first to congratulate him, while he

Just after the record runs, the team celebrated Malcolm Campbell, recovering after being badly shaken by the skid on his first run and from wrestling with the gear lever and steering wheel. When officials reported confirmation of the new 206.956 mph record, he received the news as a tonic and let the celebrations begin. Leo Villa, chief mechanic, is second from the left.

was still in the cockpit. Then, Mayor Armstrong and his wife, Dorothy, came. The siege lasted half an hour.

He told Paul Ellis he felt exhausted and had given everything he could. Then he showed his hands: steady. He was chewing gum: "Ah yes," he said, "I always chew gum when I drive. American gum. I'm very fond of it, you know."[87]

An unusual set of understatements celebrated the new record on the western side of the Atlantic: a British subject, immediately after setting a new land speed record, lauding American chewing gum as the source of his determination in driving at such high speed.

The Daytona Beach News-Journal restricted the news of the record to a single-column headline in the February 20 issue, despite the story being the jewel in the crown of a top event for the town and its citizens.[88] Yet the opening headline on the front page carried the biggest story of the day: "Triplex Driver Scalded by Steam." The daily was published in the afternoon except on Sundays when it went on sale in the morning. A basic rule of journalism is to make the biggest story the news of the day, i.e., the Triplex run. The Campbell record was already a day-old story.

23

There was jubilation on the other side of the water. Praise to the power of British technology, resources, and men. The news reached London almost immediately through the undersea cables. The five-hour time difference between Florida and London meant that the news came too late for the next day's issues of the morning dailies.

It was a different story for the motoring magazines, however: *The Motor* came out with a timely page in the February 28 issue. The headline was full of self-glorification in every letter: "Britain Shows the World. All-British Triumphs on Land and in the Air."[89]

The first part of the article had already been written to glorify the win by Sidney Webster in the S5 Supermarine seaplane in the 1927 Schneider Trophy in Venice, Italy. The lines on Malcolm Campbell were added to celebrate the achievement on land, driving a car powered by the same engine as the Schneider Trophy winner: the Napier Lion "Sprint."

The opener of the text was in tune with the booming headline: "The week which has just passed is one that will stand out in motoring history."

The Autocar was timely, too: in the February 24 issue a muted headline—"Bravo Campbell"—highlighted a feature article heavier on flourishes than on either facts or elegies.[90] The sentence about the already widespread presence of radio sets in British households is interesting to read today: "No British enthusiast hadn't gone in spirit at Ormond Beach, Florida, USA in the last days. It is probable that every reader could tell a detailed and precise narration [of the record runs] based on the news listened to on radio sets in the last weeks."

Motor Sport came a bit later with a short note in the comments page

"Rumblings and Exhaust Notes." The closing lines brimmed with a sense of British superiority: "It is possible, as we go to press, that Campbell may attempt to improve his figures. If so, good luck to him, and may he be able to keep ahead of all Americans and show that whatever else we fail to do we can still pay war debts and drive motor cars."[91]

The umpteenth example of how advertising can distort the facts could be found in a Dunlop ad in *Motor Sport*. The headline spelled Campbell's name as a teaser. The text was—allegedly—a cable the company had received from Campbell on the day after the new record: "The tires, which had a terrible gruelling, finished up absolutely cool: I didn't have to change them between the runs. I just turned round and went straight back across the line [the timing wire]."[92]

Of course, now we well know that it was a different story.

Other ads more accurately praised the Castrol lubricants and Dunlop tires. The latter is interesting as it focuses on British superiority and recalls, in a subtle, quasi-artistic way, the former record by Segrave with Dunlop tires.

Back to the other side of the water, we acknowledge how long-lasting the impressions left by Segrave on the Daytona Beach journalists and citizens were. The February 22 issue of *The Daytona Beach News-Journal* reserved the opening for Segrave: "Builds Car For Beach In Case England Loses—Will Race Motor In Daytona Beach And Boat In Miami In 1929."[93] Maybe it was a dull day for hard news so they opted for a story in the distant future.

The two American contenders had not yet tried to beat Campbell, and the Speed Trials were on

In 1928 advertising was already a reality yet was not so pervasive. Castrol Oil bought a full page in *The Autocar*'s London February 24, 1928, issue to celebrate the use of its lubricants in the new record holder, Blue Bird. A proud British company talking about a British achievement felt obliged the have the Royal Crest on top and to write "All-British Firm" beneath its name. Sir Charles Wakefield, owner of the Castrol Oil Company, was the promoter of the Wakefield Trophy, to be presented to the current land speed record holder.

the eve of the closing day. The daily unveiled the cable received from Segrave: "If Lockhart beats Campbell's record I propose to build a new car right away to attempt to regain the record for England. Preparations are already under way and the car should be ready in eight months. Please cable the full details to whom eventually gets record. Cordially, Segrave."[94]

Once again, we note that the Triplex was ignored, as usual within the British land speed record fraternity, and we can understand that the Golden Arrow program was already under way, despite the initial conditions set by Segrave.

February 22 was a U.S. national holiday, Washington's Birthday, and spectators came by the thousands to the dunes for the record runs. They were fully rewarded by the show.

The Dunlop advert page in *The Autocar*'s London February 24, 1928, issue recalls the "amazing" former land speed record held by Henry Segrave on Dunlop tires and highlights the new record set by Malcolm Campbell: "Still held by Dunlop Tyres." British superiority is further enhanced by the claim "Once again: A British Car and British Tyres!" The tag line sounds quite self-satisfied: "Dunlop—The standard by which all tyres are judged."

24

A record posted, the inevitable next stage is to beat it. Prevented by the rising tide on Sunday, February 19 after Campbell's new record, both Lockhart and White were forced to wait for low tide on Monday, February 20. The morning was for the Triplex (without official timing), the afternoon for Lockhart.

Jim White warned Ray Keech to limit the engine's revs as it would only be a trial run, and not timed by the AAA. The northward run went fine: the motors revved up beautifully and the vehicle showed good stability. The return promised a higher speed thanks to the tailwind. Everything looked good. But looks can be deceiving.

Suddenly a water hose in the front engine split. We don't know if the damage was due to material fatigue or obsolescence. A jet of boiling steam hit the cockpit (no firewall!), and Ray Keech's hip and right leg were scalded. He managed to bring the Triplex to a controlled halt, got out without assistance, and walked to the waiting ambulance, called by the operator at Checkpoint 6.[95]

He was brought to Halifax Hospital, where Dr. Guy Klock found the scalding not to be so severe but, as a cautionary measure, decided to hospitalize him for a few days. Without a driver, the Triplex was definitely out of the quest for the record and was also the reason for the organizers' decision to close the Speed Trials on Thursday, February 23.

Jim White totally disagreed. He declared that within a couple of days he would have his reverse mechanism installed, before a new record run. He forgot his earlier statement that he only needed three hours to install the reverse gear mechanism.[96]

He was completely confident of achieving the new record and shot off another of his bombastic statements, telling the scribblers that the Triplex was doing 253 mph just before the accident. This was fantasy, of course, well beyond the maximum speed possible for the car and way too much faster than Campbell's record.

He added: "We have got a machine here that will make all these boys stand up and take notice. Keech told me after the run that at the speed the motor was making only 2,300 revolutions per minute, while the maximum rating is 2,700. So you see, if the car holds together, we are going to be able to startle the world before we are through."[97]

And now to Lockhart.

He was facing severe problems with the engine: it didn't rev high enough and suffered occasional misfiring.

Lockhart began to investigate the culprit:

- Carburetors, no. Built by Zenith to his own design.
- Intercooler, no. He invented it.
- Body shape, maybe. It wasn't his design.

The wind tunnel tests didn't provide any information about the airflow inside the body. He made the decision to eliminate all openings apart from the one for entering and leaving the cockpit. Yet the Weisels opted for two small air intakes for the carburetors immediately behind the intercooler's fins. They didn't work, being in a low-pressure area just behind the turbulence created by the fins. The engine gulped for air and couldn't reach maximum revs.

Lockhart, the practical engineer, found the solution: he modified the ram tubes to the carburetors so they could breathe more easily. Some sources told of small scoops over the holes, but there is no evidence of them in any known photo. The solution added some drag, but the engine began to run smoothly.

On Monday afternoon Lockhart drove the Blackhawk to test the carburation: it worked. On a northward run against the wind he recorded 200.22 mph, a higher speed than Campbell's in the same conditions (199.96 mph). And that speed was enough for Campbell to set the record.

During final preparation for a run, Frank Lockhart watches Ray Splinder, with his distinctive bow tie, loading ice cubes into the coolant tank of the Blackhawk. A side panel has been removed to provide access to the engine. Adhering to established racing custom completely irrelevant on record runs, Lockhart carries a spare pair of goggles with dark lenses. The air temperature was quite low, as can be seen by the coats worn by the spectators.

It was late, about 4 p.m., when Lockhart completed the northward run, and the rising tide prevented the return run within the half-hour specified by the rulebook.

Lockhart said later that he didn't push the throttle over 6,000 rpm, i.e., about 1,000 rpm down on the revs needed for the record. Furthermore, at about three-quarters of the measured mile, he eased the throttle to check the engine response at high revs. He found that the clutch didn't work properly and needed to be fixed.

The Blackhawk was back in the garage, and the mechanics had to moonlight to fix the clutch. The team wanted to be ready to run on Wednesday, February 22, the national holiday promising a huge crowd.

Local cognoscenti, familiar with the beach and weather in Daytona Beach, told him that the sand would be good for two days before the wrong wind started to blow again. But by then the Speed Trials would already be over.

25

Despite the good weather forecast, on Tuesday, February 21 the wrong wind made the beach very rough. By 3:30 p.m. the AAA officials announced that the day was over for record runs. The decision stopped Wilbur Shaw in the Whippet Four just after a southward run at 106.53 mph.

In the meantime the stock cars provided a bit of a show: Gil Anderson of Indianapolis drove his Stutz at an average speed of 103.418 mph. Shortly after, Tom Rooney, out of Chicago, recorded 101.024 mph driving another Stutz stock car minus windscreen and running boards.

The fastest of the stock cars, priced over $2,000, was Wade Morton. He drove an Auburn at 108.466 mph in the fastest run.[98]

The above speeds were not a strong enough introduction to the February 22 runs with the Triplex forced to stay in the garage due to its scalded driver and the lack of a reversing mechanism to comply with the rulebook.

Campbell was asked by the organizers to be on the beach with Blue Bird at the ready, should Lockhart beat his record. He was not happy to run again, as confirmed by David McDonald, who remembered the post-record days as a time of relaxation and enjoyment.[99]

The ruthless laws of show business found one of the early applications in the motor racing world on those days in Daytona Beach. A foreign contender was needed against a native son.

The wrong wind had ruined the beach.

Rainsqualls reduced visibility.

The light was already fading at 3 p.m.

Dark clouds loomed over Daytona Beach.

Lockhart was ready to run.

Frank Lockhart's wide, boyish smile dominates one of the many portraits shot in Daytona Beach with him at the wheel of the Blackhawk. He has goggles with dark lenses pushed up onto his cap. The leather cover of the headrest provides more proof of the outstanding quality of workmanship on the beach car.

Let Paul Ellis talk. He was on the beach:

> Many thousands came for that holiday event. The stands near the timing station held only a small fraction of the people who had come from miles around, from many cities, many states to watch the day's jousting on the world's most famous speed arena. As far as you could see, north and south, there were people. They clustered thickly on the dunes, standing and sitting. Their movements were the movements of a mass. At times, you could hear their voices from near and far, a subdued chorus murmur blending with the sound of the surf. Florida's Governor John Martin was there with members of his staff. They filled a sizeable space in the middle of the grandstand. Automobiles were parked thickly the length of Atlantic Avenue, on both sides, and along the cross roads.
>
> But it was a bad day for the trials, that February 22. The sky was overcast. Mist hung low over the beach. Now and then came a light sprinkling of rain.
>
> Despite the weather, many of the stock car drivers sent their cars barking over the measured mile and back again, but obviously it was no day for a world speed record attempt.
>
> Lockhart brought his tiny white Blackhawk out early and stood by, waiting. More than once he had towed his car to the beach but each time something had gone against him. His finely designed racer had to be tuned to perfection and inevitably faults had shown up that compelled adjustments. Now, today, his car was ready. So was he, but the weather had turned against him.
>
> We could see him moodily kicking his toes against one of the tires as officials of the Stutz Motor Car Co. talked to him. We were told that they were begging him not to take a chance with his life.
>
> Once the overcast skies lifted a little, Lockhart climbed into the narrow cockpit, his crew climbed into the tow car and the cavalcade rolled to the south end of the course, near the inlet.[100]

Lockhart chose to run first against the wind, just the opposite of what Campbell had done a few days earlier and was due to do in the next runs for the record from 1931 to 1935. Segrave too, in 1927, ran southward first.

We can guess that his decision was based on the speed recorded two days before, against the wind. It would have been enough to beat Campbell as the return run would have been faster: he expected to reach 220 mph with the tailwind.

Paul Ellis went on:

> Then again the weather thickened. The afternoon wore on and the tide began to flow in. Governor Martin and his party left. Some few others followed, believing the day's running was over, but most of the people stayed on the dunes, waiting.
>
> We newspapermen had left the press table and clustered around Ted Gill, Associated Press correspondent. From there we saw two men interested in the speed trials promotion hop in a passenger car and drive south. Minutes later we heard the telephone ring in the timing stand. Hearing the jingle we agreed it meant Lockhart was telling AAA officials he had given up for the day. We swarmed back to the timing stand expecting to get the final message and go in with the day's rather meagre news report.
>
> Mears, dean of the AAA officials, was talking on the phone. His face was solemn when he put the receiver back and turned to his colleagues. Gravely he and the other officials whispered together. I saw Odis Porter wince. They nodded their heads, then Mears spoke carefully in a low voice to the man who handled the course's only public address system of those days; a huge megaphone.
>
> The megaphone man stared, nodded, then picked up his big horn and turned towards the multitude. His magnified voice boomed over the dunes: "Frank Lockhart will now go for the record."

This I knew about AAA rules: when a driver of proven experience said he was ready to drive they let him drive. So, despite their fears and great reluctance, they turned him loose. He was supposed to know what to do.

I turned to Pete Craig, United Press correspondent who had driven in many races on this beach. He whispered: "It's a murder."

Again the megaphone spoke: "Frank Lockhart has started north."[101]

26

Paul Ellis's prose is so lively and passionate it deserves continuation:

We stared in the mist. We couldn't see anything at first but soon we heard the scream of the supercharger, deep in the gray murk. Then we made out the little car, ghostly white in the fog and running towards us at a speed which seemed fantastic. By the supercharger's crescendo scream we knew Frank was coming with a wide-open throttle. We knew that nothing on wheels had ever run as fast as the little white car was running that day.

Then a scarf of light rain drifted across the beach, across the speeding car. Through the thin veil we saw the ghostly Blackhawk edging higher on the beach. Too high, into dry sand.

The same moment, as seen from Frank Lockhart's point of view: "I was going about 225 mph when I ran into a rain spot, which was hazy and which fogged my windshield. I knew I must be running pretty high on the beach and just when I broke through the hazy spot I started to turn back towards the water, but I turned too far. I could not turn it back and I knew the car was gone, so I ducked low in the car knowing that I was going to hit the water. Next thing I knew I heard the water swishing all around me and I was somersaulting and rolling at the same time. Then I was in the water again but did not believe I was hurt."[102]

The direct chronicle is very detailed and precise, as would be expected from a champion driver, able to understand, rationalize, and react to the many signals he was receiving in a fraction of a second.

Despite such a clear representation of the accident, the United Press correspondent in Daytona Beach wrote that the driver, when he spoke at the hospital, was still hazy due to the effects of the anesthetic given to him whilst his wounds were stitched.[103]

Lockhart didn't know then, and never had the chance to learn it, that the aerodynamics and the balance of the vehicle were wrong. The instability of the little white car amplified the deviation angle from the correct straight course. The driver worsened the situation when trying to correct it.

Paul Ellis:

We heard a ringing crash. The car bounced and swerved, skidded diagonally across the beach in two end-for-end loops and still on its wheels shot nose first into the ocean. It ran on its wheels until the belly hit the water. Then miraculously, eerily, like a great white pebble thrown by a superhuman hand it skipped high into the air: high and far.

As it soared it made a slow corkscrew turn. At the height of that fearsome leap, when the car was bottom up, we caught a glimpse of Lockhart's helmeted head.

Again the car hit the water, right side up. Again it soared high and far, and still a third

Lockhart's February 22, 1928 drama is unfolding. Blackhawk, over-corrected by its driver and being intrinsically unstable, spun and looped over the waves before coming to rest on the wheels in the surf. Some of the rescuers rushed to help in the shoulder-deep water with the incoming waves. There was plenty of drying and ironing to be done in Daytona Beach households that evening.

time. But now the momentum was broken. Still spinning in a corkscrew whirl the hapless Blackhawk landed on its wheels, its nose pointed directly toward the shore 200 yards away.

A heavy breaker combed over the little racer, all but hiding it from view. A low moan swept the crowd. Nobody there thought Frank Lockhart was alive.

But when the breaker flattened out Lockhart thrust his hand out of the cockpit. With one voice thousands of men and women chorused "He'll drown!"[104]

27

Newsmen had quite a story to report that afternoon. Gone was the fear that they would have nothing exciting to report. Yet *The Daytona Beach News-Journal* of the following day—Thursday, February 23—led with a full-page headline: "Shaw Drives Into Water in Flames."[105] Shaw, not Lockhart, was highlighted as having plunged into the ocean. Shaw was driving the unfortunate Whippet Four and chose to hit the water to extinguish the flames triggered by a backfire from the engine.

The minor accident happened on Thursday morning: it was the news of the day whereas Lockhart's was already a story of the previous day. The will to downplay any negative event about the Speed Trials also played a role in the editorial decision to limit the evidence of the Lockhart story.

The story had, nevertheless, the space it deserved on the front page through two articles commenting on the accident. One was about Fred Moskovics's statement that the Blackhawk would be rebuilt and request that the AAA sanction another record trial in May.[106] The other reported Lockhart's words about the accident. The sub-heading was quite significant: "AAA Heads Here Blames Attempt To Turn at 225 For Crash."

Campbell, as a professional driver, went into more detail to describe the accident dynamic as started by over-corrections of the steering wheel, but he was wrong in naming a gust of wind as the cause.[107]

Lockhart had a miraculous escape: three tendons in his left wrist were severed and two deep cuts ruined his chin, but his state of shock was due more to his irrational and profound fear of the water than to the dreadful somersaulting and rolling.

Just after the Blackhawk came to rest in the water, still on its wheels, many watchers and police officers ran to the car in the chest-deep, cold water. Gil Anderson was among the first to reach Lockhart. A driver of the Stutz stock cars, he still had his goggles and racing cap on. Alongside him ran Ray Splinder, a team member.

Looking at a well-known photo, someone mistakenly thought that the driver standing in the water, out of the wreck, was Lockhart, having somehow escaped from the cockpit.

Another dramatic photo, widely published in the period dailies, shows a close-up of Lockhart's face, with a dark blot on the forehead looking like a blood stain due to the low resolution of printed photos in those days. It was a wet wisp of the driver's wild long hair.

But who managed to undo his racing cap, and why?

The bouncing on the water had twisted the cockpit sides and bent the steering wheel. Lockhart was trapped inside; there was no way to get him out.

Lockhart, trapped inside, tries to get out of the crushed cockpit. Gil Anderson, a stock car driver, has rushed to help and is standing on the left-hand side of the cockpit. Other people are going into the surf to help and to attach a rope to the car. Gil Farrell has already jumped on the car's tail, ready to save Lockhart by holding hands over his face when incoming waves submerged the car and driver.

No human strength on the smashed body could have pushed the car and driver out of the water to the dry sand. A tow lorry already on the beach was called to pull the car out, but it took some minutes to reach the spot, while Lockhart was drowning.

Gil Farrell, a young dirt track driver, did the right thing to save Lockhart. He jumped on the tail of the Blackhawk and put his hands on Lockhart's face, covering his nose and mouth. When a breaker was coming he pressed his hands, then released them when the breaker was past, yelling, "Breathe. Now!"

A couple of brave men went underwater to wind the tow cable around the front axle. A few seconds later the car was towed out of the water.

Chisels and blowtorches were brought to cut the aluminum sheets around the cockpit. Lockhart was eased out of the car without the need of any specialized tool. He was immediately laid in the ambulance.

During the run to Halifax Hospital Lockhart was heard whispering "I feel OK" and lamenting that he felt very cold.

Gil Farrell, nearly frozen, was carried in the ambulance together with Ella Lockhart and Bill Sturm. The presence of the communications manager was needed in every circumstance including the most dramatic.

Lockhart spoke from his heart whilst in the hospital, just after the emergency care and away from the supervision and strict control of Sturm. He said that his

The tow truck has arrived. Some brave men attached the rope to the front axle: in a few seconds driver and car will be on dry land. When the surf retreats, Gil Farrell calls someone to attention. Gil Anderson is still on the left-hand side of the cockpit. A police officer appears on the scene on the right. Frank Lockhart is still trapped in the car, his wild hair so wet it partially covers his face, appearing as a sort of blot in the low-quality photograph that led many to believe it was a bloodstain.

A detail of the previous photograph highlighting that Frank Lockhart was fully conscious despite the shock and pain in his left wrist, where tendons had been severed. Note that his racing cap is missing: Who took it? When? Why? And how?

While the rescue operation was under way, plenty of onlookers came down from the dunes to the surf line and watched the ongoing drama from close quarters. On the far right the Stutz stock car in which Gil Anderson rushed to the scene is clearly visible. Still at the wheel of the car, having completed his record runs just before Lockhart's, he was the first to rush to help. When the Blackhawk was towed to dry land, helpers took a post left behind by the builders of the grandstand, levered it against the bent steering wheel, and extricated Lockhart from the cockpit. In a matter of seconds he was rushed to the waiting ambulance and taken to the Halifax Hospital together with the nearly frozen Gil Farrell, Ella, and Bill Sturm.

escape was due to three factors: a strongly built vehicle, the Blackhawk ultimately landing on its wheels, and people who ran into the ocean and kept him out of the breakers to save him from drowning. A short quote eased the drama: "I sure built the car well."[108]

Moskovics was reported as saying that the Blackhawk should be repaired within two or three weeks and would be ready to try again for the record. He

When the Blackhawk was towed back on to the beach it was not actually as badly damaged as it appears to be in the photograph. All that was needed was the shaping of new wheel fairings and straightening of the central section of the body, apart from a complete overhaul of the engine, which had been damaged by salt water. Note that the small indent on the side of the cockpit was not enough to trap Lockhart inside; it was the bent steering wheel that trapped his legs. In the big crowd watching the car, just a single woman can be seen. The kids on the beach confirm that it was Washington's Birthday, a national holiday when schools were closed.

The battered Blackhawk after the February 22 incident. One can try to understand the mounting of the front fairing around the axle: the large plate covering all but four inches of the wheel and tire can clearly be seen as well as the streamlined cover for the axle nut. The fairing, now bent away, was screwed to the plate. To change the wheel/tire, 10 screws on the central streamlined cover had to be removed, without doubt too long a job to be done four times in under 30 minutes.

added a sentence that might have sent a cold shiver down the spines of the Daytona Beach organizers: "Where we will make the new speed trials we have not considered, but if not here it will be on the dry lake beds of the west. However, the next trial will be made only when conditions are perfect."[109]

Both Sturm and Moskovics advanced a possible explanation for the outcome of the accident: the low center of gravity saved the car from overturning during the spins on the beach, thus preserving the tires, which, still being intact, eased the pulling of the car out of the water.

28

Campbell was on the beach with Blue Bird at the ready. If needed, he would set off on a record run after Lockhart. He was waiting at the north end of the course and saw the Blackhawk towed south while he was getting into the cockpit of Blue Bird. The engine was warm and he and the team waited for the start signal.

The story as told by Campbell shows some inconsistencies[110] as it was written seven years after the event. We have to forgive small errors and add-ons here and there to enhance the drama and appeal of the story. We read: "It was quite impossible for us to see anything which happened down the course because the start of the measured mile was four miles away." Obvious and correct.

"We waited there for some time and I was eventually told that I could go." Impossible: the officials would never ever have given the green light when the beach, after the accident, was filled with people and the tow truck and ambulance were still there. The officials had a direct view of the accident, which happened close to the timing stand. Furthermore, prior to starting his run, Campbell should have seen Lockhart come back to the north end and prepare for the return run.

"I was about to give the word for the mechanics to start the engine when a policeman appeared, travelling flat out on his motor-cycle. He skidded to a stop beside the car. 'For God's sake' he shouted 'There has been a terrible accident. Lockhart's dead.'" Pure fiction.

"I climbed out from the machine, jumped into another car and set off along the beach to find a big crowd gathered near the mile, where men were wading breast-deep in the sea, dragging out Lockhart's battered car. Lockhart was almost unconscious when he was dragged out, but he was not dead. In fact, his injuries were not as bad as they might have been. His arm was broken, the tendons of his wrist were cut and he suffered very severe shock. He was hurried to the hospital." Fake news.

Quite difficult to accept are the words about the broken arm because Campbell visited Lockhart in the hospital before his return to England. He therefore checked Lockhart's condition himself. And he spoke to him: "I asked him not to be in a hurry to try again, but he told me that as soon as his car was ready he would make another attempt. I could only shake hands and wished him all the luck in the world."

29

The scribblers enjoyed a festive harvest thanks to the candid interviews with Frank Lockhart in his hospital room without the filter of Bill Sturm. They wrote that he was forced to start the run against his will to comply with the pressing request of the organizers, who wanted to please the waiting crowd.

Stop it. Too much.

Bill Sturm, the spokesman, jumped in to take over the media scene. Readers elsewhere across the States needed to be told his own version of the event: unique, factually correct, undeniable. The main target was readers in Indianapolis, where Lockhart lived and where the Blackhawk was built in the Stutz plant. His key aim was to protect Stutz, killing any negative comment in advance.

The February 23 issue of *The Indianapolis News* published the feature cabled by Sturm on their front page: two large columns with the headline phrased as a trigger to read the whole story. "Car Smashed, Lockhart Talks in Ambulance of Another Trial," it blared. "Pilot, Braving Fog and Rain to Satisfy Crowd and Officials, Plunges Into Sea at 230 Miles an Hour, Fastest Auto Speed Ever Made. Youth Shocked, Bruised."

The long text opened with the glorification of Frank Lockhart: "A boy with the heart of a lion and an ambition to set a world's automobile speed record in order that America might stand in the speed forefront."

Subsequent lines mildly blamed the pressure from the Daytona Beach Chamber of Commerce on Lockhart to run on that day despite the unfavorable weather and sand conditions. Apparently, they pushed him to run to give the thousands of watchers a show worth the entry ticket.

Sturm also provided his explanation of the cause of the accident, already given to the Daytona Beach journalists: "Lockhart found that he could not see far enough ahead to tell where he was going. He probably lifted his foot and applied the brake instinctively."

A too-wrong explanation by an automotive racing expert. Masochist for a spokesman. Offensive to Lockhart, suggesting such a capital error (braking while at full speed) by a skilled, fast-reacting, rational driver. Lockhart himself never mentioned such an action when he talked in the hospital.

About the minutes between the plunge into the water and the rescue to dry land, Lockhart had said that Ray Splinder, one of his team, ran into the water and placed himself over the tail of the car to act as a human wave-breaker.

Yet Sturm wrote that he would have better known the name of the guy who jumped on the car's tail and saved Lockhart from drowning. It is more proof of how difficult it was to maintain professional distance and journalistic reporting capability when one is engulfed in a drama: that guy, Gil Farrell, was with him, Ella, and Frank Lockhart in the ambulance rushing to Halifax Hospital.

The article reported a request from Lockhart spoken just after his wounds were stitched: "Find out how long it will take to get the car in shape to try it again."

And the high-pitched final sentence was fully laudatory:

He is a great hero today as he would have been had he succeeded in completing the run on which he was travelling 230 miles an hour. Indianapolis should be mightily proud of Frank Lockhart. … Even the skill of Lockhart is futile when vision is lacking. He tried to do what he had set out to do. With even an average beach and fair visibility he would have kept the mile record in America. He never leaves matters half done. Within a year, with the same little car, there is no doubt that he will bring the record back to America.[111]

These words sealed the fate of Frank Lockhart, as we'll see later.

The news of the accident reached Europe quite soon. *The Autocar* reported on it in the first available issue. The short news was enhanced by a dramatic black line sketch, probably by de Grineau, showing the Blackhawk hitting the waves. The words placed the blame squarely on "some persons in Daytona Beach who forced the driver to run for the record despite the bad conditions of the sand and the incoming squalls of rain."

The compulsory British disapproval of everything done elsewhere colored the few words characterizing the American approach to the land speed record: "More show than technology and competence."[112]

30

Frank Lockhart's February 22 accident received wide coverage by the many photographers standing close to the measured mile, not far from the location of the accident and the final position of the Blackhawk in the surf.

The photos are, of course, still images freezing a certain moment of the event in time, not detailing how it developed. As such, they keep some doubts alive even after a technical review.

Rain. It should have been very light and only on small sections of the beach. We see many people standing at the water's edge and on the dry sand: hats and suits appear without any visible traces of damp or rain. Only one person is wearing a raincoat: he must be one of the AAA officials as he is wearing a band on his left arm. The raincoat was obvious protection for a person who had to stay still for a long time on a cloudy winter's day. Looking at the resolutions and shutter speeds of the photos, the light was good enough, meaning that the clouds were not too heavy or dark.

Gil Anderson. The presence of the Stutz stock car driver, amongst the first running to Lockhart's rescue, is confirmed by the presence of the number 6 Stutz stock car at the water's edge.

People in the water. One photo shows 20 of them, the farthest away in the water up to his shoulders and the closest ones in the water up to their waists. Only one person wearing a bathing suit can be seen: this means the air temperature must not have been too low.

Tow truck. It is clearly visible in the full frame of the photo showing Lockhart halfway out of the cockpit.

Lockhart trapped in the cockpit. A photo shows the Blackhawk under tow halfway to the dry sand. Gil Farrell is seated across the head fairing. Gil Anderson is standing on the left of the cockpit. Frank Lockhart is leaning halfway out of the cockpit and appears to be pushing his arms against the sides to help him get out of the car.

Another photo, widely published, shows Lockhart deep down in the cockpit with his hands raised to face height in an instinctive gesture to check the wounds to his chin. It is impossible to ascertain the sequence of the two photos, as the towing cable appears in both.

The right side of the cockpit appears slightly damaged. The left side shows a larger indentation but less deep; neither indentation looks deep enough to trap the driver inside. The upper section of the steering wheel appears to be in the correct position.

A source, written 29 years after the accident,[113] chronicles the event in detail, assuming that Lockhart was trapped in his car by the bent lower section of the steering wheel jammed against his legs. Ray Splinder is said to have found somewhere (maybe under the grandstand) a hardwood beam and, aided by several men, levered away at the car body until they freed Lockhart clear of the steering wheel and lifted him out of the wreckage. In those days detachable steering wheels were not yet in use.

It is quite difficult to understand how the lower section of the steering wheel was bent without hitting the driver's chest, as he was not said to have had any broken ribs.

Some photos were taken after the vehicle was towed on to dry sand and the driver was rescued. None were found showing either cuts or traces of blowtorches on the sides of the cockpit. We could, therefore, assume that no specialized tools were needed to extract Lockhart.

31

After the accident, the show went on according to schedule in Daytona Beach.

An accident, even one as highly spectacular and as full of drama as Lockhart's, wasn't enough to stop the organizing machine. Furthermore, the decision had already been made to continue the Speed Trials until Thursday, February 23.

Thursday was a working day, yet the crowd in the dunes was again substantial. The weather and sand were in good condition, and the program was quite appealing: stock car runs, the nth try by the unstoppable and under-achieving Whippet Four, Ray Keech in the Triplex back from hospital. And Campbell's Blue Bird at the ready again.

The afternoon low tide opened the roar of high-revving engines. The first excitement came at around 1 p.m. when Wilbur Shaw drove the Whippet Four into the water to extinguish the flames engulfing him and the car.[114]

Without official timing, Jim White had the Triplex on the beach and appointed five journalists and Gee Vee electricians to time the runs manually with stopwatches. Keech had now gained full command of the vehicle and had shown his indomitable courage, irrespective of any danger of being scalded again by the engine steaming coolant. Around 3 p.m. he made four runs, each within the half-hour limit of the other.

The stopwatches recorded times within three tenths of a second. *The Daytona Beach News-Journal*, once again quite positive about the Triplex, reported the precise figures for times and speeds: average in the first double run 183.89 mph; average in the second double run 203.86 mph, resulting from 209.5 mph, 17.2 seconds on the northward run and 198.67 mph, 18.12 seconds on the southward. The higher speed on the run against the wind is hard to comprehend unless it proved that White's theories on the uselessness of aerodynamic fairings were correct.[115]

The results were quite close to Campbell's record speed and faster than Segrave's.

Campbell was on the beach ready to challenge should Keech beat his record time, even if unofficially. He wasn't there only to please the crowd at the request of the organizers.

We have found a single report on the Blue Bird run, described as an "exhibition," on the day in question.[116] The speed was fractionally lower than the official record—206.793 mph—but we don't know whether it was the average of the two runs or only the one-way result. The chronicle in the February 24 issue of *The Indianapolis Star* reported Campbell's statement that he wouldn't have run for the record because the weather and sand were in poor condition.

The White Triplex being refueled directly on the beach by a Sunoco tanker from the Jacksonville Adams & Pearl subsidiary. Sunoco was one of the car's sponsors, as seen by the large poster on the side of the tanker. Jim White is second from the left in the group standing alongside the car.

Just before sunset and high tide Gil Anderson drove his Stutz Blackhawk stock car to a 106.524 mph average, beating the previous record set by Wade Morton (Auburn, 104.347 mph). When Wade Morton was again cleared to go, the tide was already washing the lower pickets of the course and the light was fading. He raced on the wet, washed beach and the wet sand made a long, rising tail behind the wheels. In such appalling conditions he didn't manage to regain the record and forwarded a protest to the officials, complaining of the excessive delay in clearing him to run.

32

After the official conclusion of the beach runs a gala dinner was held at the Clarendon Hotel on the evening of Thursday, February 23, to present the awards.

Campbell received the Chamber of Commerce Cup, presented by the president, David Sholtz. In his responding thank-you address, Campbell gave an outstanding tribute to Daytona Beach and its citizens:

> Words utterly fail me to express my deep appreciation for the extraordinary courtesy and fine hospitality that has been shown our party here. The people of your city are perfectly wonderful. I do not know how we could have been treated with finer hospitality. I think it contributes to international goodwill and especially to good feeling among nations to hold meets such as this, and I feel sure that the British people appreciate the spirit of pure sportsmanship that has been in the meet and the wonderful hospitality that has been extended to us. The members of my party shall be forever grateful to Daytona Beach and its people.[117]

Not even a skilled politician could have been so utterly laudatory. The same feelings were expressed later in Campbell's autobiography:

> After the run, I was fêted [by the Americans] to an embarrassing extent, and it was the more difficult to accept these congratulations since I appreciated that the success was not due to myself alone. Behind me were the engineers and scientists, the designers and the workmen who had constructed the car, while I owed more than it is possible to express to the loyal work of Villa and Leech, and the rest of my mechanics; it would have been impossible to find a keener and more efficient little group of men.[118]

Even following such praise of the value of teamwork and of America as a whole, Campbell privately harbored a negative opinion of the Daytona Beach venue, subject to the unpredictable beach and sand conditions and first and foremost to the vagaries of the weather, which forced him to waste days when everything was ready to go.

In the following year, 1929, Campbell snubbed Daytona Beach and went to Verneuk Pan, a dry lakebed in the middle of nowhere in South Africa, to avoid the vicissitudes of the beach. As is well-known, the record attempt was a failure, and Campbell, lured more by the money offered than by the beach and weather conditions, came back to Daytona Beach four more times to establish four more records. Such behavior, too, is customary for a skilled politician.[119]

A prize for Lockhart was presented at the banquet. Bill Sturm accepted it on behalf of Ella Lockhart, who declined to be present despite having earlier confirmed. The silver cup was filled with roses (a homage evidently chosen for her) and was brought to the driver at Halifax Hospital. David Sholtz conveyed best wishes from everybody in Daytona Beach for a full and speedy recovery.

A smaller cup was presented to Jim White as a sign of appreciation for having been there with the Triplex.

The festive party was entertained by music and a closing show reported as "unique" in the chronicle.

Leo Villa, free from any role of having to please anyone and being ready to praise the event, wrote that he had very good whiskey, carried in by the police officers themselves, despite America being in the depths of Prohibition. He remembered that it was the best drink he enjoyed in Florida.[120]

Campbell left Daytona Beach on Saturday, February 25, for New York, accompanied by his manager, Girard Hammond, and Eugene Pulliam, editor-in-chief of the local daily, who was to interview him in a special broadcast on Sunday prime time by a local city radio station.[121]

Before leaving Daytona Beach, Campbell knew he had won over the city and the citizens, unseating Henry Segrave from his glorious pedestal as the first land speed record holder there. The local police chief, Guy Hurd, who had dismissed him as "That Englishman" on seeing the February 16 accident, awarded him the badge of honorary police officer no. 49. (The city was too young to have heroes, events, or historical records after which to name a civic award.)

Campbell won the hearts and goodwill of the police force, presenting a box of cigars to those who served on the beach, on foot and on bikes. As an additional present, Officer Patterson was given a pair of goggles. Sergeant Locke got a set of racing plugs, Sergeant Cupernall a racing cap.[122]

Even an Albion gentleman like Malcolm Campbell had to bow to American publicity rules: In the February 25 (the day of his departure from the city) issue, *The Daytona Beach News-Journal* published a large photo of him standing by the side of the car said to have been selected as his personal vehicle during his stay in Florida: a Chevrolet Coupé. U.S.-made.

3

Intermission—March

1

They left him alone at the hospital.

Everybody had gone away: Campbell and the British party, White and Keech, Shaw and the stock car drivers, AAA officials and timekeepers.

The roses in the chamber of commerce cup were wilting (despite the care of Ella, to whom they were addressed).

Frank Lockhart recovered from the shock quickly. His left arm bandaged in a sling was not enough reason for him to stay at Halifax Hospital.

Dr. Klock and the nurses, together with Bill Sturm, had to work hard to keep the flurry of journalists at bay on the day of the accident: everyone wanted to hear live from the protagonist how it went and how it was going. It was certainly an intriguing bit of news to hear the subjective narrative of such a scary accident.

By now even the wire agency correspondents had left.

The Daytona Beach News-Journal felt a professional obligation to keep interest in the facts and the person alive. On Saturday, February 27, a front-page article appeared under a typical no-news headline: "Lockhart Defends Racing as a Scientific Necessity." The sub-heading offered a bit of interest for the future: "Is Coming Back; Asks May Beach Conditions."

Everything worth reading was already in the sub-heading. The text opened with a short recap of the facts, reporting the alleged speed of the accident as 235 mph, though Lockhart had repeatedly said that, looking at the rev-counter, he estimated his speed was 225 mph.

The text dealt with the question of beach conditions in May and added another statement from Lockhart: "I really expect I can have the car ready before my wrist is entirely well. I understand the car is not hurt much. Sure, I'm coming back."

The headline was linked to another statement from the driver: "Ninety per cent of the improvements made on family cars have been developed through racing as tests. The 500-mile race at Indianapolis each year is attended by every automotive engineer and the data gathered just adds to the safety of all automobiles in spite of the hazards of the race itself."

The sincere and noble character of the man was clearly visible, even without the filter and guidance of his manager, in the final lines where he praised Dr. Klock: "He was on the beach when I crashed and was one of the first men to get to me. He stayed with me in the ambulance, and has stayed right with me here in the hospital, all through it. I have the utmost confidence in him."

He added his thanks to Gil Farrell, who saved him from drowning and then fell exhausted when he and the Blackhawk were pulled out of the water. Excusing himself, he said that he only originally mentioned Ray Splinder as the first to reach him because he had known him for a long time. He said: "I sure am thankful to Farrell."

On Monday, February 27, the Blackhawk was crated and loaded on the train to Indianapolis. Jimmy Lee, Jean Marcenac, and Ray Splinder, the members of the Lockhart team, left Daytona Beach on the same day to drive to Indianapolis by car.

They knew well that weeks of hard work were awaiting them to fix the Blackhawk. They certainly knew that it was impossible for Lockhart to wait until May to return to Florida and try for the record again: May was the month of the Indianapolis 500, and Stutz had already pre-entered the two Miller-Lockharts as Stutz Specials, one for Lockhart and the other for Tony Gulotta.

That crazy record business had to be accomplished during April.

On Tuesday, February 28, Frank and Ella Lockhart and Bill and Teressa Sturm left Daytona Beach by train on a Pullman sleeper for Indianapolis.

The local daily, in a farewell article, published additional words by Lockhart, saying thanks to Dr. Klock and every other person who helped him to escape from his "watery grave."[1]

The article closed by noting that neither vacation nor convalescence was awaiting Lockhart in Indianapolis. He would join his team in the Stutz workshop to fix the Blackhawk.

2

Malcolm and Dorothy Campbell, the team mechanics, and their party of British friends boarded the *Berengaria* moored at Pier 24, the Cunard Line berth on the Hudson River harbor.

The huge crate containing Blue Bird was chained to the bridge, as on the outward crossing.

Looking at the published photos,[2] the crate appears to be covered in graffiti, quite unusual for the period. There were ad-like scribbles: "Dunlop for Ever" and "Speed 214 mph." The biggest one read: "Come Again. Daytona Beach Police Dept." and was followed by the signatures of Guy Hurd, Chief of Police, and E.R. Hall, Chief of the Firefighters Department. It confirmed that Campbell was not only awarded the badge of honorary Daytona Beach police officer no. 49 but also had left a good image of himself behind.

The crossing was quiet but with a major unexpected problem: an epidemic of flu jumped on to the ship from New York City, where it was quite widespread. It became so virulent that the crew and the passengers, including the Campbells and their team, suffered badly.

Malcolm, looking extremely ill, had to be back on his feet when the ship arrived in Southampton. The welcoming committee was headed by the mayor,

Mrs. Lucia Foster Welch. Campbell had to play the role of guest of honor at the welcoming receptions.

He then had a couple of hours to relax on the train to Victoria Station, London, where he was once more in the midst of congratulations, cheers, parties, people to welcome, speeches to deliver, hands to shake, dinners to share, and telegrams to answer—too much for a man who was still recovering from the flu.

The climax of the festivities was the gala dinner organized by Sir Charles Wakefield for some 500 guests, including Sir William Johnson Hicks, secretary of the interior. According to *The Autocar*, Campbell "deserved considerable sympathy as he had to contend with all the events without having to deal with them in bed when one is feeling ill."[3]

No way to avoid the celebrations. It was the return of the hero who had crossed the water to reaffirm British superiority at the pinnacle of speed on land. By the way, Campbell came as the second man to do so: the second to speed beyond 200 mph, the second Briton to clinch the land speed record in a foreign land. In comparison, the welcome given to Henry Segrave in 1927 was warmer and shared amongst a wider circle.

Such a comparatively lukewarm (for him) welcome gave a further boost to his will to retain exclusive hold on the land speed record going forward. As it happened, the rivalry with Segrave, who took the record from him and Ray Keech in 1929, concluded on June 13, 1930, when Sir Henry met his fate while attempting to gain the water speed record on Lake Windermere, England.

Enter the 1930s: the first five years of the decade became Campbell's own hunting ground for the land speed record.

He was the first man to achieve over three miles per minute in 1927 in one of the runs on Pendine Sands, on February 4 (record average speed 174.883 mph).

On February 5, 1931, he was the first to exceed four miles a minute in Daytona Beach (speed 245.736 mph).

He wrote in his autobiography:

> It promised much in personal achievement if I could be the first to reach five miles a minute on land. I wanted to do it because I felt that once the goal of 300 mph had been reached, there was a possibility that the record might stand for England for some time to come. It would then be a mark of the excellence of British engineering. It would be unwise to suggest that any new record could not be beaten, or that the speed on land would rise to a particular figure and then remain stationary.[4]

Many years later, in 1949, Donald Campbell sketched a portrait of his father: "Dad couldn't stand to be thwarted. Once he'd got the World Record and had it taken away from him then his one idea was to get it back again. I think this game must be a disease in the blood."[5]

3

It was a long journey by train from Florida to the Midwest with many changes of locomotive as the Pullman sleeper was switched from one railroad company track to another. The sleeper left Daytona Beach early in the morning and arrived at Indianapolis's Union Station after midnight—too late for the welcoming program. Lockhart and the party spent the night on board the sleeper.

At 7 a.m. on Wednesday, February 29, 1928, Stutz employees gathered in front of the gates to the plant on North Capitol Avenue without going through. It was not a wildcat strike but the signal to start a 300-automobile cavalcade across town to Union Station. They woke up the whole city center, moving around with blaring car horns.

Lockhart was due to leave the train at 7:30 a.m., but the crowd jammed the stairway to the platform and an extra half hour was needed to get everybody in.

Frank appeared at the rear of the Pullman car, cheered loudly by the crowd. Many tossed their hats into the air. He peered out at the huge crowd and drew back immediately as though he was scared.

The Indianapolis News reporter relayed the comment of a Stutz worker who had contributed to the construction of the Blackhawk: "He is a modest guy."[6]

His face lit up and a boyish grin spread over it when he appeared again, standing on the small observation deck at the rear of the car. The cheering reached its climax. He was elbowed by Lee Busch and Tom Brady, Stutz plant supervisors, to a waiting open car—a Stutz, of course. They took care not to hurt his bandaged arm, still in a sling. Everyone saw the pair of bristly scars on his chin.

Colonel Gorrell, Stutz vice president, was already in the car along with Bill Sturm. They drove off at the head of the cavalcade to the Stutz plant, where Colonel Gorrell read the official welcome speech in the absence of Fred Moskovics, still travelling from Florida and not expected until the next day.

Ella Lockhart received a huge bouquet of roses, flowers not easy to find in winter in the Midwest. Frank got a gold medal with the Nike of Samothrace and a dedication: "Undaunted. Daytona Beach, 1928."

It's funny to note that *The Indianapolis News* reporter, very precise in the chronicle, did not dare to display his shaky knowledge of ancient Greek art and described the image on the medal as "a winged headless woman." (The Nike of Samothrace is also known as the "Winged Victory of Samothrace.")

Bill Sturm had to recount every detail of the accident again and again. Once more he forgot to mention Gil Farrell and promoted Ray Splinder as the main rescuer, he who protected Lockhart's face from the incoming waves.[7] Asked about the Blackhawk, due back in Indianapolis in a couple of days, he answered that it would be ready again in six to eight weeks, adding that preliminary agreements had already been established for the AAA sanction on a new record attempt.

He didn't miss an emphatic conclusion, as expected from a PR professional: "[Lockhart] will go back to Daytona Beach to prove that he has the fastest car in the world."

4

Jim White was in better shape than Lockhart. The Triplex was still working perfectly after extensive tests and many trial runs. The reverse motion mechanism was still missing from the vehicle. Ray Keech's commitment lasted until the end of April. Furthermore, the contract included a substantial bonus should he win the new record.

We don't know how long the Triplex stayed in Philadelphia, probably for fitting the reverse motion mechanism. White mentioned in his *Motor Age* story[8] "the large sum spent to comply with their [AAA's] request." He added that he had to spend another huge sum to have the AAA-approved timing system installed on the beach. He asked for, and actually got, the system used by the Indianapolis Speedway. He wrote that the daily rental fees amounted to $300 in April.

For him it was a welcome relief that Willys-Overland decided to run the Whippet Four again—driven, as before, by Wilbur Shaw—to seek the elusive record for a four-cylinder engine. Shaw agreed to share the costs with Lockhart and the Stutz, too. As defined by the agreements, the total cost was split among the three record-seekers. The Daytona Beach Chamber of Commerce had already paid for the February Speed Trials and only offered the services of checking and patrolling the beach during the new record runs.

The record business had to be concluded within April because drivers, mechanics, timing system and AAA officials had to be back in Indianapolis by early May, the month reserved for the 500-Mile Race. The trouble was that the beach was spoiled by the wrong winds and tides for the whole of March. The first half of April had already passed because of the unsuitability of the sand for high-speed runs.

The Daytona Beach News-Journal reported on April 2 that the Triplex was already in Daytona Beach's Fernwood Garage on jacks whilst a reverse motion mechanism was fitted to comply with the AAA rules. No technical details have ever been released by any period source: even today we do not know how the RM gear worked with the three driving gears on the rear axle and, apparently, only one clutch on the front engine.

We understand from the local daily that the installation was "virtually completed" on April 4: the Triplex couldn't go for the record because of the poor condition of the beach, as per a quote by Keech.[9]

The article also said that AAA officials would arrive on the afternoon of April 5 to examine the Triplex. The vehicle received a new name—"Spirit of Elkdom"—perhaps in honor of the Elks Lodge, quite powerful in Florida.

Lockhart and Shaw were expected on April 8. Maybe.

With no real news and a too-long intermission, some cheap literature was published about Ray Keech, presented by the local daily as a solid Eastern driver, open and friendly, who showed proof of undaunted bravery when he was scalded by boiling steam on February 20 yet managed to bring the Triplex to a regular stop after a painful three-mile run.

When we read the whole story we have to overlook the confusion of names and historic figures: "Keech has captured the imagination of the speed bugs in this city. They liken him to Ben Hur and Caesar, perhaps because of the carefree style of his pose at the wheel and the firm set of his jaw as he guides the monster annihilator of space. ... Despite his narrow escape, Keech is once more eager to trust his life to the mercy of the huge mass of steel and rubber on which he bases his record hopes."[10]

5

Malcolm Campbell enjoyed his days regaling the British media with interviews and bylined articles. He was the hero of the day, the most revered authority on the highest speeds on land, the British citizen who had shown his country's superiority over those faraway colonials. He was the idol of every British boy, much more so than Henry Segrave, his competitor who claimed more wins yet cared far less about self-promotion and PR exercises.

Campbell wrote a lot and gave his name to many stories and books written by other authors, addressed to boys and adults. When he came back from Daytona Beach, he opened the media's eyes to the emotional and exciting value of high speed: soon 200 mph in a car seemed to belong to the unknown territory beyond the borders of what a human being could reach. No grand prix racer even approached such a speed. Everyday family cars could reach 40 to 50 mph on the poor roads of the time, if everything ran smoothly.

Segrave had already written a detailed account of his over-200 mph record in bylined articles[11] and in his autobiography.[12] In precise, cold, and very technical prose, he sketched the sensations at that speed as "very hazy."

In his second run on Thursday, March 24, 1927, the Sunbeam 1000 HP skidded and hit the wooden pickets delineating the course on the ocean side, cutting them off like a razor blade. Despite the excessive reduction ratio at the steering wheel, Segrave managed to absorb the skid and align the car on its correct course again. He wrote: "The skid covered perhaps 400 yards of actual distance travelled. It was over so soon that I had not the time to think about taking my foot off, or do anything but wrestle with the steering wheel: and by the time I began to think that I might be getting into difficulties and that I had better take my foot off, the car was back again on its original course."

Words and thoughts so normal that they were forgotten the following year when Malcolm Campbell's new record was celebrated.

We know that Malcolm Campbell remembered the skid during his February 19 record run as "the worst experience of all [his] life."[13] We also know what he wrote about the physical effort being so demanding as to block any possible mental strain or any related and articulated thoughts.

The best-loved question of the scribblers centered on his feelings at 206 mph, imagined as akin to immersion in an alien world of superhuman mystery. Of course Campbell was the second man to go beyond 200 mph, furthermore a speed then largely less than the limits set by the winning seaplanes of the last Schneider Trophy: close to 300 mph. But such factual background could be obscured by sensational prose.

Campbell's matter-of-fact answer: "I hardly know. My whole mind was concentrated on the task in hand and my faculties were so riveted on one problem—keeping the Blue Bird on her course—that I had no time for outside impressions. ... I scarcely noticed the exhaust noise and the whole run was one tremendous sweep over the sand which I hardly felt, with a hurricane wind seeking to wrest the car from my control."[14]

Question: "What do you see at 200 mph?"

Answer: "On the beach rushing to meet me, everything [was] forming a blurred kaleidoscope which raced past me on either side of the car. I could not distinguish anything I passed, except as merged and hazy shapes of different shades. I kept my eyes focussed directly ahead, to infinity, and the objects which I was able to pick up—seen from the corners of my eyes—became vague as they rushed towards me, merging into a shapeless blur which constantly streamed by."[15]

Had Campbell been one of the Italian artists of the "Aeroart" school, he could have transferred those words on to canvas.

6

Frank Lockhart was too optimistic. Just after the February 22 accident, he cabled Fred Moskovics from Halifax Hospital asking him to forward a request to the AAA to sanction another attempt at the record within 30 days.[16]

On March 7, already in Indianapolis to work on the Blackhawk, he found enough time to give an interview to a local radio station, widely broadcast over Indiana, about the car being repaired quickly and about he himself being perfectly fit.[17]

Dr. Edmund D. Clark, who cared for him in Indianapolis, consulted with Dr. Klock in Daytona Beach to get details of the surgery on the tendons of his wrist. He informed his colleague that the tendons were uniting and were almost safe from infections. As said by Dr. Klock earlier, Dr. Clark confirmed that Frank Lockhart would soon be able to drive the Blackhawk and any other street or racing car on tracks or normal roads.[18]

The whole of March went by doing repairs to the Blackhawk and waiting for the driver's wrist to heal. A small yet significant improvement on the car's body was to modify the air intakes for the carburetors.[19] The whole body was reshaped and straightened by Myron Stevens, the team's body-builder.

Mr. N.H. Pearson of the Willys-Overland concern managed the contacts with the AAA and Jim White, on behalf of Wilbur Shaw, who was once again to be at the wheel of the Whippet Four. Pearson informed Mayor Armstrong and the Daytona Beach Chamber of Commerce that the two drivers (Shaw and Lockhart) and their cars would be in Florida for Sunday, April 8. Keech and the Triplex were already in town. Only Jim White and the AAA officials were still not there.

The day of arrival was delayed to Tuesday, April 17, when Bill Sturm detrained in Daytona Beach. Wilbur Shaw and the Whippet Four team had arrived the day before.

Sturm released a statement to the local daily[20] saying that Lockhart was perfectly fit and was due to reach Daytona Beach driving his own car the following

The Blackhawk, fixed and ready to run again, was back in Daytona Beach by train on the morning of Thursday, April 19. It was unloaded from the closed baggage car of the train on to a flat truck to take it over the bumpy path on the tracks. Some kids are watching, perhaps having skipped their school classes.

The Blackhawk back in Daytona Beach in April and ready for the compulsory photo op. The differences from February can be seen in Frank Lockhart's wilder hair and the lighter clothes of the men watching; one is in a bathing suit. Jean Marcenac, in white overalls, stands in the middle with Bill Sturm on his right. Two ladies look on from the back.

day. The journey from Indianapolis was a distance of some 1,000 miles: it provided some indirect proof of Lockhart's recovery.

He added that they would wait until the sand and the weather were perfect prior to launching the Blackhawk on another record bid. No more runs to please the crowd. If the wait had been more than 10 days they would have been forced to go back to Indianapolis and postpone the record runs to the following year.

The Blackhawk arrived in Daytona Beach by train in the early morning of Thursday, April 19. Frank and Ella Lockhart and the mechanics arrived in the evening of the same day. Lockhart said that the Blackhawk was ready to run, only needing the ice and fuel tanks to be topped up. From the Clarendon Hotel garage he would bring it to the beach only for a trial spin, not for the record even though the AAA officials were already on duty and the timing and telephone systems were checked and ready.

4

Act Two—April

1

Jim White was no longer an "outlaw" racing outside AAA rules and sanctions. His Triplex, now equipped with a regular reverse motion mechanism, had been approved by Odis Porter of the AAA Technical Board. His new runs for the land speed record could be staged under AAA Sanction #1959.

There was something else about the friendly relationship between Jim White and the AAA: he paid to have them in Daytona Beach. And, as always and everywhere, the scent of the dollar is powerful enough to smooth over any obstacle.

It was a lot of money. No report exists on the actual amount paid but, as a comparison, for the 10 days of the February 1928 Speed Trials the AAA issued a $4,700 invoice to the organizers, including $1,000 for the telephone system (money that remained in Daytona Beach as the contractors were local) and $200 for the timing wire devices.

At sunrise on Thursday, April 12, the Triplex left Fernwood Garage to be towed to the far northern end of the course.

The police had cleared the beach of the few early morning wanderers. Timing devices and a telephone network were installed by the contractors, who had been very early risers.

The daily chronicle indulged in a bit of poetry: "The officials stood at the judges' stand admiring the sunrise effect on the ocean."[1] The sun was slowly burning away the misty patches.

At 7 a.m. the mechanics started up the Triplex. Only a few minutes later the ring of the telephones announced that Keech was heading south.

The noise of the engines became louder along the four miles of the approach to the measured mile. Just after the car crossed the entry wire everybody noticed problems with the engines, their exhaust note intermixed with bangs and misfires. A thick black cloud came out of the right rear engine, mixed with bursts of flames—evidence of severe miscarburation.

White had just reached the judges' stand when Keech started his return run, immediately after his first run. Once again the noise and black smoke signaled that the carburation was still out of tune.

The two-run average was quite slow: 149.87 mph, due the rear engines misfiring and not yet at the right temperature. White informed officials and timekeepers that the runs were finished for the day. Everyone was about to leave when White reversed his decision and said that the problems were quite minor and that Keech was ready to start another run.

There was scarcely time to refit and re-check the timing system before the Triplex entered the measured mile going south: 146.57 mph. One of the engines was still misfiring.

In the meantime the tide had risen so rapidly that the mechanics didn't have enough time to check the engines properly before the new run. The day's program was over. It was a pity because sand and weather conditions had improved in the previous weeks.

The day after—Friday, April 13—in the early morning, Keech and Triplex were again on the beach. White had already informed pressmen and officials that he had to leave in the afternoon. So did Odis Porter, called back to Washington on some urgent matter.

Keech held his speed below 117 mph despite the engines running smoothly, much better than the previous day. Yet the sand was in worse condition, crossed by ridges that forced the driver to wrestle with the steering wheel to maintain his correct course.

The mechanics discovered the cause of the misfire: sand entering the carburetors. They cleaned them and understood that, somehow, filters should have been useful.

While the Triplex was crossing the measured mile a funny event occurred, prompting the few bystanders at such an early hour to laugh: a creative snapper had placed his camera, half-buried in the sand, in the middle of the measured mile, hoping for a shot from a very low angle when the car passed over. The car, running slowly and snaking, hit the camera and smashed it to pieces. The film and remains of the camera were strewn across the beach for several yards.[2]

2

The appeal of the April runs was fading. They felt like déjà-vu all over again. Daytoners were no longer excited. Furthermore, the supplement to the February Speed Trials was a competition without international contestants.

Malcolm Campbell, the Briton who had beaten both the American contenders, was a long way away in London. He was busy with celebrations and improvements to Blue Bird. He was also sketching the requisites of a new record site away from the Florida beach and its uncertainties about wind and sand.

The Daytona Beach News-Journal duly reported a detailed chronicle of all the runs, despite the scarcity of people on the dunes to watch them. Nobody ever thought to ask for their entry ticket.[3]

The daily used all its journalists' skills to raise the image of both cars and drivers. Lockhart's Blackhawk was the "aerodynamic wonder"; Keech's Triplex was "powerful." The co-star, the Whippet Four, warranted nothing more exciting than the comparatively cold "special."

On Friday, April 20, Keech opened the afternoon runs. The top speed of the four ways was 204.62 mph, an average of 201.11 mph—the highest speeds so far reached by the Triplex. They gained the honor of the leading headline on the front page of the local daily.[4]

The beach was perfect. At 3:58 p.m.[5] Lockhart started his first run: he could use the beach, reserved for White, thanks to his permission. It was more than a kind gesture, as Lockhart and Stutz shared the costs with White.

Remembering the February 22 accident, Lockhart raised his speed more conservatively. Furthermore, he was dissatisfied with the performance of the engine. In between the two runs (the second one northbound) he had the 16 spark plugs changed. The top speed was timed at 4:53 p.m., northbound into the wind: 200.33 mph. Not bad, yet not good enough for Lockhart, worried by the shaky carburation of the engine.

Wilbur Shaw and the Whippet Four, so far delivering disappointing performance, were on stage too. On Sunday, April 22, the morning paper reported: "The beach is expected to be in good condition at low tide, 3.25 pm, and it is believed by those who have been watching the trials closely and who know the power in the three special creations, that before sunset today two new records will have been set up, one by Shaw and one by either Keech or Lockhart, and American cars and drivers will reign as the fastest drivers in the world."[6]

A quasi-precise forecast.

3

A warm, glaring sun rose from the ocean on Sunday, April 22 and quickly lifted the mist. A gentle southeasterly breeze was in the air. The beach was smooth.

People didn't care about the Whippet Four, buried in the garage again to change another burnt-out piston. They felt that something exciting was in the air. By midday cars jammed Atlantic Avenue en route to the dunes: the queue stretched for three miles. At last the record runs had awakened the Daytoners.

The afternoon was Lockhart's and Keech's. The former opened the runs, yet he knew well that the engine was still out of tune. On the first northbound run he reached 201.455 mph, while on the return run he didn't make it past 84.152 mph due to the carburation problems. Anyway, it was a good opener to the feature runs of the day, starring the Triplex.

Ray Keech launched the Triplex southwards at about 4:30 p.m. The light was fading and the tide was coming in, reaching the pickets on the lower edge of the course.

The Triplex made such a thunderous noise that it drowned out the sound of the sea lapping on the shore. Against the wind it was timed at 203.96 mph, a good start towards the record. Keech didn't change his tires at the south end of the course: he and Jim White trusted the Firestones, which had a price tag of $1,300 for the four.

Turn the car around.

Start northwards with the wind.

Enter the measured mile in a cloud of black smoke, exhaust noise masking the cheers of the people gathered on the dunes, who felt that they were watching history in the making. And the story of the new land speed record was 100 percent American.

The chronicle:

> Keech had come south against a strong wind. As the powerful Triplex thundered over the speedway the crowd which had packed the sand dunes cheered madly, for they felt sure the big car was making a higher speed than before, somewhere close to the record. When the time was announced as 203.96 mph the crowd broke into delighted shouts, for at last it seemed that Keech was going to make it.
>
> Keech's return was awaited breathlessly and shortly afterwards the great car thundered north again at a terrific speed, its motors roaring perfectly, just a green bluff that whizzed past the pits. Tense with excitement, feeling a new record had been made, the crowd awaited the result.[7]

When Odis Porter emerged from the judges' stand he "was at a loss" (words by the chronicle) to account for the unbelievable failure of the timing wire at the entry to the measured mile. No passage was recorded and, as a consequence, no time was taken and no record was set.

Later on Keech said that the wind forced the car to zigzag along the course and, maybe, the Triplex missed pressing the timing wire.

Odis Porter, quite confused, did not provide an explanation for the failure. He added, hoping to absolve himself of any guilt, that they had checked the system immediately before the run and just after it: it worked perfectly. The exit wire had always worked with no fault. He declared that never in his life had something similar happened and he would "give five hundred dollars out of [his] pocket had it never occurred."[8]

Thinking about the failure again, AAA officials and timekeepers found a likely explanation in a jump of the car due to a ridge close to the wire: the car could have "flown over" the wire without a single wheel pressing it.

Three months later in his article in *Motor Age*, Jim White displayed not the slightest glimmer of diplomacy:

> The AAA timing device clearly demonstrated its inefficiency for beach conditions. I paid enough money for the rental of the Indianapolis track timing device to build several more suitable devices for the beach. The darn old trap went back home after failing to record when it was vital.
>
> The personnel of the AAA are mighty fine but, as I have said, I think their rules are antiquated, and I have ample reasons to find fault with their equipment and their attitude.[9]

He was even too polite after having spent his own money on the timing system, fees, and AAA officials' expenses in Daytona Beach.

What about Keech, after such a blow?

It is hard to trust the narrative, invented by some unknown author and reprinted many times,[10] that Keech stopped the car in front of the timing stand and, incensed, told the judges and timekeepers that he would go for the record again immediately and that they should take good care of their f****g systems.

We know that to stop and restart the Triplex was a long and complex action; thus Keech never brought the car to a standstill in between the runs.

The chronicle reports that Keech went by the front of the timing stand slowly while heading back south. The writer noticed that he had a forced grin on his face and gave a halfhearted hand signal.

When he reached the south end, close to the mouth of the Halifax River, he turned the Triplex around and headed northwards again as the light was fading and the haze was thickening. The official half-hour interval had passed; everything done before had to be scrapped.

4

Acceleration: regular.
Engines: synchronized.
Exhaust: black smoke, as usual.
Rev-counters: clicking around 2,500 rpm.
Keech pushed the throttle pedal to the floor: it was now or never.
The Triplex pressed the measured mile traps regularly.
The crowd on the dunes was cheering louder than before, awaiting the result. The system had worked correctly: time 16.83 seconds, speed 213.90 mph.

Keech started the return run southwards immediately, against the light wind. The chronicle reported that the engines suffered some misfiring; the exhaust smoke was blacker than ever and became useful for signaling the approaching car in the haze of the sunset.

A short wait for the result: officials and timekeepers now had to buy some benevolence after the previous failure. Time: 17.86 seconds; speed: 202.567 mph; averages: 17.34 seconds, 207.552 mph. New record. Malcolm Campbell beaten. Keech displayed a broad grin when he drove slowly back to the grandstand. The sentence to be written in the history books was quite simple and straightforward: "Boy, howdy! I never did so much running in all my life."[11]

As he left the car two strong boys carried him on their shoulders to the judges' stand. He accepted the congratulations coolly and quietly. He dismissed with a deprecating gesture a slightly burned arm caused by an engine backfire.

He said that he could have reached a higher speed if the wind had not picked up, pushing the car off course towards the dunes and forcing him to correct the steering, losing traction and speed in doing so. Pointing to the Triplex, he had words of thanks for the car: "And there she stands, not a serious break on her yet. The car has a lot more speed in her yet."[12]

Arriving back at the hotel Keech found a cable from Malcolm Campbell: "Bravo. Heartiest congratulations. You thoroughly merit success."

The day after, encircled by journalists, he dismissed the trite question about

Frank Lockhart (left) congratulates Ray Keech on his setting the new record on April 22, 1928: 207.552 mph driving the Triplex. The brave achievement by Keech deprived Lockhart of the honor of being the first American to win back the land speed record for America. Yet he carried on with the Blackhawk: he wanted to prove to the whole world that a small, light, scientifically designed and built vehicle could go faster than the behemoths like Triplex and Blue Bird. He was wrong.

how he felt being the new speed record holder, the first American driver to take the record from the Britishers: "Exactly like yesterday."[13]

The two British drivers deeply engaged in the land speed record play were asked to comment on the American achievement. Words by Malcolm Campbell and Henry Segrave were relayed from London to America. *The New York Times* published them despite being traditionally loath to report about technicalities and facts within the motoring world. Both quotes were bloated with nationalistic pride.

Campbell: "Congratulations today to Keech. He deserves his success if ever a man did, but I shall certainly make another attempt with the Blue Bird. Britain must win back the record."

Segrave: "We cannot allow Americans to hold this record long. I am waiting for Frank Lockhart to create a new record with his wonder car and expect him to add at least ten miles per hour. I am building a new car."[14]

Campbell went on to say once again that he disliked Daytona Beach as a record venue, dreaming about sites already proved to be grossly unsuitable: Pendine Sands and some mysterious "Sands in Denmark."

The background of such strange theories was quite stingy: "It is too expensive to cross to America again." Once again, Malcolm Campbell used words to disparage Daytona Beach and the Americans, who had welcomed and honored him as well as paying his expenses. Three years later and after the failure of his South African venture in 1929, he returned to Daytona Beach to win more records and money.

Both comments praised the driver (it was the bare minimum to be expected from sportsmen everywhere) but ignored the vehicle. Segrave went beyond Keech and the new record to accept a new record being established by Frank Lockhart in his Blackhawk as the natural outcome, the only American contender deserving of British respect and mention.

5

And now what, Lockhart?

He suffered a major blow to his technical and design principles. The Triplex—brutal, heavy, powerful, and primordial in technology, construction, and handling, the exact opposite of his car—had won the land speed record for America.

Lockhart had invested a large chunk of his personal finances and nearly a year of his life in the Blackhawk. He came close to ending his life on February 22. And now he was back in Daytona Beach to prove that his idea was not just a silly dream.

He had distilled in the Blackhawk the best of period know-how, engineering, parts, and materials. Every small detail has been thought up and designed by him and the Weisel brothers, assisted by suppliers and the small team of specialists who built the car. Fred Moskovics raised and managed the funds needed to complete the project and offered the whole power of the Stutz Company and the state-of-the-art facilities of their Indianapolis plant.

The land speed record was not the paranoid obsession narrated by Borgeson[15] and the authors who, for decades, copied him. Furthermore, Lockhart was in absolutely no need of additional money. He was well aware that his time in Daytona Beach was sliding by quickly towards the end of April. Only one week was left before he had to return to Indianapolis.

In February an Englishman had won the record. Now the honor of the first American driver and car to win it went to the Triplex and Ray Keech, for him a second-tier driver whose path he only crossed when lapping him on track.

Keech went through the ritual celebrations. On Monday, April 23, he was the guest of honor at a dinner in the Clarendon Hotel: he was awarded a gold watch

A close-up of Frank Lockhart shows his tense look in April, quite different from his smiling demeanor of February. The bandage under his chin to cover the two scars left from the February accident is clearly visible. Myron Stevens did another of his wonder-jobs straightening the cockpit side panels to be perfectly flush.

in front of 230 guests and everyone important in the city and across Florida. The watch meant the appreciation of the chamber of commerce and the municipality for being the first American to clinch the record, beating the British drivers who had held it for so many years.

Lockhart may have feared the repetition of events he already knew well. The new record had been achieved once more on a Sunday in front of a festive crowd. Maybe he also felt a vague recollection of Mrs. Means's prophecy when she had read his palm.

Monday came, and he was still fighting against the out-of-tune engine. Even the God of Weather was against him: the sand had worsened and the sky was loaded with dark clouds. Rain soon came. Though Lockhart had announced that he would take the Blackhawk onto the course, at 3 p.m. AAA officials and timekeepers closed the beach for the day: no runs.

On Tuesday, April 24, Frank Lockhart was ready for a trial run early in the morning to take advantage of the low tide, calm wind, improved visibility with the sun to the side, and the absence of any mist lingering on the early morning beach, dissipated by the higher April temperatures.

Jim White insisted on attacking the AAA officials: he mentioned the February agreement signed by him, Campbell, and Lockhart in the chamber of commerce, stating that no runs for the record would be allowed within 30 days of a new record being set. The reason was to have time for the promotion and publicity of the new record.

Arthur Means answered, on behalf of the AAA, that the agreement was limited to the February Speed Trials.[16] Lockhart could run, sharing the sand with Shaw and the Whippet Four.

The beach was theirs.

6

It was as though he hesitated to go for a record that was already in American hands. As though he feared he would be perceived as engaging in fratricide.

On Tuesday, April 24, Lockhart was ready with the Blackhawk at 6 a.m., just after sunrise. He knew that the early hours were best for sand, tide, a gentle breeze, and light on his side without any danger of being blinded by heading into the sun.

He recorded a 180.090 mph average over the two runs between 6:32 and 6:52 a.m. Before starting the southwards run at 7:33 a.m. he had the ice tank topped up. Maybe, in less than the half-hour interval, he changed the front wheels/tires because, for the first and only time, he drove the mile without the front wheel fairings. Speed southbound: 191.693 mph, the fastest of the day. Average: 182.048 mph.

The speed reached without the front fairings could have opened some doubts about their effectiveness as well as the impossibility of completing the wheel/tire

The only known photograph of the Blackhawk without its front wheel fairings, taken during the second southwards run on April 24, the third run of the day. The car reached a speed of 191.693 mph, the fastest of the day. Despite such a good performance without the fairings, Lockhart and the team raised no concern with the problem of changing the wheels/tires in less than half an hour. Between the earlier run at 6:52 a.m. and the third run at 7:33 a.m., 41 minutes had elapsed, and the car had to run again without any front fairings. Lockhart and the team were focused on fixing carburation problems. They did it later in the day, pushing the issue of wheel/tire changes back.

change in the half-hour allowed between runs. Lockhart was concentrating on the engine, still out of tune, as evidenced by the black exhaust fumes. He tried again in the late afternoon, past 6 p.m., and recorded 181.177 mph average. The highest speed was on the southbound run: 184.620 mph. Maybe he reckoned the engine carburation was correct after the hours spent in the garage tuning it.

Gar Wood, the famous motorboat record-holder and Henry Segrave's fiercest competitor on water, was there on the thinly populated grandstand on the dunes. Bill Sturm watched from the air, from a plane flying over the beach.

The next task for AAA officials, policemen, and people was at 6 a.m. the following day. It meant another very early wake-up for the contractors installing the wiring systems.

7

The Daytona Beach weather report for Wednesday, April 25 was for a clear sky, a light southeasterly breeze, and temperatures ranging between 65°F and 75°F. April 26 was forecast to be partly cloudy, with possible showers and gentle variable winds.[17]

Wednesday, April 25, 1928, dawned in Daytona Beach with clear skies, a light southeasterly breeze, and a minimum temperature of 65°F: a nice spring day in Florida. Frank Lockhart and the Blackhawk were on the beach very early in the morning to take maximum advantage of the low tide. At 6:35 a.m. Lockhart started his warm-up run southwards: the sun was rising over the ocean on his left side. Speed: 147 mph, just a good, final check of the whole package.

At 7:08 a.m. on April 25, Lockhart started his return run northbound. Once again more than 30 minutes had elapsed yet we don't know whether they changed the wheels/tires: the evidence from the narrative of the day suggests that they didn't. The speed on the return run was recorded as 167.169 mph.

7:32 a.m., April 25: In less than half an hour Lockhart started southbound again, against the wind. Ice tank refilled, wheels/tires untouched. Speed: 203.504 mph. The result was a good building block for the new record: the return with the wind would have guaranteed 214 mph, more than enough for the record.

7:59 a.m., April 25: With Blackhawk untouched at the southern end of the course, Lockhart commenced his return run. Acceleration was regular, no carburation problems, no side wind forcing the car off the correct course. The photograph was shot some distance from the measured mile. It is one of the last showing Frank Lockhart alive: disaster struck about 500 yards before the entry to the mile.

It was a nice spring day in Florida, while in New York the temperature was 40°F and Indianapolis was still in the grip of winter at 36°F. The figures explain why rich Easterners came to Florida in the first months of the year: warm and nice climate when it was still hard winter at home.

The southeasterly wind wasn't ideal to smooth the sand, yet it was blowing when Keech made his record runs, too. Lockhart didn't feel the sand and wind had been a problem on the previous day's runs.

Nobody checked the sand: it was too early in the morning to do so. Nobody had ever done it before the record runs.

Writers telling the story of the day some years after the event wrote that the beach was in perfect condition. The chronicle in the local daily, the only one to be trusted, mentioned many small ridges in the sand, to be expected with a southeasterly wind.

Lockhart was quite determined to go for the record. The engine was running smoothly albeit not 100 percent perfectly: anyway, it delivered the expected power when pushed to the 7,000 rpm needed for the record.

At 6:35 a.m. Lockhart started southwards for a trial run. At a speed of 147 mph, it was just a warm-up for both driver and car. A skid, rapidly corrected, sent the car 10 yards towards the water's edge.

7:08 a.m. Return run. Average of the two runs: 167.169 mph.

We ignore the controls done in the 20 to 25 minutes between the runs at the southern end of the course. For sure the wheels/tires were not changed nor the ice tank topped up: the latter operation was possible only at the northern end, where the local ice company's van was waiting.

Lockhart had to correct some skids during the return run, too. *The Daytona Beach News-Journal* wrote about a 25-degree deviation, a frightening figure if correctly reported.

In view of the gentle breeze, such a skid should have triggered a reconsideration of the conditions of the sand, as only a high ridge could have initiated the skid. Maybe it would have been wiser to postpone the record runs, but of course it's easy to be wise 94 years after the event.

At 7:32 a.m., in less than half an hour, Lockhart set off southwards again. Ice tank topped up, wheels and tires untouched, full confidence in the stability of the car despite the skids, faith in the condition of sand and wind.

The result—203.504 mph against the wind—was relayed to Lockhart while he waited at the southern end. He correctly thought that it was a good cornerstone of a new record. The return with the wind, even though a gentle breeze, would have guaranteed a 214 mph speed, more than enough to get the new record.

Lockhart and the mechanics at the southern end performed a visual check of the car. No one looked at the tires or inside the fairings to see if humid sand encrustations could unbalance the wheels. The final section of ground to the Halifax River was made up of a different sand from the longest stretch of the beach: it was reddish and damp, layered down the centuries by the river and covering the silicate surface pummeled by the eternal ocean waves.

The reddish sand stuck to the tires and covered the treads.

At 7:59 a.m., vehicle untouched, Lockhart started his return run. Telephones along the acceleration miles rang to signal that the run was underway.

The whine of the supercharger had a higher pitch than the exhausts and filled the air, drowning out the gentle lapping of the ocean. Very few people shared the moment: the grandstand in front of the measured mile was host to only a few dozen people.

Six cars were parked there, at the edge of the dunes. Two belonged to electricians, two to the course surveyors; one was driven by Means as a reserve car for the AAA officials and one was owned by a Mr. R.O. Simms of Daytona Beach, standing by if needed. Some yards away Ella Lockhart watched from another car together with her friend Jeanne Pringle, an actress from Pittsburgh.[18]

No ambulance was present on the beach at the request of Bill Sturm, who was afraid of the negative psychological impact on the driver.

220 mph was the estimated speed when the Blackhawk approached the measured mile, some 500 yards before the entry timing wire.

8

Let the period chronicle talk: "The Stutz Blackhawk Special went out of control five hundred yards away from the beginning of the official mile start, turned

The wreck of the Blackhawk, stationary after somersaulting seven times following the blowout of the right rear tire. Before the last jump, the body of the driver was thrown out of the cockpit. He came down on the sand, face down, arms by his side, in front of the grandstand and close to Ella Lockhart, who was among the first people to rush to him. He was dying.

sideways and hurtled thirty feet through the air. It went more than a hundred yards, turned down and came down on the beach broken in pieces."[19]

The more complete Associated Press story, published in Indianapolis, quoted Odis Porter: "On Lockhart's run north, about 500 yards from the grandstand I observed that his right rear tire blew and his car kind of sank. Then swerved one way and then the other, then rolled north about 350 feet, left the ground and bounced sideways. The car hit the ground about 550 feet north, bounced again 300 feet and threw Lockhart out. The car landed upside down."[20]

More dramatic and detailed was the story published on the front page of *The New York Times*, based on the AP report and completed by editorial lines:

> The light Stutz racer blew out a tire as it approached the measured mile timing wire and smashed to pieces in a 1,000-foot leaping skid. Lockhart was thrown limp and inert from the hurling car near the end of his maverick plunge down the beach, after it had jumped four times in the air, whirling and rebounding with the terrific momentum of its 200-mile an hour charge upon the beach course. The beach course was not in first-class condition for fast driving. Scarcely perceptible ridges made by the sea at high tide ran parallel to the course and made steering at high speed difficult.[21]

Such a precise witness was acknowledged by the Arthur Means report to the AAA Contest Board, dated May 1, 1928. Rushing to the sand before the rising tide washed all marks away, Means, other AAA officials, some policemen, and

The wreck of the Blackhawk raised the interest of the few bystanders, growing in number as the day wore on and the news spread all over Daytona Beach. It was anyway an easy task for police officers to keep the few people at bay. Frank Lockhart was carried by private car to the Halifax Hospital where he was declared dead at 8:35 a.m. on April 25, 1928. He was 18 days past 25.

journalists did a survey of the beach to find and measure the signs left by the car:

> The car seemed to take a course with the beach when suddenly the tracks left the ground completely for a distance of 57 feet. At the point where he landed first there were three very decided wheel marks gouged in the sand in a parallel position to the course.
>
> He again hopped into the air for a distance of 33 feet, there being three distinct wheel marks deeply gouged in the beach where he next landed, apparently indicating that the car did not land squarely but partially at an angle.
>
> He again hopped 36 feet and while in the air evidently turned crossways as he hit a ridge in the soft sand 20 to 24 inches high and gouged two very deep holes in this ridge, approximately 30 inches deep. The car at this point was sideways, the holes being at least 10 feet apart and about 5 inches wide each.
>
> He then made a very high bounce in the air travelling 140 feet before again making contact with the sand.
>
> He landed apparently sideways directly on the electric wires carrying the electric circuit from the trap to the timing instruments between the anchor post, for taking up tension on the starting wire, and the post carrying the marker indicating the start and finish of the mile record distance point. There were two deep impressions in the sand at this point, approximately 10 feet apart, indicating that the car landed crossways on the beach.
>
> He next bounced 120 feet and apparently landed on four wheels again, as at this point there were four distinct impressions in the sand, the two forward ones being considerably deeper than the two rear ones.

The left rear tire was still inflated after the disaster. The bodywork was wrecked, yet the engine didn't suffer any major damage and was salvaged when the wreck was taken back to Indianapolis. Bought and revised by Riley Brett, it was fitted to the S.M.I. Special, built by Myron Stevens and entered in the Indianapolis 500 in 1939, 1940, 1941, and 1946. Its best classification was sixth in 1940, driven by Bob Swanson.

The next bounce was 75 feet and the car evidently landed on its side or top as there was but one large irregularly-shaped hole in the sand approximately 10 feet wide, 5 feet long and 16 to 18 inches deep.

The next bounce was 41 feet, when the car came to rest. This entire accident happened directly in front of the judges' stand.

Note the quite uncommon use of "he" referring to the car: the Blackhawk was so closely tied to Frank Lockhart that it took on his gender.

The few bystanders on the beach were sparse in the grandstand. Ella Lockhart was close, seated in her car together with Jeanne Pringle.

Hans Orte, a snapper from the local LeSesne photo agency, was struck by a piece of the wheel fairing and had to be hospitalized to have stitches in a badly lacerated right hand. George Cash, a member of the team of electricians, was immediately discharged by the hospital having been only slightly hurt by another scrap of metal cutting his coat.

Sergeant Ernest Cupernall, patrolling the beach together with Sergeant Sandy Hager and Officer Adams, were in danger of being hit by the car jumping towards them and managed to dash out of the way: "When we saw that a crash was imminent, we darted out of the way. The car passed directly over my head, missing me [by] about two feet as it hurtled through the air. It seemed almost as if

In the aftermath of the February 22 run that ended in the ocean, Lockhart had said, "I sure built the car well." The Blackhawk, strong enough to survive the first crash, which spared the life of its driver, was still quite recognizable after the terrible jumps of the fatal accident on April 25. The tail cone was intact, as was the cockpit: the latter acted as a safety cell, despite such a concept still being far in the future. The lack of safety belts meant the driver was thrown out of the car. It would in any case have been impossible to survive the sudden decelerations from the heavy impacts on the hard sand.

I felt the breath of a living demon as the car hurtled overhead, the engine roaring and the wind whirling."[22]

For sure, both scribblers and policemen had the knack of poetry on that day in Daytona Beach.

9

Sergeant Cupernall identified the cause of the disaster immediately: "After the accident we examined the car's tracks on the beach and plainly saw marks that showed that the right rear tire was worn badly."[23]

We continue to read the impassive, detailed, and legalistically phrased report by Arthur Means:

> The cause of the accident has been attributed to a blown out right rear shoe. The deduction for this is placed upon the following investigation: the assistant surveyor of the course, Mr. G.H. Asbell, noticed, as did many others, that there were distinct impressions on the sand showing a fracture or break in the tread. He followed the course of the car north on its first run to the point where the brakes were applied to slow down to make the turn for the second, southerly run.
>
> Immediately after the impression in the sand indicating where the brakes had been released, two small fractures about the size of a silver dollar [diameter 1.5 inches] showed

The worst impact against the hard sand was inflicted on the front of the car. Front axle, wheels, and fairings were torn off the body together with the steering arms; one is visible close to the blown right rear tire. The front wheel fairings took the impact of the bounces on to the sand and left the front ice tank, made of steel rather than aluminum like the rest of the body, untouched.

up on the beach, while a third spot about the size of a dime [10-cent coin, diameter 11/16 inches] also eventually showed. The spots continued to the point where he made the turn for his second southerly run and the car departed on the southward trip with these spots plainly apparent.

It completed the southerly run of approximately 9 miles and the spots gradually increased in size until at the southern turn for the trip north the two spots the size of a dollar had grown to about 4 inches long.

Mr. Joseph L. Allen, Chief Judge, and Mr. L. Warren Baker, Assistant Timer and operator of the calculating machine, having noticed the spots in the sand also, secured a photographer and proceeded to the southern end of the course and had a series of photos taken. They plainly indicate the fractured tread and are submitted as part of this report as evidence that the tread of the tire had worn off.

On the return north, the size of the fractures continued to increase and at the point where apparently the tire blew out, the cord marks of the carcass were plainly discernible on the beach.

At the point where the fracture marks disappeared, the track broadened out plainly indicating that the tire had blown.

After the track flattened out, the car continued on an absolutely straight course for 100 feet before going in the skid described previously.

The deductions as outlined above were drawn from the actual marks on the beach. A diagram was made of every mark indicated in the sands, and attached to this report is a blueprint showing these marks as accurately as they could be paced and measured.

The car after the accident was a complete wreck. An inspection of the right rear tire at the garage immediately following the accident disclosed what apparently seemed to be a blow out. The hole was approximately 10 to 12 inches long and the cord carcass frayed all around the opening.

Pieces of the inner-tube were picked up for fully 100 feet along the beach, many of the pieces being found in the course where the car was still maintaining a straight line, although the impressions on the beach plainly indicate that the tire was flat.

Unfortunately the photos and the blueprint did not surface together with the written report. It has to be said that the diagram of the accident published by Borgeson[24] and other authors is rather too simplified to be relied upon.

Another report by the Society of Automotive Engineers (SAE)[25] was circulated; it confirmed that the damage to the right rear tire happened at the end of the northbound run when the driver applied the brakes. We have to remember that the brake pedal acted only on the rear wheels. According to the report, the braking action was excessive and lowered the tire deep into the sand, where it was cut either by a fragment of shell or by some other hard and cutting object buried below the surface.

The SAE report also explained the reason for the skid towards the dunes, i.e., on the opposite side of the blown tire: inflated at 125 psi, the tire stuck to the wheel because of the beading. The diameter grew due to the centrifugal growth of the sides and, as a consequence, the wheel increased the rotational speed and caused the skid on the other side.

On May 3, 1928, a photo was published on the front page of *The Daytona Beach News-Journal* showing the Blackhawk with three wheels in the air, the body pointing upwards, the right rear wheel deep in the sand to the lower edge of the fairing. A static image cannot explain the instantaneous forces acting on the vehicle.

A short movie[26] taken by a brave operator from the grandstand in front of the measured mile shows the accident from a few seconds after the blowout until the very end.

The first frames provide a confirmation of the Means and SAE explanations. At the end of the straight course after the blowout, the Blackhawk made a series of little jumps due to the ridges in the sand, assumed an upward trim and, out of control and subject to forces unknown to us and uncontrollable by Lockhart, pointed left to the dunes.

10

To provide a different angle to the story of the accident, we can quote the post, signed by Daniel Strohl, which appeared on *hemmings.com* on April 25, 2018, 90 years after the accident.

The author proposed a new theory to explain the facts, quoting the late Gordon Buehrig (1904–1990), a great automotive designer and technician, who designed the stock Stutz cars in the 1920s. According to what is reported as the Buehrig opinion, the cause of the accident was the seizure of the crown and pinion gears in the car's final drive. It had been taken out from regular Stutz production and it was well known that such a gear arrangement was a weak point in the cars of the marque. The seizure was caused by the engine suddenly stopping when it ran out of fuel.

The theory is nonsense, plainly contrary to proven facts, and against the reports from experts, officials, witnesses, and the direct checks on the beach. By the way, it is impossible that the tank was empty: 40 gallons could not have been used after only 22 miles running on the beach, plus warm-up time. And Sergeant Cupernall clearly told of the roaring engine when the car jumped over his head. We know also that the gears were purpose-built and carefully tested by Timken.

Another explanatory theory for the cause of the accident was reported by Zenas Weisel in a letter to his brother, John, on July 24, 1942. The text of the letter, published here for the first time, was mailed to the author by Jim Weisel, John's son, through Tom Kinney, in 2003.

Zenas Weisel wrote:

> I got to talking with a flyer by the name of H. Wilson Cain and showed him a picture of the straight away car. He surprised me by saying he was down the beach that morning and saw the accident. He said the run was made early in the morning just after dawn and that Frank had already made a run at 237 miles an hour. He was at the starting point and asked Frank how it handled and he said Frank said: "She's a honey."
>
> This flyer said the accident was all Frank's fault because he refused to take time and change tires. He said the cords were showing and that Frank saw them, but didn't want to take a chance of not getting the tires changed in time. He had made a good fast run and was going to sort of loaf on the way back so decided to take a chance.
>
> He said he had practised changing tires a lot and that because of the wheel fairings they had not been able to finish the job quick enough always.

He said Frank had stated he had made the prior run at about 260 judging from his tach speed so there must have been a lot of wheel slip.

He said that Frank said he wasn't going wide open, that there was a lot left under his foot.

The above lines report on words said by a third person 14 years after the event. Yet the letter was mailed by one of the designers to his brother, the other designer of the Blackhawk: for this reason it deserves the highest attention and the presumption of truth.

The words by H. Wilson Cain show a logical contradiction: he was at the southern end of the course and, as an obvious consequence, he couldn't have witnessed the accident 3.5 miles north of his vantage point. Yet it could be a simplification of the narrative.

A huge discrepancy emerges from the two figures about the speeds on the southward run, the second of the morning: Lockhart is reported as saying 237 mph first and 260 mph later, based on rev-counter readings. We know that the timed speed was 203.505 mph. Wheelslip eating up 14.3 percent of the related speeds seems too high even though we only consider the claimed figure of 237 mph. The 260 mph speed was outside the performance envelope of the car, and Lockhart knew that perfectly well.

Malcolm Campbell, by the way, in the four records he achieved in Daytona Beach from 1931 to 1935, complained about wheelslip as the cause of the differences between the readings on the rev-counter and the actual speeds. In the 1933 record he wrote of having read 328 mph on the rev-counter whilst the timed speed was 272.116 mph, i.e., a 17 percent difference due to wheelslip—a figure rather close to Lockhart's.[27] The sand was the same, yet nobody ever measured the coefficient of adhesion.

If the story were true (and it's a big "if"), Lockhart's decision to take such a chance on the return run would have been sheer folly after having seen the poor condition of the tires.

It was quite difficult either for Lockhart or for anyone else to visually check the tires. The open section of the tire under the edge of the fairing was about eight inches long at the tread. As a consequence the probability that the damage was in exactly that section was 8.4 percent. Furthermore, the tread was covered by the reddish humid sand picked up over the final yards of the course.

Should we take Means's report for granted (we do not have any reasonable doubt about doing so), we read that signs of the carcass cords appeared in the sand only from the point of the blowout: it was therefore impossible that the cords would have been visible when the car was standing at the southern end.

If Lockhart had seen the worn condition of the tire, as reported by Mr. H. Wilson Cain, he would have decided to start the third run completely contrary to his belief, his character, his attention to detail, the mental lucidity needed to go for the record, and the basic skill of a racing driver.

In the words of Mr. Wilson Cain, the issue of the wheel change—a job too long to complete within half an hour—surfaces again.

Should we assume that Zenas Weisel somehow agreed with those words?

He and his brother John were the designers of the mounting system for the fairings. The system demonstrated the practical impossibility of performing the wheel-change in less than half an hour. It could be the distant origin of the accident and death of Frank Lockhart.

Maybe Zenas Weisel hoped, at last, to wipe out some personal feelings of guilt, placing the disaster on the driver's shoulders for having made an irrational and foolhardy decision. Then as now, dead people cannot defend themselves.

11

And here an aside about a mystery still unresolved today: who supplied the tires to Lockhart in February and in the fatal April runs?

Many facts about Frank Lockhart in Daytona Beach and details of the Blackhawk are well known, but we do not and never will know the brand of tires fitted to the car.

Commenting on Frank Lockhart's trip to Daytona Beach, *The Indianapolis News* published a detailed article on the car's characteristics, listing the main parts and components and their suppliers. Regarding the tires, however, the article only mentioned the diameter (30 inches), adding that they were tested up to 3,000 rpm. Nothing else. The tires are the only component of the car without any mention of the supplier.[28]

Tom Kinney, a resident of Indianapolis, historian, and scholar of Frank Lockhart, discovered a long (five pages) typed report on Firestone letterhead[29] written by Mr. C.D. Smith of the development department of the company, to inform his colleague Mr. E. Waldo Stein, the company representative in Indianapolis, about the tire tests he supervised together with Lockhart.

He also wrote about "new tires" purpose-built for the Blackhawk, to be forwarded later to Indianapolis for tests on the dynamometric rig at the Stutz factory. The date of the report is January 23, 1928. When it was read in Indianapolis there were less than three weeks to go before the Blackhawk was due to be shipped to Daytona Beach.

We do not know anything about the tests of the "new" tires or if they were ever performed. We know nothing of the reasons that led Firestone to the decision to stop development and construction of the tires for Lockhart's beach car.[30]

We know nothing about what led to Lockhart discarding the Firestones, tires he knew well through their widespread use in track racing. Firestone was the trusted supplier of the tires for the Millers he had driven since the 1926 Indianapolis win.

Mr. Smith detailed the January 12 tests at various tire pressures and speeds to assess the centrifugal growth: at the highest pressure, 110 psi, the growth didn't exceed 30 millimeters. Such a figure guided the design and construction of the wheel fairings on the Blackhawk.

Test number six in the report dealt with Lockhart firing a 12-caliber rubber shot against a tire rotating at 3,000 rpm. The rubber bullet tore a hole from bead to bead and destroyed it.

Today it is difficult to understand the rationale behind such a destructive test as it was obvious that it would end in disaster: the rig was torn away from the floor whilst pieces of rubber, concrete, and metal were blown all around the room. Only a few small remains of the tire were left on the wheel rim.

The test was later exploited by some authors who built the Lockhart myth as a portent of what was to happen on the beach.[31] They quoted Lockhart as saying: "Now I know that I'm done if there is a blow-out."

The most likely explanation for the halting of additional tests, even though it might look too simplistic, was the lack of time to perform the tests required by Firestone and requested by the driver. Mr. Smith's report, very precise, detailed, and clinically technical, closes with the following words: "As far as blow-out is concerned, it hardly seems as though there is much danger of that, and I certainly

The outcome of the test on the experimental Firestone tire on January 12, 1928, on the Stutz dynamometer, which was able to spin a wheel up to 3,000 rpm. Frank Lockhart shot a caliber 12 rubber bullet at the tire spinning at maximum speed. As might be expected, the test ended in disaster: not only was the tire destroyed, but also the whole rig was torn away from the floor. Such a foolish experiment, with the cooperation of the Firestone specialist then working with Lockhart, was later cited as a premonition of what happened on April 25 (original by Jim Weisel; from Tom Kinney collection).

don't know what we can do to further minimize any chance of an occurrence of this kind."

Furthermore, adding to the lack of time and the forecast of significant capital investment by Firestone (they would have supplied the tires free of charge), a key role might have been played by management wanting to avoid any risk associated with Lockhart's venture. The company had already sold tires to Jim White for the Triplex; maybe they didn't want to supply two competitors, both Americans, chasing the same goal.

The second component of the mystery concerns the Mason tires supplied to Stutz for its mass-produced cars, including those shipped to Daytona Beach for the February 1928 stock car record runs. Without cross-referencing the sources, it was too easy for some authors to assume that the same brand of tire was used on Lockhart's beach car.

On such a theory—never checked against the facts—was built the myth of the $20,000 offered to Lockhart to select the company's new experimental high-speed tires. The myth was further dramatized by hypothetical lucubrations on the difficult financial situation of the driver: it was written that Lockhart was forced to accept the offer to avoid personal bankruptcy and the total failure of the program. All false.

The Dickinson Cord Tire tires sold by United Tire Corporation of Pottstown, Pennsylvania, advertised as "Every Dickinson tire is a racing tire," are the third component of the mystery.

Myron Stevens, builder of the Blackhawk body, sent a signed letter to the author on February 6, 1977, writing: "As for the tires, they were built by a relatively unknown company who would pay for advertising if the record run was successful. I can't say it for sure but I believe the name of the tires was Dickinson."

About 50 years on from the events it is quite normal for having some uncertainties. Furthermore, Myron Stevens, in his letter, did not mention the February runs, just April's.

Sarah Morgan-Wu and James O'Keefe, who authored the best and most complete biography of Frank Lockhart,[32] dug out a Dickinson ad published in the June 1928 issue of *Popular Mechanics* and bylined by an E.L. Merriman, retailer in Pine Plains, New York. The cover date of the magazine is two months after Lockhart's death.

The headline showed a lack of respect and civility: "Spectacular Performance of Dickinson Tires Wins Enthusiastic Endorsement of Foremost Race Driver."

The text was a letter supposedly mailed to the company by Frank Lockhart, who died on April 25 due to the blowout of a tire during his final record run at Daytona Beach.

In the letter Lockhart praised the Dickinson tires used when the accident occurred on February 22: "The tires stood up and it was fortunate for me that they did it as they permitted the car to slide. But had one of them gone far from sliding there would have been only one result. But they held and when the car was pulled from the water they carried approximately the full pressure as when I started the run."

We have to believe that such a letter was a fake due to the unbelievable bad taste contained in it. The closing lines are even more disgusting after the death of the driver: "I see no reason why Dickinson tires would not carry my life in another attempt to the world's record as soon as my hand heals. No tire would have served me better."[33]

Were we to trust such a despicable document by a cynical seller and an unethical ad-man, we could deduce that Lockhart used Dickinson tires in the April runs too.

Neither evidence nor documents have been discovered to support this hypothesis.

The truth remains buried. We will never find it.

12

Before the final hop of the Blackhawk, Lockhart was thrown out of the cockpit. No safety belts in those days. He came down on the sand some 30 feet ahead, in front of the grandstands, face down, arms by his sides.

Some of the few bystanders rushed to him. Someone even tried to resuscitate him. Blood was pouring from his nose, mouth, and ears. Ella Lockhart was among the first to reach him: her husband's body was thrown quite close to her car.

No doctor on duty. No ambulance. Mr. Simms's car was called in to rush him to Halifax Hospital. Ella Lockhart, Arthur Means, and a Mr. Ira A. Wharton, a Daytona Beach resident, jumped in the car. Bill Sturm wasn't there.

"Mrs. Lockhart, of course, became somewhat hysterical and although the writer tried to comfort her and assure her everything was all right, the trip to the hospital was a most gruelling experience," wrote Arthur Means in his report.[34]

When the car reached the hospital Lockhart had no pulse.

Dr. Klock was called to Halifax Hospital immediately and arrived in 10 minutes.

He could do nothing but confirm the official declaration of Dr. C.C. Bohannon, chief of staff, who pronounced Frank Lockhart dead at 8:35 a.m. on April 25, 1928. He was 18 days past 25.

13

The Associated Press network relayed the news across America immediately. Ted R. Gill, the special correspondent on the beach, had a narrow escape when the Blackhawk, out of control, passed over his head—impossible to be a closer witness than that.

Odis Porter, in his explanation of the accident to *The Daytona Beach News-Journal*, said that Gill went to Lockhart's body, then rushed to his car and zoomed away to find a telephone booth to communicate the news, as was his professional duty.

The news went out through the transatlantic cables and reached the UK quickly.

The Daytona Beach News-Journal missed reporting directly on the most significant local event of the year. They had no reporter on the beach that morning, incredible for a daily covering facts and gossip surrounding the record runs in detail.

Being an afternoon paper, they had enough time to cover the event and devote the entire front page to it. The leading headline gave a crude synthesis: "Stutz-Lockhart Crash—Driver Dead." The news article was the Associated Press dispatch dated Daytona Beach, April 25, quite strange for the local daily.

The first column listed the early comments from Daytona Beach, Indianapolis, and London, also publishing the immediate reactions of some VIPs. The editor, Eugene Pulliam, was away, travelling across Indiana, and the column opened with his message of sympathy cabled to Ella Lockhart: "Terribly shocked by tragic news of Frank's accident. He was a wonderful boy and I admired him sincerely. You have my heartfelt sympathy." Quite a stale cliché for such a message.

Fred Moskovics issued a better phrased statement from Indianapolis, where the Stutz factory closed as a mark of respect: "It is only fair to say now that he should not have gone to Daytona Beach at this time. His hand was not cured from the first accident. It still was weak. I did all I could to dissuade him from going and begged him to take no needless chance, for if ever there was an event where a driver needed every physical resource to attain success, this was the event. Yet he tackled it with a crippled left hand because it was in his blood to get that record."[35]

As the boss of the Stutz concern, Moskovics was pestered by reporters chasing his comments, better if exclusive. *The New York Times* published these words: "(I consider) Lockhart the greatest mixture of driver and mechanic in the world today. I believe in him to such an extent that I have given him every aid possible and taken him as a member of Stutz's engineering staff. Our problem with him is to let him off the job. He would work all of the time if we'd let him. He never drinks, never smokes and doesn't swear."[36]

We have to note that Moskovics talked about Lockhart using the present tense as though he were still alive. The words display further strong proof of the deep affection he held for Lockhart.

Arthur Means added a statement he attributed to Fred Moskovics in his report, no other mention of which has been found in any Daytona Beach or Indianapolis paper:

> Mr. Moskovics was of the opinion that the blowout did not cause the accident but that Mr. Lockhart had lost control and gone into a skid, causing the tire to blow as a result of this skid, rather than the skid resulting from the blowout.
>
> At this writing [May 1, one week after the event], the report of investigation which he intended instituting at Indianapolis with several of the prominent automotive engineers has not come to hand. However, it is the opinion of those present at the beach that the accident was the result of a blowout and not the result of any physical deficiency on the part of Mr. Lockhart.[37]

Means's words are for sure the most credible among the deluge of theories and petty explanations issued after the accident. They place a tombstone on the insinuating words of Moskovics, if indeed they were ever uttered. Words impossible to be vested with justification from a top manager who trusted Lockhart completely and, as in the statement to *The New York Times*, provided finance and counsel, was always at the forefront, and rushed to Daytona Beach to handle the rites. Once again, we have to repeat that to blame a dead person was and still is the most common procedure.

No documentary evidence exists on the manufacturer of the tires fitted to the Blackhawk in April, yet the corporate defense by Moskovics charging Lockhart as solely responsible for the tragedy raises some suspicions: Stutz used Mason tires as original equipment on their production cars.

Perhaps, could it be that there was some vestige of truth in the tale that Mason offered Lockhart $20,000 to use their tires on the Blackhawk in April? A successful record run would, of course, have boosted the Stutz image.

With no evidence and factual checks many authors have written the tale.[38]

14

> Look you and see friend
> By the gray light of dawn
> Where a conqueror of speed
> Has conquered and gone.
> A slave of the ambition
> A hero of might
> Has passed to eternity
> As passes the night.
> Gone, aye, forever
> In the space of a breath.
> Builder of Science
> But conquered by Death.

The verses written by Ethelyn Towner, junior at the Mainland High School, Daytona Beach, had the honor of leading on the front page of the local daily focusing on the accident, even before the series of comments and words of sympathy.[39]

Ray Keech: "There is only one way I can feel. Frank was a wonderful boy and a great driver and you can truly say that the automobile world has lost one of the most promising youngsters seen to touch a wheel. My sympathy goes out to Mrs. Lockhart and Frank's entire family and I only hope that they feel as I do, that Frank was trying to help the world in general when he met his death seeking new automotive speeds."[40]

At Brooklands, Malcolm Campbell said: "He was very keen on his job and was one of the first to congratulate me when I set my record figures in my Blue Bird. The motoring world has suffered a great loss in his death."[41]

Campbell supplemented his typically egocentric statement with some more suitable remarks to London dailies and correspondents of the American press:

"His death is a great loss. He belonged to the best type of American young manhood and resembled Colonel Lindbergh in many ways. He was very quiet and lived for his job. After his smash in February I advised him not to try again until he was quite well. I am afraid he did not wait long enough."[42]

Henry Segrave in a statement published in *The Daytona Beach News-Journal*: "America has lost her greatest racing driver. I cannot say how sorry I am. His little car must have been far too light for such speed. Lockhart put heart and soul into his machine. It is awful to think he has been killed after his providential escape in February. I am left without words."[43]

Segrave's statement released to the London dailies and relayed to *The New York Times* was shorter and stronger: "It is dreadful, absolutely dreadful. Lockhart was one of the heartiest and jolliest boys you could meet, full of brains, and one of the pluckiest men I knew. America has lost her greatest race driver in Lockhart."[44]

Both the great British drivers praised the human side of the fallen driver alongside his unbroken skill in racing, yet their different attitudes display clearly and straightforwardly their different approaches based on family heritage, education, and racing business.

Wilbur Shaw, who was on the beach and was among the first people to get to Lockhart's body and to check the marks left in the sand: "The accident was not the fault of the beach, not the fault of officials and occurred because of the little oversight in checking the tires. It is perhaps a lesson to all other drivers. Together with Floyd Smith and the whole team of the Whippet party, I can only express our sincere sympathy [to Mrs. Lockhart] for the loss of her husband. Small consolation can be gained from this, but if there is any to be gained, she shall know that her loss is ours."[45]

George Souders, driver and competitor at the Indianapolis Speedway and on tracks across America: "Frank Lockhart was the greatest driver the world has ever known. And he was more than a speed wonder. Lockhart was an automotive engineer of unusual ability and a designer as well. Racing and developing racing cars was his chief aim in life. He was as devoted to this work as Lindbergh is to flying. The game has lost a wonderful performer, a clean driver and a young man of the finest character."[46]

Theodore E. "Pop" Meyers, Indianapolis Speedway general manager: "Lockhart was a mighty fine type of young manhood, a sensational driver and a true sportsman. He came here in 1926, a modest unassuming boy. Success did not change him. Lockhart had rare gifts as a practical mechanical engineer. His end undoubtedly cut short the career of a mechanical genius."[47]

Edward H. Armstrong, mayor of Daytona Beach: "WHEREAS the city of Daytona Beach is deeply grieved at the tragic accident that cost the life of a courageous pioneer of the racing world AND WHEREAS it is fitting and proper that our citizens show the highest respect in which they hold the memory of Frank Lockhart NOW THEREFORE I E.H. ARMSTRONG, MAYOR OF THE CITY OF DAYTONA BEACH, FLORIDA, by virtue of the authority in me vested do hereby declare a period of public mourning for two full days, Wednesday and Thursday, during which time the American flag shall be lowered to half-mast throughout the city."[48]

5

Epilogue—May

1

Poor Lockhart. His death opened up a Pandora's box of fake news and lies. The perversion of creating scandals and thrillers around the tragic end of a well-known personality blew up everywhere across the United States, California being the main source.

The origin was an Associated Press dispatch from Los Angeles on April 26, 1928, the day after the tragedy.[1] The text included a quote by Carrie Burgamy Lockhart, Frank's mother: "I begged him to stop trying for records. I told him it could end only one way. And, well, it has."

To add credibility and substance to the short text, the opinion of Harry Miller was also included: he aired his belief that Lockhart had invested every penny of his money in the Blackhawk and was therefore financially pressed when he drove it to his death. Miller added: "He raced in Daytona Beach before his hand was healed from a previous accident. He hoped to establish a new record and relieve his financial situation."[2]

Harry Miller's quotes are questionable despite his authority and personal credibility because it was well known that he didn't like Lockhart, guilty of having successfully modified racing cars that he, the great Harry Miller, considered already so perfect as to make any improvement sacrilege.

Carrie Burgamy Lockhart had lived in respectable misery at 1033 West Sixth Street, Los Angeles since being widowed by the death of Caspar Lockhart, 49, on March 31, 1920. She made her life as a seamstress and, using what little money she had, she contributed towards the cost of Frank's early cars to race on the Californian dirt tracks.

Another AP dispatch from Los Angeles[3] relayed the story that the furniture in Carrie's home had been mortgaged to pay for the tires used by Frank in his final runs in Daytona Beach. Fake news, born of a perverse attempt to make the story more intriguing for readers.

Carrie was also reported as having said that she didn't have enough money to pay for a train ticket to Indianapolis for the funeral, accompanied by her other son, Robert. Furthermore, she said she didn't have the funds needed to pay for Frank's burial in Los Angeles.

Here might be the source of the legend of the delirious cable from Frank to his mother: "Ma, I have the world by the horns. You'll never have to push a needle again. I'll never have to work anymore."

The text was published by Borgeson[4] as the answer to a letter from Carrie mailed in early April to Frank care of The Clarendon Hotel, Daytona Beach, asking for 10 dollars to stay afloat.

Nobody ever saw either letter or cable, yet they were the basis of the false story[5] that Lockhart died "penniless," i.e., cash-strapped, having burnt all his own money on the Blackhawk, and that no one in the family had the funds needed for the funeral and burial in California.

The next step was spared us by Borgeson, yet it was to circulate a lot because once again in 1994 two authors in Daytona Beach repeated it in a book on the history of racing on the beach and on the Trioval. Other pages in the book are nevertheless factual and reliable.[6]

Their dirty story tells how the Daytona Beach citizens had started a generous money-raising program to pay for Frank Lockhart's last rites. They were said to have given the collected sum (which was never disclosed) to Ella Lockhart, who, in the dirty story becoming dirtier, fled the town with the money, leaving Frank's body in the Beach Street Funeral House.

A new money-raising program reached a positive conclusion and, after a few months, his body could be moved to California for burial, close to the birthplace of his mother, brother, and Ella.

The above-mentioned lines report a sequence of lies. Someone already back in the 1920s wanted to titillate the inclination towards gruesome stories that a lot of people like (though they're reluctant to admit it).

The documented facts tell another story.

2

Fred Moskovics, accompanied by his wife, rushed to the Southeast on board the first available express train leaving Indianapolis. He reached Florida in the late evening of April 26 and disembarked in Jacksonville, where he was met by one of the team mechanics, who drove him by car to Daytona Beach.

Ella Lockhart, described by the local daily as "the brave Californian girl who witnessed her husband's death," was a guest of Dr. Guy Klock and his wife, who cared for her at their home.

Moskovics immediately took charge of the rites and arrangements. With Ella Lockhart's consent, he managed to change the preliminary program to have the body taken to Los Angeles, where Frank's mother lived. He said that Frank Lockhart was an Indianapolis citizen and there the last rites had to be celebrated.

Hundreds of citizens of Daytona Beach paid their last respects to Frank Lockhart, the "intrepid young driver" described by the *Daytona Beach News-Journal* in the April 24, 1928, issue. The bier was in the funeral chapel of Bingham and Maley on Second Avenue.

On Saturday, April 28, the bier, covered by flowers and with Arthur Means and Odis Porter as escort of honor, was moved to the railway station and aimed at Indianapolis, between two lines of silent, grieving people. The silence was broken only by the hum of an aeroplane piloted by a Mr. Lindley, a local aviator. He flew over the short cortège throwing flowers.

Ella Lockhart, "pale but composed and gracious in her bereavement as always, holding a bouquet of flowers,"[7] boarded the last car of the train to Indianapolis. With her were Mr. and Mrs. Fred Moskovics; Mr. and Mrs. Bill Sturm; and Mrs. Julia Burgamy, Frank's aunt, who had arrived from Cincinnati, Ohio.

The farewell from the city of Daytona Beach was delivered by Mayor Armstrong, who opened a week of wakes to be celebrated in every local church. The Kiwanis Club announced a series of conferences open to boys of all ages to praise the sacrifice of another boy, Frank Lockhart, who gave his life to scientific progress through automobile racing for the glory of the country.

There was no doubting that the citizens of Daytona Beach shared the deep sadness of Frank Lockhart's death.

A local newspaperman wrote a few lines full of sweet poetry, which took away any scent of racial discrimination from the definition of "negro" (at that time not considered in any way offensive): "The many who lined the streets waited until the train had vanished, then silently turned away and left the station. A negro boy walked toward one of the fallen flowers, paused for a moment, then walked around it leaving it there unmolested. Overhead the hum of the airplane died away into silence. The body of Frank Lockhart has gone."[8]

3

The train reached Indianapolis's Union Station around midday on Sunday, April 29. The scenario was different from that in February. No parade of cars, no horns blowing: only a hearse heading for the Flanner & Buchanan Funeral House, 23 West Fall Creek Boulevard.

The Reverend Doctor Lewis Brown, rector of St. Paul Episcopal Church, was appointed to celebrate the rites.

Theodore "Pop" Meyers selected the pallbearers from racing VIPs: Earl Cooper, dean of the drivers who raced in the Indianapolis 500; Peter de Paolo, reigning AAA National Champion; Tony Gulotta, driver, Lockhart's friend and wingman-to-be; George Souders, winner of the 1927 Indianapolis 500; Lora L. Corum and Gil Anderson, Stutz stock car drivers; and Jean Marcenac, member of the team who built the Blackhawk and who was in Daytona Beach in February and April.

The rites had to be postponed to the afternoon of Tuesday, May 1, waiting for the arrival of Carrie and Robert Lockhart from Los Angeles. Carrie fell ill during the journey and was hospitalized in St. Louis, Missouri. She never made it to Indianapolis.[9]

The Stutz factory closed during the rites.

The mayor of Indianapolis, Mr. Lemuel Ertus Slack, attended the funeral service. Eugene Pulliam was appointed as the official representative of the Daytona Beach Municipality: he was already in Indiana for tasks related to his job as editor-in-chief of *The Daytona Beach News-Journal*. The message cabled by Mayor Armstrong appointing him closed with the following words: "The city of Daytona Beach bows with humble spirit today at the bier of the boy whom we learned to love."[10]

Dr. Brown's sermon was broadcast by a local radio station. What he said may today appear unimaginative and somehow obsolete, closer to the European rhetoric of the period than the American factual objectivity: "He was a martyr to science as surely as any man who ever gave himself to science. He gave himself completely to his machine, to the definite purpose for which he was striving. He died as nobly as any soldier on the battlefield and in this spirit he should be remembered. His life should be a beacon to all who strive for high achievement."[11]

Ella Lockhart sent a message of thanks and respect to Daytona Beach citizens through Eugene Pulliam. She said, between sobs: "Please tell the people of Daytona Beach that I can never express my appreciation for their wonderful kindness and words of sympathy."

The long article in *The Daytona Beach News-Journal* from Indianapolis praised the wonderful courage shown by Ella Lockhart despite the deep sorrow of the tragedy.[12]

The casket was placed in a private mausoleum until it could be taken to Los Angeles for burial.

Frank Lockhart now rests in the Forest Lawn Memorial Park, Glendale, Los Angeles County.

4

After the emotion of the rites, mundane facts had to be dealt with and agreed upon.

The wreck of the Blackhawk was unloaded back in Indianapolis on May 4 to go through detailed checks either to confirm or deny the Moskovics theory on the cause of the accident. No report on such a check, if indeed it ever took place, exists.

Bill Sturm said that he had the intention to rebuild the car to prove Lockhart's theory that a scientifically designed and built car with a small engine could go faster than all those vehicles relying on sheer power alone. He affirmed: "Someone should perpetuate his interest and ability by taking up the work where he left off."[13]

Ray Keech answered, saying that he was available to drive the rebuilt Blackhawk. He added: "I believe that the car is the fastest car in the world and capable of travelling 225 miles an hour. I want to see the car repaired and personally I'd like to take it back to Daytona Beach and drive it."[14]

Fred Moskovics stated that, should the Blackhawk be rebuilt, it had to be done outside the Stutz facilities and without his personal commitment.[15]

Lockhart's will wasn't signed, so the value and distribution of his estate had to be ascertained. Malon E. Bash, judge in the Indianapolis Court of Justice, appointed Fred Moskovics as administrator of the estate, which was tentatively valued at $10,000 plus the two Miller-Lockhart racing cars ready for the next 500-Mile Race on May 30, 1928.

On May 7, Louis Chevrolet and Charles Merz, drivers and important persons in the racing fraternity, submitted their appraisal of the goods in the estate[16]: the bank account contained $5,725.85; credits due were $1,974.33, including reimbursement of the entry fees for the Indianapolis 500. The value of the insurance policy for the February 22 accident still had to be ascertained.

The most valuable goods were the two Miller-Lockhart racing cars, by far the absolute best in America and, as such, in strong demand. They were conservatively valued at $3,000 for the first and $5,000 for the second. Spare parts and tools were estimated to have a value of $5,068.

Goods, cash, and credits totaled $27,033.93—certainly not the amount left by a "penniless" man.

The first racing car was left to Ella Lockhart, who expressed the intention to enter it in the Indianapolis 500, to be driven by Tony Gulotta in the name of Frank. It was set off against her share of the estate.

Debts against the estate totaled $22,302.67 including claims by Curtiss Aeroplane Company for the wind tunnel tests ($689.48), the Daytona Beach funeral home bill ($458), two large amounts totaling about $8,000 made by the Stutz Motor Car Company for travel and expenses in Florida and for the Indianapolis funeral.

After all claims had been settled, on June 11, 1929, Ella Lockhart retained ownership of the first racer, valued for the estate at $3,000, and received $7,606.99 cash. Carrie Burgamy, Frank's mother, received cash for her quarter of the assets, worth $3,935.66. It was a significant sum at that time ($64,349 in early 2022 value), which reimbursed her for every dime she had put into Frank's early racing cars. She could then live a quieter life.

Ella Lockhart returned to California at the end of June 1928 and again took up her job as switchboard operator. Just after World War II she remarried and moved to Oregon, returning to California after the death of her second husband. She died in 2002 at age 101. She rests together with Frank in the Glendale cemetery.[17]

5

It's nonsense to call "penniless" a man who left an estate worth $27,000. Yet some narrow-minded West Coast hacks much preferred the fake news of a mother in need, impoverished by the folly of her son and his racing cars, leaving her destitute without even the money to travel to his funeral and bury him in California, close to home.

The story, relayed by the wire agencies, appeared in many papers in the Los Angeles area and reached Daytona Beach.[18]

Too much.

On May 15 Bill Sturm could no longer bear to see such a barrage of fake news and issued a statement to the Indianapolis offices of the wire agencies, also repeated in Daytona Beach:

> She [Carrie Lockhart] never had a dime invested in the car and there is absolutely no need for her to have any funds to bring Frank's body to Los Angeles. Mrs. Frank Lockhart is able to take care of that.
> There have been so many misstatements since Lockhart's death that in justice to Frank they must be cleared off.
> There never has been a bit of truth in the statement that Frank's body was held at Indianapolis and could not be shipped to a heart-broken mother in Los Angeles until his debts were settled. Mrs. Frank Lockhart wishes it distinctly understood that she wanted his body brought to Indianapolis because Frank's life centered here.
> At Indianapolis he had met people who appreciated his ability to the utmost. Fred E. Moskovics, president of the Stutz Motor Company, could not have treated Frank any better had he been his son. Frank Lockhart's wife is the one to be considered. Whenever Mrs. Frank Lockhart gets ready to take Frank's body west, she will do so.

And finally the strong denial of the "penniless" rumor:

> Frank did not die penniless, regardless of reports to the contrary. When Mr. Moskovics will conclude his trust and the estate finally is settled, his mother will have her legal one fourth, even though in a will that was not signed Frank left everything to his wife.
> Mrs. Frank Lockhart will be able to live without asking charity of anyone.
> It is about time that western newspapers and others ascertain the facts before they publish misleading statements. The true facts can be obtained only by Frank Lockhart's widow.

At the conclusion of such strong and clear words against un-named journalist colleagues, Sturm reiterated his praise for Lockhart, already published elsewhere:

> I repeat emphatically Frank Lockhart was as fine a character as I have ever known. He was fair to everyone. It is a pity that he cannot now be here to speak for himself.
> If Daytona Beach will always remember him as a straightforward little gentleman in every particular, Daytona Beach will make no mistake. No mother or father in Daytona Beach should ever wish for a finer boy as a son.[19]

6

The Blackhawk was never rebuilt. The engine was recovered and revised by Riley Brett, who later had it fitted in the S.M.I. Simpson Motor Special, built by Myron Stevens to be raced in the 1939 Indianapolis 500, driven by Bob Swanson, 26, who qualified 22nd and was forced out on lap 19: final classification 31st.

The car/engine package did better in 1940, driven by Bob Swanson again: 20th on the grid and sixth at the checkered flag, four laps behind winner Wilbur Shaw driving the Maserati Boyle 8CTF in his second win in a row. The car was entered in the 1941 race to be driven by Deacon Litz, 42: he qualified 29th and

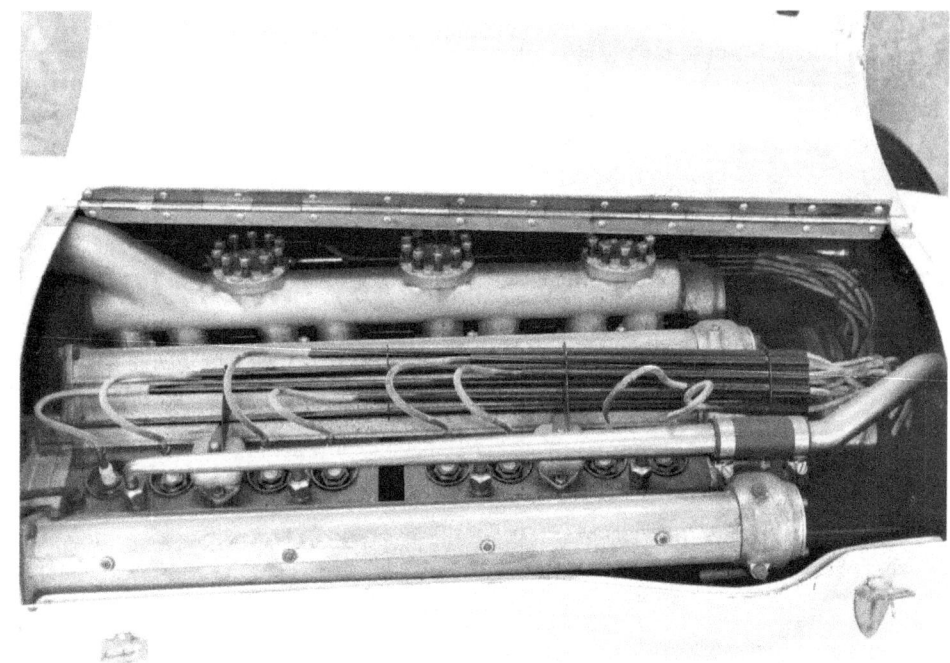

The 1939 S.M.I. Sampson Motor Special has been preserved in the Indianapolis Speedway Hall of Fame Museum, in its final trim as modified by Gordon Schroeder. The engine, photographed in 1975, shows the craftsmanship and precision of Frank Lockhart. The upper tube from the supercharger is linked to the inlet valves. The lower tube is for the cooling fluid connected to a traditional radiator (author's photograph).

was out on lap 89, 22nd. In 1946, when racing at Indianapolis resumed after the break due to the war, the car was modified by Gordon Schroeder and driven by Sam Hanks, 32. He qualified for the race on the outside of the front row yet only lasted 18 laps in the race: 31st.[20]

The first Miller-Lockhart was entered in the 1928 Indianapolis 500-Mile Race by John Burgamy, Frank's maternal uncle, for driver Tony Gulotta. Tony should have been Frank's wingman in the Stutz Team racing the two Miller-Lockharts. Gulotta had the racing No. 8 instead of the No. 2 given to Lockhart, who had ranked second in the 1927 AAA National Championship: racing numbers followed the previous year's final classifications in the championship.

Consciousness of fair competition rules, the well-known speed of court ruling, the costs of a legal action (which they would certainly have lost), and the egocentric and temperamental attitude of Harry Miller pushed the Stutz Company to publish on May 29, 1928 (i.e., on the eve of the race) a large ad in *The Indianapolis News* to clarify the whys and wherefores of the presence of Tony Gulotta's No. 8 racer, entered as the Stutz Special.

Headline: "A Statement to the Public in the Interest of Fair Play."
First section of the text:

> Sincerely believing that where credit is due, credit belongs, the Stutz Motor Car Co. Inc. desires to announce that the Stutz Special (racing car No. 8) which Tony Gulotta will drive

in the 500-mile race at the Indianapolis Motor Speedway is not a Stutz product. Basically, it is a Miller-built racing car—into which have been incorporated a number of very vital changes. These changes—and they are considered to be improvements—came from the hand and mind of the late Frank Lockhart of our engineering department, who had expected to drive the Stutz Special in the 1928 race.

Two columns followed listing the 19 changes Lockhart had made. Then a carefully worded explanation of the company's interest in racing:

> Our interest in professional racing was entirely due to the fact that we wanted to enlist the genius and the ability of the late Frank Lockhart, realizing that his experience with the small, high-efficiency engines would keep our organization fully alive to all the niceness of design and precision workmanship—with the idea that these qualities must inevitably reflect themselves in our everyday production.
>
> We were certain that these highly-stressed mechanisms held the secret to long life, SAFETY and smooth handling—and that the regular Stutz organization would be bettered by that knowledge.
>
> This knowledge is now reflecting itself in the greater care and painstaking effort with which Stutz cars are produced and the desire for the attainment of an ideal which permeates our entire organization.

The word "Safety" is in uppercase in the original. The closing copy was printed in lower case, due to the shortage of paid-for space, yet it brought home the key message: "With the passing of Frank Lockhart, we withdrew from active racing—and Tony Gulotta's car is designated Stutz Special because of our knowledge that it was the wish of Frank Lockhart—and the racer is not so-named from any desire upon our part to sail under colors that rightfully belong to another."

Byline: "Stutz Motor Car Company of America, Inc."

Tony Gulotta qualified fourth in the 1928 Indianapolis 500 at 117.031 mph. Pole went to Leon Duray, front-wheel drive Miller, 122.391 mph. Gulotta was in the lead at 450 miles but 18 laps (i.e., 45 miles) before the checkered flag he had to pit to clean the clogged fuel line. He finished 10th at full distance.

The second Miller-Lockhart with spares and tools was bought in early May 1928 by Ed and Maude Yagle from Philadelphia. They paid $14,800, a price much higher than the value assessed within the estate and close to the regular market price tag of a 91 Miller racer. The added value came from the Lockhart-made improvements.

It was driven by Ray Keech, who qualified 10th and finished fourth in his debut Indianapolis race.

In 1929 Keech started from the outside of row two in the same car and won the race. A fortnight later, on June 15, 1929, he died on the Altoona, Pennsylvania, board track.

On March 13, 1929, in Daytona Beach, the Triplex runs on the sands ended up totally wrecking the car, causing the death of the driver, Lee Bible, and a cameraman, Charles Traub, who was filming too close to the course.

Two of the 1928 Speed Trials vehicles finished as wrecks.

Two protagonists of the 1928 story met their deaths in cars either built or modified by Frank Lockhart.

7

What was left of the 1928 Daytona Beach Speed Trials after such a tragic end?

The event unlocked the golden age of the land speed record, which lasted for a decade before World War II. In the 1930s the land speed record was a British-only business: Malcolm Campbell, Kaye Don, George Eyston, John Cobb.

The competition between the last two drivers pushed Eyston to the 357.49 mph record on September 16, 1938. Cobb had the last hurrah of the Golden Age, clinching the record again on August 23, 1939 (one week before World War II started), at 368.85 mph.

In the 1930s, the only record retaining a bit of magic, the only record that involved the breaking of a mythical barrier, was Campbell's five-miles-a-minute in 1935.

Members of the general public were not moved to any deep emotional feelings by the achievements by John Cobb, a wealthy British gentleman seeking higher speeds at the wheel of an exotic vehicle far removed from the common perception of a car, speeding in the middle of nowhere.

John Cobb's return to the Bonneville Salt Flats in 1947, when he was 48, was seen as a snobbish and obsolete gesture by a man past his prime. However, he raised the record to 394.20 mph on September 16 driving the same vehicle of 1937 vintage, which had been mothballed in America during the war. What emotion could be raised by a burly Londoner driving his vehicle in a no-no land, powered by engines designed 30 years before?

In the same year jet airplanes flew much faster than was possible with traditional piston engines like the ones used by the land speed record seekers. In December 1947, news of an aircraft breaking the sound barrier was released: a U.S. experimental rocket plane, the Bell X-1, had recorded the Mach 1.06 speed on level flight, i.e., 700-plus mph, over 300 mph faster than the fastest period car.[21] It took another 50 years for a land vehicle to reach the same goal.

At the time of the 1928 Daytona Beach Speed Trials the scenario was very different: the land speed record generated deep fascination, interest, and emotion. It was a key issue of the whole automotive scenario.

The British media promoted the quest for ever-higher speeds, building on the fame of Malcolm Campbell and Henry Segrave, the country's speed heroes.

In April 1928, *The Autocar* published a full page focusing on the future of land speed records, ennobled by the adjective "great." The piece began with discussion of Lockhart's and Campbell's vehicles. As customary with the British media, the Triplex was ignored, even though it was the record holder, having bested Campbell.

Issue no. 1: car weight and stability at 200-plus mph speeds. Many doubts still lingered within the inner circle of experts about the architecture, weight, and aerodynamics of the record car. The article advanced the four-wheel drive option as the solution to reduce the effects of the side-wind and make the vehicle stable. Doubts about the tailfin surfaced again.

It was taken for granted that the Daytona Beach sandstrip was the only available site for the record. The mile speed record-seekers had to wait seven years to "discover" the Bonneville Salt Flats, Utah,[22] as the site of choice for land speed records: a smooth surface in a site wide, free from obstacles in any direction, windless (under certain conditions and at certain hours), and enjoying quite stable and predictable weather.

Campbell's Blue Birds kept rear-wheel drive until 1935, as did George Eyston on his 1937 Thunderbolt. John Cobb's Railton had four-wheel drive.

Issue no. 2: engine. According to *The Autocar*, the engine for a record car should be one built for aeronautical use, being already fully tested and tuned to deliver peak power at low rpm, and so avoid the skyrocketing expense of a purpose-built engine. The latter item was proven dramatically by the huge failure of Kaye Don's 1930 Silver Bullet, powered by two purpose-built engines of Sunbeam design and construction.

Issue no. 3: downforce.[23] The article presents a few lines that are well ahead of their time and appear today to be a precursor. It speculates on flat surfaces to be mounted on the sides of the vehicle to improve the pressure of the tires on the sand to reduce wheelspin. But, then, materials and tire construction technology did not cater for additional load, by the way quite difficult to define and compute theoretically. A few words, apparently added without any depth of knowledge of the matter, said something on the additional effect of stabilizing the vehicle on the runs. How and why was not written.

At the conclusion of the story of the 1928 Daytona Beach Speed Trials, closed by two new land speed records and one death (two more were to be recorded in 1929),[24] one can agree with the closing words of the article: "One thing is certain. A definite programme in which attempts to beat the world's land speed record become a race meeting is, to the last degree, unwise. The entire possibilities of record-breaking depend on a man being able to challenge only when his car is absolutely ready and the circumstances entirely favorable."[25]

6

Aftermath—1929–1935

1929

After all the upset and emotion of Lockhart's death had subsided, the 1928 Speed Trials went on record as a great success. Crowds of wandering souls looking for adrenalin rushes invaded Daytona Beach and spent money in local shops, hotels, and restaurants. The result sanctioned not only a set of speed records but also an effective promotion of the recently incorporated municipality: Daytoners pushing hard for a front-row seat in the fast expanding offers of tourism across Florida.

The municipal government, the chamber of commerce, and other local businesses agreed unanimously to continue the event in 1929 and beyond.

They knew well the uniqueness of the beach and sands as a site that was ideal for high-speed racing.

They knew that a promising new land speed record car was ready in England, to be driven by their preferred driver: Henry Segrave.[1]

They knew that the American record holder, Jim White, owner of the Triplex, was ready to defend the title and the honor of America.

They raised the money needed to engineer the beach and provided time-measuring equipment, lines of communication, and police to patrol the beach, the dunes, and the streets. A new way to inform the crowd—loudspeakers—became available and was installed along the course. The AAA sanction was easily granted on the guarantee of full coverage of the expenses of officials and timekeepers.

As before, stock cars were called to offer a sideshow in the name of the progress of the American automobile industry.

The safety of drivers and the public became a concern following the Lockhart tragedy in April 1928, the first death in 25 years of safe driving and racing on the sand. No one was permitted within 12 feet of the lower edge of the dunes, which offered a vantage point along the whole nine miles of the course, rising up to 12 feet above the highest ocean waves. No entry ticket was needed apart from for the grandstands close to the timing towers at either end of the measured mile. The ticket price was quite cheap: 50 cents, as in February 1928.[2]

On January 31, 1929, Henry Segrave, the designer Captain John Samuel Irving,[3] Mrs. Doris Segrave (*née* Stocker), and a team of six mechanics sailed from Southampton on the White Star liner *Majestic* bound for New York. The car, the

"Golden Arrow," was also on board.[4] It had been built in three months of frantic work by a group of specialized British companies enrolled in the enterprise by the generous sponsorships[5] won by Henry Segrave and the promise of additional publicity and glory: such was the impetus for Dunlop, providers of wheels and tires, and Napier, offering the latest version of the Lion Series VIIB broad-arrow aero engine, now rated at 938 HP @ 3,300 rpm using a special BP fuel of 75 percent petrol, 25 percent benzole, and a small percentage—10 cubic centimeters per gallon—of tetra-ethyl-lead additive. Such a fuel was not used on the actual runs in preference to alcohol instead, which produced a lower output (925 HP @ 3,000 rpm), but which had other advantages—such as acceleration from low speed, cleanliness of the spark plugs, and better cooling—that outweighed the loss of power output.[6]

The final assembly of the car was completed on board the ship, adding the surface radiators between the wheels. The builder, Gloucester Airplane Company, followed the solution already used on the Schneider Cup racing seaplanes: cooling water circulated between two thin copper foils, the outside one corrugated to a depth of three millimeters with a six-millimeter pitch. The weight of each radiator was 94 pounds, contributing to the total dry weight of 7,814 pounds.

Though these were an improvement on the surface radiators used by Malcolm Campbell on his 1928 Blue Bird, which were a failure, Captain Irving retained doubts about their efficiency and opted for a backup tank to be filled with ice or,

The Irving Napier "Golden Arrow" at Daytona Beach in February 1929. Objective: to win the new land speed record in the name of Britain. Driver: Henry Segrave. Vehicle: designed by Captain John Samuel Irving. Power: Napier Lion Series VIIB engine, the same as used by Malcolm Campbell in 1928, 938 HP @ 3,300 rpm. Body: good aerodynamics due to its reduced cross section further improved by the surface radiators between the axles, lowering the drag from the wheels.

better, some heat-absorbing chemical. If needed, the coolant could enter the radiators through special thermostatic valves. It was never used on the beach, when the engine temperature at the end of each run was only 165°F; i.e., too cold.

The 20 gallons of water in the engine and radiators were refilled at the end of each run. On record day the mechanics even forgot to put the ice in the auxiliary tank.

When arriving at Daytona Beach by train, Segrave was given a hero's reception: "The whole heart of America opened to him."[7] No surprise. He had been the favorite driver of Daytoners since his successful 1927 run, when he raised the record beyond the mythical 200 mph "barrier" and, first and foremost, had started the close association of Daytona Beach with the highest speeds on land.

In 1929 everything went right for him, even though the Golden Arrow had not yet covered a single inch under its own power.

Weather and beach, on the contrary, were not at their best: wind blowing from the wrong quarter, ridges in the sand, and streams of water across the beach. Nevertheless, Segrave went for a trial spin on Monday, February 25: he easily reached 180 mph and was completely satisfied with the reactions of his car.

It is nice to note that Segrave referred to his car as "she," like a ship. Was it because Golden Arrow was "true as steel, easy to control, very expensive and very fast"?[8] Today we can forgive the anti-feminist stereotypes embedded in the statement since that was the common culture of the day.

The adverse weather cycle forced Segrave into a long wait, whilst he was anxious to go for the record. On Monday, March 11, he decided to wait no longer: the wind had subsided to a slight breeze, the sand was reasonably smooth with only sparse puddles of water.

Starting from the north station, he covered the course at 177 mph,

Henry Segrave (left) was so brave as to wear a bathing suit despite the cold weather of the late winter days in Daytona Beach. Bill Sturm (right), who acted as his manager, had a differing view of temperature and dress. Segrave, 34, looks older since he began balding at an early age. Bill Sturm, 45, carries the camera from which he was inseparable.

saying that it was "a slow run in order to mark the path which I intended to follow on the record run."⁹

After a quick change of tires (Dunlop guaranteed them for only 25 seconds at maximum speed) and refilling the cooling system, he started northbound for the record. He had asked for a big bullseye sign and a powerful light to be installed across the start and finish lines of the measured mile.

The main difficulties in driving in a straight line on the beach were the glare and the mist, which reduced forward visibility to half a mile. Furthermore, the width of the course was confined to about 50 feet from the flags marking the border of the ocean's reach. Steering either towards the water or to the soft sand on the inner side could, at the very least, be extremely dangerous.

Segrave pushed hard on the throttle following the marked path still visible in the wet sand. His goal—and the car's design objective—was four miles per minute (240 mph), yet he recorded 15.55 seconds over the mile, 231.362 mph.

To him it looked like a failure: "I had missed the programmed average. I had known, ever since the car first began to take shape in the blueprints, that she would do the calculated speed. And here we had failed."¹⁰

Fourteen minutes later the car was ready to go southbound in front of a crowd optimistically reported to be 100,000.¹¹ The still air failed to push the

Segrave is joined by his wife, Doris (*née* Stocker), 42, a theater actress in her younger days. Theirs was a happy life together, from their wedding on October 4, 1917, until the untimely death of Sir Henry on Lake Windermere on June 13, 1930.

6. Aftermath—1929–1935

Golden Arrow beyond a return time of 15.57 seconds, 231.214 mph. Seldom had such a balanced result in both directions been recorded on record runs: proof either of unusually calm air or the car having reached its limit. The average, and the new record, was 15.56 seconds, 231.362 mph, 23.810 mph (11.5 percent) higher than Ray Keech's performance a year earlier.

Segrave reflected: "I had a feeling of relief after I finished a job of that sort. But it is not the sort of relief that makes one vow never to do it again, for it was my firm intention to try again in a day or so. I knew I would have gone 240 miles an hour."[12]

There was never another run: the Trials were ended after the death of Lee Bible in the White Triplex on March 13.[13]

The Golden Arrow never ran again, having covered only 40 miles under its own power. Henry Segrave never took the wheel of a racing or record car again in the few months he had left to live.[14]

Despite the understated reaction of the protagonist, the whole of Britain went wild over the announcement that the land speed record was once more in British hands. And with such a margin as to discourage every likely

A rare portrait of Lee Bible, the Tennessee-born mechanic and occasional racing driver who was so brave, maybe even too reckless, to drive Jim White's Triplex in 1929 as the defender of Ray Keech's record of the previous year. Keech and other top-tier racing drivers had refused to drive the car again, so Bible was the only one available to White. He passed the tests required by AAA officials and on March 13 was given permission to go for the record. On his first run at full power, he lost control of the Triplex, which skidded violently and was completely destroyed, taking the life of the driver and a cameraman, Charles Traub.

foreign challenger. The money and the honor of the Wakefield Trophy were back home.

When the Segrave party disembarked in Southampton on April 12, 1929, from the White Star transatlantic liner *Olympic*, a flurry of celebrations began to unfurl in a rapturous vein. On the previous day it had been announced that a knighthood would be conferred on Segrave, who once again had beaten Malcolm Campbell: the latter was presented with the same honor only two years later.

The first celebration gala dinner was given by the Royal Automobile Club on Monday, April 15, 1929, in London in the presence of His Royal Highness the Prince of Wales (later to briefly become King Edward VIII before abdicating the throne). The prince paid a great tribute to British ingenuity: "The Golden Arrow was more than a motor car. It was a challenge to the world. Every item was manufactured in this country and it demonstrated what British craftsmanship could accomplish."[15]

At the dinner given by Sir Charles Wakefield on Tuesday, April 23, 1929, the home secretary, Sir William Joynson-Hicks, congratulated Segrave on his record, magnifying it into "the greatest achievement in the way of speed the world has ever seen." He went on in this laudatory vein, adding: "We had shown the world not only that we possessed a Segrave but that we were pre-eminent in engineering."[16]

Was the subject worthy of such a fuss? Everybody celebrated the return of Britain to the top of land speeds, an endeavor that Britain assumed it would dominate despite having been unexpectedly bested by the Americans using a monster of a car that boasted none of Britain's scientific and technical know-how, engineering, and design finesse. Segrave reinstated everything to the natural order of things—as seen from the British Isles.

Yet the glory years of land speed records as a source of national prestige were approaching the end. Prestige had a different meaning in the 1920s: it meant national achievement at a time when Britain still had an empire, a strong currency, and the world's mightiest navy and was the dominant power in Europe, having won the Great War. The land, air, and water records were proof of the worldwide leadership of British creativity and engineering.

Foreign challengers disappeared (to return 30 years later when they were all American). So did the power of the appeal to national pride in manufacturing a new car specifically for the record.

The attention of the man in the street diminished abruptly, to rate the whole business of land speed records as the obsession of Malcolm Campbell and, later on, as the self-maintained objective of wealthy drivers like George Eyston and John Cobb.

1930

The Daytona Beach organizers didn't notice the change of attitude on the other side of the water. They were focused on the marketing side, to promote the city, and carried on with the Speed Trials in 1930, proclaiming: "The event would be perpetuated for the ensuing ten years on the same dates each year [i.e., from March 15 to 30]."[17]

The decision to fix a date for the speed record attempt was a big mistake because of the vagaries of weather and the position so clearly expressed by the Britons, the main contenders for the record.[18]

Of course everyone in Daytona Beach concurred with the organizers: it was a matter of city marketing to improve everybody's business.

By early June 1929 they could claim to already have 10 tentative challengers for the 1930 event. The list included some unknowns: a Mr. Jimmy Sockwell of Miami, Florida, who claimed to have the engine already and be ready to build the vehicle, and a Mr. Herman Finke of St Louis, Missouri, whose sole qualification was "inventor." One then unknown Aussie driver, Norman Smith, motoring editor of some Australian newspapers, was also mentioned as a likely contender.[19]

From the British side of the water, Henry Segrave, the defender; Malcolm Campbell; Kaye Don; and Charles Amherst Villiers were mentioned. Villiers (who, as a matter of fact, was one of the designers of the early Blue Birds) was reported as having a six-wheeler under construction to go for 400 mph. Jim White was also said to be preparing a new vehicle to vindicate the Triplex.

While Harry Hartz was mentioned in passing as having an eye on going for the record, Ray Keech was reported as having gone into deeper detail. Meeting the press at the AAA championship race in Cleveland on June 2, 1929, i.e., 13 days before his untimely death in Altoona, he said he intended to drive a new car to break Segrave's record. He didn't provide any hints about the nature of this dream vehicle, and the scribblers focused on a funny detail: in order to reduce the cross section of the vehicle he would stay put inside the body and steer through a periscope. The submarine-like idea was sold as the way to gain further speed by disposing of the windscreen.[20]

At the opening of the 1930 Speed Trials only Kaye Don[21] showed up with a sleek 31-foot-1-inch-long new vehicle, appropriately called "Silver Bullet" by Sunbeam, the manufacturer. Louis Coatalen was the designer, yet the whole car demonstrated that he was, unfortunately, past his prime[22]: it was too complicated and full of untested components, including two purpose-built V12 engines, each of 1,416-cubic-inch capacity and claiming to produce 2,000 HP each. A figure to fool the media, whilst the output on the dyno had barely reached 1,350 HP.

Beyond comprehension was the angle of 50 degrees between the two rows of cylinders instead of the usual 60 degrees. To keep the cross section within a reasonable width, the two engines were installed in tandem, an additional source of potential mechanical problems.

Total dry weight was reported to be 10,800 pounds, making Triplex, 1928 Blue Bird, and Golden Arrow comparative featherweights. The design maximum speed was 280 mph.

Some features were really innovative and paved the way to the future. To allow the lowest possible seating position for the driver (Kaye Don had a tall and bulky figure), the transmission shaft was doubled to run alongside the driver, a

The Silver Bullet on the Daytona Beach sands in March 1930. The Sunbeam car was powered by two purpose-built V-12 1,416-cubic-inch engines, each one said to deliver 2,000 HP. On the dyno they hardly delivered 1,350 HP and were quite distinctive and very difficult to tune properly. Kaye Don, the Irish driver, never managed to get them to run smoothly.

solution later (1933) used by Vittorio Jano on the Tipo B Alfa Romeo Grand Prix racer.

The tail was topped by two vertical fins, a layout later (1932) used on Norman Smith's "Fred H. Stewart Enterprise" Australian record car. The two tailfins of the Silver Bullet were joined by a horizontal plate that could be raised by the driver to act as an air brake at the end of the mile. Reid Railton copied this feature on the 1935 Blue Bird. The variable-angle rear "wing" was much later adopted in F1 to make overtaking possible; i.e., the exact opposite of the job it was designed to do on the Silver Bullet.

Instead of a traditional front radiator, a double skin along the body sides acted as a surface cooler. The solution was clever, yet the car performed so poorly and for such short periods that a real-life test was never possible.

The heavy mass was also due to the presence of armor grade sheets surrounding the driver to protect him from being hit on the lower side. The bottom was completely flat as far back as the rear bulkhead of the cockpit. The curious explanation for such an aerodynamically disastrous solution was to allow the car to float on the waves should it be forced into the ocean: Lockhart's surfs and jumps in February 1928 had left quite an impression on Coatalen.

At least the tail had a raised lower profile to facilitate the extraction of air trapped between the sand and the underside of the car and to increase the downforce of the horizontal plate on the rear wheels. Yet these considerations were still far ahead of the acquired know-how of the designers of high-speed cars.

6. Aftermath—1929–1935

Kaye Don, six mechanics, Louis Coatalen, Kaye's sister Rita Liversey (he was a bachelor), and an unknown number of friends boarded the liner *Berengaria* on February 26, arriving in New York on March 4. They reached Daytona Beach on Saturday, March 8, just in time for the Speed Trials.

The first week had already passed when the Silver Bullet first hit the sand on March 15 for a trial spin, to be repeated the following day. Without official timing (the instruments were to be ready by March 17) manual stopwatches recorded a 144 mph average over the mile.

The weather was against Don. The rough beach forced him and the Silver Bullet to remain idle until Monday, March 31, when he dared to sprint on the beach. The scheduled time of the Speed Trials had already passed, but the AAA officials, backed by the organizers, assured him that he could stay and try for the record for as long as he wished.[23] A new record by the Silver Bullet was the only hope of overcoming the gigantic failure of the event. Once again, the records by stock cars had no appeal to the crowd, and the whole business of the city suffered.

Nothing good came out of the runs: 186 mph average, the fault of the very rough sand with many ridges. One of them bumped the driver hard in the cockpit (don't forget that there were no safety belts then; the first to wear one was Malcolm Campbell in 1933).

Kaye Don, in dark pinstripe suit and hat, checks the sand on the Daytona Beach record course. Bad weather (25 rainy days) and rough sand prevented him from going faster than 186 mph, quite a long way short of the 231.362 mph record set by Henry Segrave in 1929.

On April 10 (33 days since arrival) the beach was in acceptable condition, yet the engines misfired badly in front of a meager group of onlookers, said to be about 1,000.[24] The highest officially recorded speed was 182 mph.

That was it. Asked about plans for the coming days, Don answered showing typical understated British humor: "I shall certainly go home before Christmas, as I already have an engagement for a party then."[25] The British group confirmed their reservations to sail for England on Wednesday, April 16. William Sturm, who acted as Kaye Don's manager, was due to return to Indianapolis on April 11.

The last nail in the

coffin of failure hitting Daytona Beach hard, too, was the statement released by Kaye Don to an Associated Press reporter in New York on the eve of departure for England: "Had I not believed I could exceed the present record of 231 mph I would not have spent $50,000 on the trip here. Naturally I am coming back next year to make a new try. If the machine had worked perfectly we could not have made the run because of the condition of the beach. Of the 31 days we were at Daytona Beach, 25 were rainy."[26]

How did his fellow Britons take such a heavy hit to their national pride? They reported the words of the unlucky protagonist on the unsolved problems of the engine: carburation and supercharger. Strangely enough, they downplayed the effect of the rough beach and the bad weather. Yet Kaye Don added: "I'm determined to find a suitable place elsewhere. I don't think Daytona Beach is suitable any longer."[27]

Who else said roughly the same words? The one who went to South Africa in 1929 and then returned four more times to Daytona Beach: Malcolm Campbell.

Campbell: "The bitter experience I met with at Verneuk Pan in 1929 had given me to think that it is probably better to deal with the devil you know rather than with the one you don't. That is why I chose to go to Daytona Beach for so many successive years. At least I knew what the difficulties to be encountered there were like. The sands of Florida had served their purpose, but speeds had outgrown their capacity: under its best conditions the beach was so uneven that we suffered terribly from wheelspin."[28]

Once again Malcolm Campbell concealed the fat purse he received from the organizers in Daytona Beach every time he returned there.

1931

The organizers wanted to go on with the Speed Trials despite the failure of the 1930 edition, and Campbell was the only brave man left in the whole world aiming at the land speed record via a properly studied and structured approach, carrying along the promise of a new limit. The other few having surpassed 200 mph on land were all gone: Henry Segrave, Frank Lockhart, Ray Keech, and Lee Bible (maybe).

Details of the 1931 expenses were published by *The Daytona Beach News-Journal*: Campbell was awarded $4,000 out of the profit gained on the fully paid budget of $11,000 and expenditure of less than $4,000, including $2,076 to the AAA for their fees and expense accounts, $250 to cover meals and lodging of the six mechanics (quite restrained chaps indeed!), and $250 for William Sturm's professional fees in his role as Campbell's manager and simultaneously acknowledged by the municipality as an effective promoter of the town.

The cost was about one third of the previous year's, when there was no new record and the whole affair was a complete flop in terms of people watching the runs. The 1930 costs were said to have amounted to between $20,000 and $26,000. The reason for such a big reduction in costs was said to be the new structure implemented by the city to manage the event.[29]

Though he was a wealthy man, Campbell became well aware of the mounting costs of chasing records, which had to take into account the extra costs of unforeseen delays in the attempts. Daytona Beach provided guaranteed coverage of the transportation and running expenses on site, but the monetary burden of building the record vehicle was down to Campbell. He had to rely on contributions from third parties as he didn't have a motor company behind him like Henry Segrave in 1927 and Kaye Don in 1930.

Campbell knew that, after Segrave's record, his old yet revamped Blue Bird was history. Ending his long relationship with Joseph Maina, he charged Reid Railton[30] with building a new car able to regain leadership. Railton was chief engineer at Thomson & Taylor, whose factory was on the Brooklands estate, where Campbell had a personal shed for his racing cars.

To reduce costs, Campbell opted to re-use as much as possible of the old junk. Railton would of course have much preferred to start with a clean sheet of paper, yet he complied. In the end, the only major parts of the old car that survived were the front axle and brake gear, the steering gear, and the glorious frame side members, built by Vickers in 1926. The engine was the new supercharged Napier Lion VIID: 1,450 HP. Total dry weight of the car increased to 7,950 pounds; lightness was not the main concern of Reid Railton, backed by Malcolm Campbell, who couldn't forget Lockhart's Blackhawk and his own comments on the too-low mass of that car.

A welcome addition to the budget of the rebuilt Blue Bird was the £10,000 contributed in 1930 by Miss Betty Carstairs,[31] who had a record in high-speed motor boat regattas and was often seen at Brooklands with Malcolm Campbell.

The small team of mechanics travelling to New York with Campbell on the liner *Homeric* in January 1931 included Harry Leech, Leo Villa, Joe Coe, and Steve McDonald (a.k.a. Dunlop Mac), who were the trusted staff of every record attempt by "The Skipper," as they called Malcolm Campbell.

The weather in Daytona Beach was, for once, rather friendly: Campbell arrived by train on January 29 and two days later managed to make a trial run without suffering any mechanical setbacks.

On February 5 he was ready to go for the record: he won it at 245.736 mph, a sound margin (14.374 mph, 6.2 percent) over Segrave's. More good news was that, at last, the organizers had agreed not to repeat the folly of imposing fixed dates for the record runs.

Blue Bird was not alone that year. Campbell, being a true patriot, believed in "All-British and Best" and took a lightened little Austin Seven to America to win the 750cc Class mile record. He drove it on the beach to an average of 94.031 mph, greatly improving on the existing record of 86.76 mph.

1932

Prospects for 1932 were uncertain. The Daytona Beach Racing Association had been established to back the municipality in the organization and management of the Speed Trials. Mr. Cassie Wingate was appointed chairman.

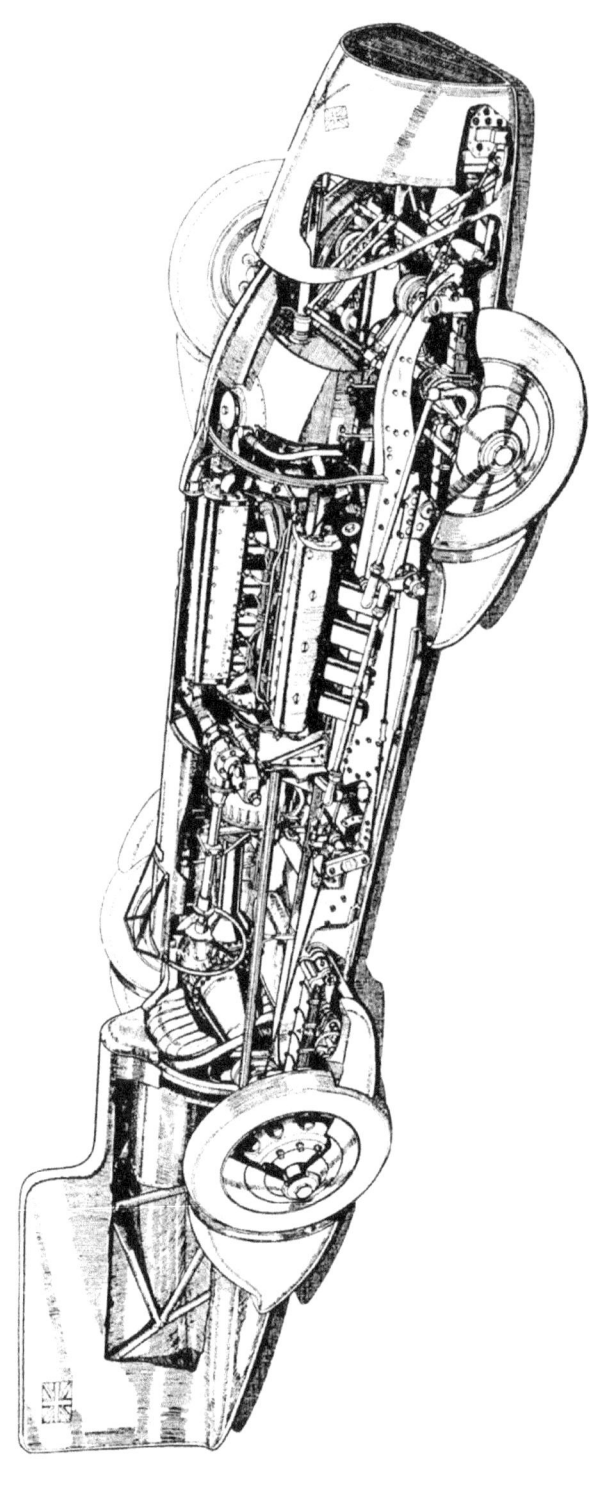

A clear cutaway of the 1931 Blue Bird, published in the French motor magazine *La Vie Automobile*, Paris, March 10, 1932, page 94. The vehicle was a complete redesign by Reid Railton around the Napier Lion Series VIIB engine. Only a few parts of the earlier car were used in the new one (*La Vie Automobile* magazine).

Top: The 1931 Blue Bird under construction at the Thomson & Taylor workshop at Brooklands. Ken P.T. Taylor peers around the tailfin, held in position by some workers. Malcolm Campbell looks at the seating position. The workshop doesn't convey an image of cleanliness and order. *Bottom:* On February 5, seven days after disembarking from the train in Daytona Beach, Malcolm Campbell was ready to raise the land speed record to 245.736 mph, a sound margin over Segrave's run. He also drove his small Austin Seven to a new Class H (up to 750 cc) one-mile record at 94.031 mph.

The Association was charged with the quite difficult task of assembling the money needed to fund the event. They launched a crowdfunding program that by the end of January 1932 had reached $1,604. A Mrs. Lilian B. Dana was so generous that she was given a mention in the local daily: she gave $10.[32] Problems arose with the largest city businesses: the Chamber of Commerce, Merchants Association, and Hotelmen's Association refused to contribute with paid advertisements in the printed program. The outcome was that no program was published at all.

Campbell was a sure participant due to the princely sums he was expecting to receive, yet what about the challengers? Just after the single-staged 1931 show an article promptly appeared in the local daily touting the prospect of a royal group of contenders. Billy Arnold and Harry Hartz, fresh from their stock car records, were reported as saying they were planning a 300-mph supercar to give the British racers plenty of competition. Truth be told, it was more speakeasy talk than serious plan.[33]

Campbell said he would return if his record were broken. Kaye Don in London didn't refrain from telling everybody that he would take the glory away from Campbell, driving a modified Silver Bullet.

Norman Leslie Smith, the Aussie land speed record-seeker, enters his Fred H. Stewart Enterprise car on the Ninety Mile Beach in northern New Zealand. He was nicknamed "Wizard" after many transcontinental runs at record speed (days and weeks, not hours or minutes!) and the unofficial long distance records set in his "Anzac," a special vehicle built on a Cadillac frame with a Rolls-Royce engine. He never made it to Daytona Beach despite invitations from the municipality.

6. Aftermath—1929–1935

The third foreign player was Norman "Wizard" Smith who, on a bumpy, flooded, and isolated beach in the north island of New Zealand, was trying to get his record car "Fred H. Stewart Enterprise" to run at a decent level of performance and reliability. The car was a poorly executed copy of the Golden Arrow powered by the Napier Lion engine, loaned by the British government.

Soon after New Year's Day, 1932, Campbell received a cable from Florida: "The City of Daytona Beach invites you and offers every co-operation to further your attempt to create a new world record."[34] He accepted the invitation and informed the organizers that he would only return if a modified course would be provided to gain a longer run to build up speed before the mile. Daytona Beach duly obliged: they opened a wider gap in the trestle under the pier crossing the beach at the northern end and wired two different measured miles to allow a five-mile acceleration run both ways.[35]

Blue Bird, thanks to Reid Railton, the designer and race engineer (to use current F1 jargon), and the new supercharged Napier Lion VIID engine, was ready to go for the record on February 24, 1932. And Campbell did it facing a 40-mph wind blowing southwards: 253.968 mph was the new record resulting from the first run with the wind at 267.459 mph and into the wind at 241.773 mph. The improvement on his own record was 8.23 mph, 3.3 percent.[36]

Blue Bird 1932 being unloaded from the baggage car at the Daytona Beach depot. As in the past, it raised widespread interest. Note the "road" tires mounted for transportation and transfers to and from the beach. The beach tires had a very thin, smooth tread that we would describe as "slicks" today. They were unsuitable for road use.

The crowd was said to number 10,000. The special correspondent of the London daily newspaper *Daily Herald* was unaware of the size of past audiences and defined the thin smattering of people along the dunes as "huge." He wrote: "This huge crowd, brought here by Campbell, saved the city from financial chaos. That was why Campbell was asked to make the attempt: to attract visitors. They came and he saved Daytona."[37]

So long the myth of record-setting, the enhanced national pride gained by Britain, the paeans to the superiority of British engineering and automotive design.

1933

In December 1932 Reid Railton was again busy modifying Blue Bird to accommodate the longer (84-inch), heavier (1,600-pound), more powerful new Rolls-Royce R–Type engine developed to propel the British seaplanes to their definitive victory in the Schneider Trophy. The power output, 2,450 HP @ 3,000 rpm, brought the sought-after dream of Malcolm Campbell into the realm of the possible: five miles a minute—i.e., 300 mph—on land.

Sir Malcolm's intense look before a run in Blue Bird in 1932. He received a knighthood from King George V on his return from the 1931 record. The new supercharged Napier Lion Series VIID propelled the vehicle to a new record: 253.968 mph, an 8.2 mph (3.3 percent) improvement on his previous performance. In 1932 Campbell was again the lone record-seeker in Daytona Beach.

Once again, Malcolm Campbell was the only pretender to the World Land Speed Record, despite rumblings in the local press[38] about letters of invitation mailed to Norman Smith in Australia and André Stapp[39] in France. A theoretically more credible challenger was Barney Oldfield, who bombarded the American media with stories of a land speed record vehicle designed by the great Harry Miller.[40] The challenge remained on paper and in the scale model.

On February 2, 1933, Campbell was again in Daytona Beach. He wrote: "The City surpassed itself by its welcome when I stepped off the train. There was an enormous crowd waiting at the station, headed by police, city officials and members of the Racing Association, accompanied by a band. The band marched at the head of a procession to the hotel, where I found my room filled with flowers sent by friends I had made in America."[41]

He had to wait 14 days for the beach to be in acceptable condition prior to driving on a test run. The sand was so rough and bumpy that the gear lever dropped out of top gear. In forcing the lever home, he strained the tendons of his left hand and wrenched muscles in his forearm. Nevertheless, Blue Bird reached 227 mph over the mile, confirming that the more powerful Rolls-Royce engine was doing its job.

When the wind was not too strong, a small plane was kept ready on the beach to fly Leo Villa to the other end of the course to supervise operations in between

Sir Malcolm and the new Blue Bird were back in Daytona Beach on February 2, 1933, yet they had to wait 14 days to go to the beach for a trial spin on the rough sand. The right day dawned on February 22, three days after the fourth anniversary of his first record in Florida. The new record was raised to 272.116 mph, 18.15 mph (7.1 percent) beyond the old one: the engine was doing its job.

runs. Another example of American state-of-the-art care when organizing the event.

On February 22 the car was back on the beach. The sand was still rough, and there were shells on the beach that might cut the tires. The first run was timed at 273.556 mph, a much higher speed than the record set the year before. The rev-counter had shown a speed some 50 mph higher; the difference was due to wheelspin.

In 20 minutes the wheels, weighing about 200 pounds each, were changed (the tires were badly cut by the shells, as expected), the tanks were refilled, and Campbell had his painful arm massaged. Despite easing the throttle to three-quarters and wrestling against a vicious tendency of the car to snake along the course, he managed to drive at 270.676 mph. The average was 272.116 mph, obviously a new record, 18.15 mph (7.1 percent) more than the 1932 one.

Campbell was not satisfied with the result: he had seen a higher speed on the rev-counter. The rough sand and its low coefficient of adhesion were a strong handicap to achieving his coveted goal of five miles a minute.

1935

Blue Bird had to be rebuilt again to increase grip and aerodynamic stability. Reid Railton worked on it. It took the entire year of 1934 before it was ready. The new car retained the Rolls-Royce engine, now tuned to deliver 2,500 HP @ 3,400 rpm. Such stressed performance was assumed to be sustainable due to the very short period— just a few minutes—operating at full power.

The body was redesigned to enclose the wheels, except at the top and sides. Twin rear wheels were used in the hope of reducing wheelspin and improving traction.

The final result was a heavier car: 10,450 pounds, an increase of 1,500 pounds over the 1933 model. As an additional measure to reduce wheelspin the rear axle was loaded with 1,500 pounds of ballast. The target speed was computed at 335 mph.

Air brakes were mounted just behind the rear wheels to aid in slowing the car down after the mile and help it stay within the limits of the beach, which furthermore was no longer completely straight due to coastal erosion.

Alighting from the train at Daytona Beach on January 31, 1935, Campbell asked for a line to be drawn on the sand to serve as a guide where the course deviated from straight. A similar line had been used in 1929 at Verneuk Pan, and it became normal when the record runs moved to the Bonneville Salt Flats. The officials agreed and marked the beach with a two-foot wide line made from a mixture of burnt motor oil and lamp-black. During the runs the oily line had the unpleasant effect of being splattered on the windscreen by the front wheels, partially blocking the driver's view.

The beach remained in poor condition, restricting the trial run on February 14 to only six miles. After another long wait until March 2 the course was cleared and deemed good enough for a record run. Never before had Campbell had to wait so many days in Daytona Beach.

A problem arose with the engine cover being displaced by the pressure of the wind at speed and partially covering the exhaust ports, diverting fumes into the cockpit. Campbell had to lift off, reducing speed to about 200 mph.

At last, on March 7, after 35 days and three trial runs, the right day finally dawned: the sand was smooth; the strong wind was from the right quarter; visibility was good under a clear, sunny sky. The first run into the wind was 272.72 mph, only a quarter of a mile an hour faster than the existing record. The return run was timed at 281.03 mph, thanks to the tailwind.

The average speed was 276.816 mph, a 4.37 mph (1.6 percent) improvement.

There was complete disillusionment after having spent so much time, money, and expert effort redesigning and rebuilding the vehicle. The long march towards the coveted 300 mph mark was becoming drawn out and difficult.

"It was obvious that the fractions of a second which stood between us and complete success [i.e., reaching 300 mph] were entirely due to the conditions of the beach and were not the fault of the car. We had created a new record but we had not done the 300 mph which I was convinced was possible. I know that Blue Bird can do the speed."[42] So wrote Campbell just after returning home.

Such specific blame on the Daytona Beach sands was smoothed in the long and detailed articles written seven months later for *The Motor*, when he explained

The 1935 Blue Bird after being towed under the Daytona Beach Pier. The vehicle had been extensively modified by Reid Railton to achieve Sir Malcolm's lifelong goal: 300 mph. The body was flatter and wider to enclose the wheels, except at the top. Twin wheels to improve traction were mounted at the rear, in front of air brakes (here seen in the raised position). The front radiator had a shutter (here closed) to be used on the mile run to reduce drag.

Blue Bird on the beach on March 7, 1935: at last, a run for the record after 35 days of waiting and three short trial runs. The turbulence created by the sand thrown upwards by the rear wheels proved that the aerodynamics had some major drawbacks (original from Rolls-Royce Limited).

Blue Bird approaching the end of the mile. On March 7, 1935, the record was raised to 276.816 mph, a disappointingly small 1.6 percent improvement. The rough sand was seen as the culprit, having induced too much wheel-spin: going by the rev counter, Sir Malcolm reckoned his speed to be 330 mph. The main problem was later identified as the engine not receiving sufficient air due to the incorrect positioning of the supercharger intake at the top of the radiator outlet.

that the disappointing results in Florida were due to intrinsic faults in the design and positioning of the air intake for the supercharger, resulting in the engine not "breathing" well enough.[43]

Anyway, the time had come to abandon the sands of Daytona Beach, the warm and friendly Floridian hospitality, the generous purse they provided.

Campbell turned 50 on March 11 without the gift of the 300 mph record to crown his land racing career.

The time had come to follow the advice of Ab Jenkins, the record man from Utah, who was promoting the Bonneville Salt Flats as the site of choice for record runs.

Describing the feelings of the first drive on the Salt Flats on September 1, 1935, Campbell wrote an inspired piece of poetry:

> It was the most wonderful sensation I ever felt. Here we were, skimming over the surface of the earth, the black line ever disappearing over the edge of the horizon, the wind whistling past like a hurricane and nothing in sight but the endless sea of salt with the mountains 50 miles away in the distance. I felt highly elated when I jumped out of the car. The course seemed to be perfect, the car was running magnificently. I felt that, given any degree of luck, we should reach our coveted goal.[44]

And so it went:

September 3, 1935.

Bonneville Salt Flats.

Average speed over the mile: 301.129 mph.

The first comment by Malcolm Campbell, just out of the car and still covered in salt, was short and rhetoric-free: "Bloody good show, chaps!"[45]

Later on, back in England, he had plenty of time to build up a noble narrative for the motoring magazines: "And now, after all these years, I have said that I am retiring. I do so with the utmost regret, but having made a promise I intend to keep it. It is not easy to tear oneself away from an almost lifelong hobby, but we must all be philosophers and realise the fact that all things must at last come to an end."[46]

Appendix 1

The Aerodynamics of the 1928 Vehicles

A Parallel Overview

Three thinking heads, three different approaches to the aerodynamics applied to a land speed record car aimed at over 200 mph, a speed then thought to be the upper limit of the possible, hit only once by Henry Segrave in the Sunbeam 1000 HP record car in Daytona Beach in 1927. The car was nicknamed "The Slug" by the snobbish British writers and "Mistery S" by the creative American scribblers.

The period knowledge of aerodynamics focused on the reduction of drag in a straight line. The studies and experiments of pioneers like Paul Jaray, Gabriel Voisin, and Harry Miller proposed teardrop shapes inspired by aeronautical experience, more pleasing to the eye than effective. Wind tunnels were already in use for airplanes and fast cars. Designers were not yet thinking in depth about lateral stability, aerodynamic drag, or aerodynamic lift. *Downforce* was an unknown word.

The relative position of the center of gravity and the center of pressure had scarcely begun to be considered: some ideas had already surfaced, yet the lack of mathematical tools and knowledge for solving the problem and the scarce experimental evidence brought in contradictions and major differences among the land speed record vehicles, where the issue was of primary importance.

We have to consider the period know-how when discussing the aerodynamics of the three cars in Daytona Beach in 1928. It is clear that what we today consider to be erroneous, sometimes lethally erroneous, was accepted as correct then.

Blue Bird

Malcolm Campbell had a long background in record cars and knew well how to exploit the national know-how and experience gained from the Schneider Trophy winning seaplanes: light, compact, and powerful engines, and aerodynamic finesse.

The sleek profile of the 1928 Blue Bird on the Daytona Beach sands. The aerodynamics were honed in the Vickers wind tunnel managed by Reginald Pierson. The open wheel layout was agreed by Campbell and designers Joseph Maina and Charles Amherst Villiers to avoid the problems that arose on the 1927 Sunbeam 1000 HP record car. The fairings close to the wheels were adopted to reduce drag: it was already known that open wheels contributed 60 percent of total vehicle drag. What they didn't understand was the downforce created by air escaping upwards from the rotating front wheels: Malcolm Campbell complained about the heavy steering.

The UK also had a wide-reaching industrial structure and world-class test centers, including reliable wind tunnels.

Campbell, born of Scottish heritage, paid for his cars himself—at least so the self-built myth says, confirmed by so many authors and witnesses. He had a conservative approach to selecting designers, materials, suppliers, and builders. He aimed at recycling and reusing materials wherever possible. He himself and his small team of mechanics, led by Leo Villa, did some work and the car's final preparation in the garage of the family's Povey Cross estate, south of London.

It may be true for racing cars, driven at Brooklands, but it is less credible for land speed record cars, much more complex and expensive.

It has been written that the 1928 Blue Bird cost $65,000.[1] The British Air Ministry gave Campbell the free loan of two 950 HP Napier Lion Series VIIB "Sprint" engines with an agreement to keep the innards of the sealed engines out of sight. The Lion "Sprint" was still on the Air Ministry's secret list. One engine was installed in the vehicle whilst the spare never came out of its original crate.

The 1928 Blue Bird was the first almost completely new car in the series. Designed by Joseph Maina and Charles Amherst Villiers, it was built on the frame of the 1927 car[2] by Napier at their Acton Vale factory near London, to maintain the secrecy of the engine. The body was shaped by Barker & Co., London.

With a wheelbase of 145.5 inches, a front track of 65.25 inches, rear track of 57 inches, and overall length of 181 inches, the broad-arrow engine did not allow much room for streamlining. The fully enclosed bodywork was discarded to keep dry weight quite low: 5,200 pounds. The driving position was high with the seat on top of the bulky Maina-designed gear-case and transmission. Such a seating

Appendix 1: The Aerodynamics of the 1928 Vehicles

position forced a large cross section and was also the cause of severe problems in the runs on the beach.

The open wheels didn't cause the tires to overheat, an advantage over the fully enclosed body used on the 1927 Sunbeam, designed by Louis Coatelen and Captain John Samuel Irving. Its additional mass and cooling problems negated the aerodynamic advantage of enclosing the wheels.

Wind tunnel tests managed by Reginald Pierson (1891–1948) at Vickers convinced Campbell to add streamlined fairings behind the front wheels and ahead and behind the rear ones. It was already known at the time that the wheels contributed 60 percent of the overall drag.

Guided more by intuition than the scientific method, Campbell opted for a tailfin, fitted behind the cockpit, hoping that it would help to stabilize the car at high speed.

He provided input to a technical article published on the eve of the ocean crossing to America: "Novel features are the fitting of a gigantic tailfin or plane to ensure directional stability."[3] Two sizes were built; the smaller one was to be used in windy conditions, i.e., the usual beach environment everywhere on the coast of the ocean. Furthermore, should the crosswind be too strong, no tailfin would be used—quite a strange way of thinking indeed.

On the record runs Campbell used the smaller fin, irrelevant for stability when the wind had a significant lateral component. Open wheels and a small tailfin were the cause of the wrestling he had to go through to maintain a straight course, fighting with all his might against the tendency of the car to snake from left to right.[4] He explained later: "There was just the possibility that the airstream past the wheels was having an effect which had not been considered or realised beforehand."[5]

What neither he nor anybody else at the time appreciated was the downforce on the front wheel induced by air escaping upwards.

The uselessness of the tailfin was further worsened by the radiator blocks placed on the sides of the tail, screening the fin. The basic idea was to avoid the great additional resistance of a conventional front-mounted radiator. Experiments conducted by Fairey Aviation on fast bombers for the Royal Air Force showed the efficiency of side radiators, yet flying conditions are quite different from those to be found on the beach in Florida.

The blocks consisting of two sets of tubes formed four practically independent interchangeable radiating units. Each unit was four feet seven inches long and one foot seven inches high. Pipes running from the radiators to the front of the engine through the cockpit made it uncomfortably warm despite rubber protection. Photos show a crude arrangement of tubing and mounts.

In Daytona Beach it was discovered that the radiators worked in a partial vacuum and were, as such, ineffective. They cost nearly £450 and were eventually sold for scrap metal for £5.

Eager to project the image of a winning driver-designer, Campbell wrote: "I'm quite certain that this method of directional control [i.e., the steering gear duplicated according to the Marles scheme] together with the tailfin tremendously increased the stability of 'Blue Bird' at these speeds."[6]

One of the many journalists who interviewed him when he arrived back in Britain had nothing personal to defend and kept a well-studied balance: "Nothing very definite can be said as to the real value of the fin, though everything points to its having been useful."[7]

Campbell relayed to Reid Railton his doubts on the usefulness of the tailfin in 1931 when Blue Bird was heavily modified by Railton and fitted with the more powerful Napier Lion Series VIID supercharged engine: 1450 HP vs. 950 HP.

Railton wrote: "So long as the fin was quite vertical, it did not much matter where it was placed in relation to the tail, since it did not operate unless the car turned from the straight."[8] The fin was offset to be flush with the headrest of the driving position on the right side and not in the middle of the tail, as it had been before.

While the words dealing with the vertical position of the tailfin are senseless, the note on it acting like a rudder when the vehicle deviated from straight is basically correct, yet he failed to understand that the effect of a tailfin was to position the center of pressure well behind the center of gravity to make the vehicle intrinsically stable.

Campbell was not alone in his doubts about the tailfin and its value in pushing the center of pressure towards the tail: at a conference at the Institution of Automobile Engineers in December 1933, Railton (to whom Campbell had entrusted the design of the three Blue Birds from 1931 to 1935) said: "I personally cannot follow Capt. Irving's argument on the relation of the centre of gravity and centre of pressure. I do not think that the centre of pressure should be behind the centre of gravity. Indeed, I do not consider it a very important point." He was completely wrong when he added that, under the effect of a side wind, the tailfin would have enhanced the dangerous movement of the car into the wind: "The greater the tail-fin, the greater will be this effect."[9]

Nevertheless, Railton agreed to mount large tailfins on the Blue Birds he designed. He saw them more as a smooth continuation of the headrest than an aerodynamic device. Applying such a basic, erroneous concept, he didn't dare to offset the tailfin from the geometrical center of the vehicle. Not by chance, his land speed record masterpiece—John Cobb's 1937 Railton—did not have a tailfin.

Campbell's synthesis in an interview with *The Autocar* was: "I think that future record cars will pay a lot to aerodynamics for their speed. They won't simply look like a bullet, but being scientifically designed."[10] It was a forecast of a new road to follow, still unknown and very long.

Triplex

One of Malcolm Campbell's American challengers in 1928 had a contrasting vision about land speed record cars and aerodynamics. Jim White, a rich wire industrialist from Philadelphia, fond of fast cars, wanted to take the land speed record away from the British and bring it back to America.

Appendix 1: The Aerodynamics of the 1928 Vehicles

When he had the Triplex record car built, this was his thinking:

> The principal reason for building the Triplex was that I could never be reconciled to the streamline theory. My idea of piercing the air is simply that the maximum size to open the air is your obstacle. The wind offers a resistance increasing with speed, to overcome which the vehicle must have power and weight sufficiently fully to utilize the power, and the surface to run over at high speed must be extremely smooth to ensure contact. The Triplex eventually demonstrated to my satisfaction that my idea on piercing air is correct.[11]

The Triplex was built on those principles: highest possible power on a sturdy frame (three L-12 Liberty aero engines, cumulative power 1,200 HP), free hand on the weight (estimated 8,000 pounds[12]), longest possible wheelbase (175.5 inches), body reduced to a chisel-shaped front covering the front engine, flat sides covering the rear engines, and the cramped cockpit inserted between the front and rear engines without any firewall shielding the driver. A piece of metal with a rectangular hole offered a primitive windshield for the driver's head.

White refused to use a wind tunnel. The Triplex did not run for a single yard before leaving for Daytona Beach in February 1928. White's explanation: places for safely testing the car didn't exist outside the Florida beaches.

Jim White arrived in Daytona Beach and delivered the first of his many bombastic statements to the local daily: "This is a purely sport proposition. We have built the car but have never driven it. We don't even know whether or not it will run, but as a sporting proposition this run for us is $20,000 worth of fun. Major Segrave said that half of the 1,000 HP of his engines were used to overcome the wind resistance only. At the same speed the Triplex has about 1,000 HP to spare."[13]

Two mechanic-builders worked for two years in White's workshop at 11th and Olive Streets, Philadelphia, to adapt a sturdy lorry frame to the mounting of the three Liberty L-12 engines, 1,649.3 cubic inches each. The engines were built by the tens of thousands during the Great War years. Now obsolete junk, they were put on sale—pennies on the dollar—by the administration, yet they refused to sell them to White as they were expected to be used for experimental purposes: the land speed record was not thought to be one of these.

White found three units modified for marine use elsewhere. One was, in his words, "abused." He had them rebuilt and tuned to deliver some 400 HP @ 2,500 rpm.

The use of aero engines, even obsolete ones but delivering high torque at low rpm, led to the decision to connect the transmission shafts directly to the rear axle through the usual crown and pinion gears—crude yet simple. No gearshift was installed so there was no reverse gear, which every racing and record car had to have in those days to comply with the international AIACR rules, agreed to by the AAA.

No technical details on the Triplex have been written and passed down over the decades. No report exists on the procedure for starting the car or warming up the engine. The car itself was a total wreck in 1929, and no significant part of it survived the crash.

The Daytona Beach News-Journal wrote[14] about the lack of a clutch.

A few enlightening lines came from Leo Villa, an expert beyond any possible doubt. He wrote[15] that only the front engine had a clutch. It was the first to be fired up and was powerful enough to move the car. As soon as the car started moving, the driver switched on the ignition of the two rear engines, which fired up due to the rigid link through the rear axle. Thanks to the high torque and low revolutions per minute of the aero engines, it was possible to keep them all running even when the car was moving at low speed. The engines had to be switched off when the car came to a standstill.

The above explanation could mean that the rear engines had to be warmed up on the runs on the beach prior to opening them up to full power. Such a routine, even though dangerous for the metal in the rear engines, is consistent with the many miles (450) covered by the Triplex on the beach and the low speed recorded on the early runs of every day.

British writers and cognoscenti, standing high on the platform of recognized masters of the land speed record, discredited the Triplex, naming it a monster, behemoth, nightmare, brute-power junk. Yet, for the very first time, the Triplex brought the land speed record to America, beating the most revered British speed champion, Malcolm Campbell.

Campbell, who had watched the Triplex closely and who had been defeated by it, failed to comment. He went back to work on his Blue Bird to win back the record once again.

Blackhawk

Frank Lockhart's Blackhawk was described by Malcolm Campbell as "a triumph of scientific design and ingenuity." "It was beautifully built, painted white, streamlined to the last degree with every projection faired off," Campbell continued. "It was obviously the result of much careful work and fine designing."[16]

The car, if the truth be known, had some basic design faults due to miscalculations and aerodynamic errors due to the period lack of know-how, which ended in the fatal outcome on April 25, 1928.

Campbell again: "The Blackhawk is a beautifully-made car and Lockhart is a very brave and able driver, but the car is very light. You need a heavy car for high speeds. I am very fond of Frank and I pray he doesn't have a mishap."[17] A scale model of the Blackhawk body was tested in the Curtiss Aeroplane and Motor Company wind tunnel and verified in the wind tunnel of the Army Air Force at Wright Field in Dayton, Ohio. It was checked against the model of the 91 Miller driven by Lockhart at Muroc Dry Lake, California, on April 11, 1927, when he recorded the 164.009 mph average over a flying mile, reaching 171.021 mph on the fastest run.

Extrapolating the aerodynamic data (C_x Blackhawk 0.061; C_x 91 Muroc Miller 0.168), it gave a theoretical 230 mph maximum possible speed for the Blackhawk, thanks to the more than double power produced and the lower drag. Such a very

Appendix 1: The Aerodynamics of the 1928 Vehicles

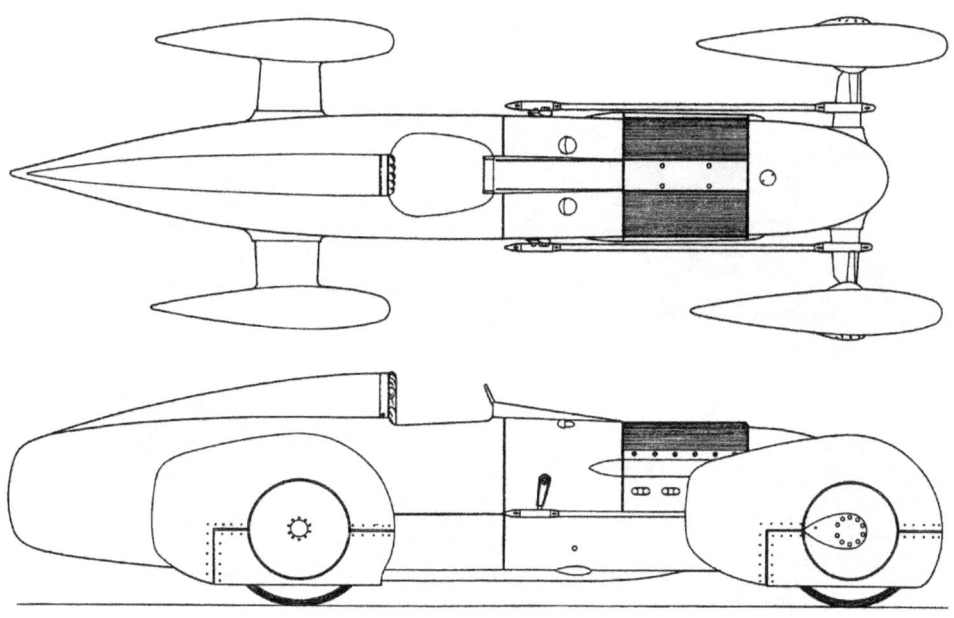

Side and top view of the Blackhawk. The finned area on top of the engine cowling is the intercooler, one per supercharger. The engine exhaust ports were flush with the body, good for streamlining but ineffective—perhaps counterproductive—for fume extraction.

good theoretical result put an end to the costly and time-consuming tests in wind tunnels.[18]

Many years later, Myron Stevens, the body's master panel-beater, expressed some doubts[19] on the size of the model of the 91 Muroc Miller: maybe it was made on a different scale from the Blackhawk's and, as such, recorded larger (and wrong) drag measures. Checking the actual speed of the Miller against the wind tunnel data, the theoretical maximum speed of the Blackhawk was computed to be higher than was actually possible.

Since the early design sketches, Lockhart had decided on a longer wheelbase than the 91 Miller, to improve directional stability. Perhaps he was too conditioned by the sacred 100-inch measure of the single-seater Miller to change it to a much longer wheelbase, which would have resulted in a safer and better vehicle. He could have feared becoming a sort of sacrilegious villain for modifying the accepted measure too much and selected 112 inches— a measure that ruled the design of the whole vehicle.

When looking at the car Campbell noticed from the very beginning that it was too small and too light, thanks to the widespread use of aluminum in the engine and body.[20]

Even more serious was the mistake of fully covering the wheels with streamlined fairings: the shape was aerodynamically perfect to reduce drag at the cost of a complex and delicate construction. The center section was cast in aluminum, and the panels were shaped from aluminum sheets. The center section

154　　　　Appendix 1: The Aerodynamics of the 1928 Vehicles

The simple yet sturdy frame of the Blackhawk during construction in the Stutz workshop. The two U-shaped rails made from nickel steel were arched over the rear axle and joined together at the rear by a forged fitting. The three steel supports for the light aluminum body contributed to the rigidity of the "fuselage" of the vehicle (original by Jim Weisel; from Tom Kinney collection).

covered the nut screwing the wheel to the axle. The fairing was screwed to a central plate of such a wide diameter to cover the whole wheel disc apart from four inches.

The photos make it difficult to understand the mounting of the fairings. A circle of bolts appears on the outside of the front ones, screwed on the center section of the fairing covering the hub. The inside mount looks more difficult to understand: in some photos two large screws appear, and they could be bolted to another central plate around the axle.

Front fairings were stationary and the narrow steering angle (0°6′) made it possible to reduce the cross section.

It is even more difficult to understand the mounting of the rear fairings. From the photos, even taking into account the distortion of the lenses, section and profile appear different on each side. It could be a mistake, as they were shaped by hand and eye. Nevertheless, the effect of this possible asymmetry, if any, would have been negligible compared to the intrinsic instability of the car.

The wheel fairing solution was aerodynamically clean, even though the use of regular rivets instead of flush ones when joining the panels appears rather hard to

Appendix 1: The Aerodynamics of the 1928 Vehicles

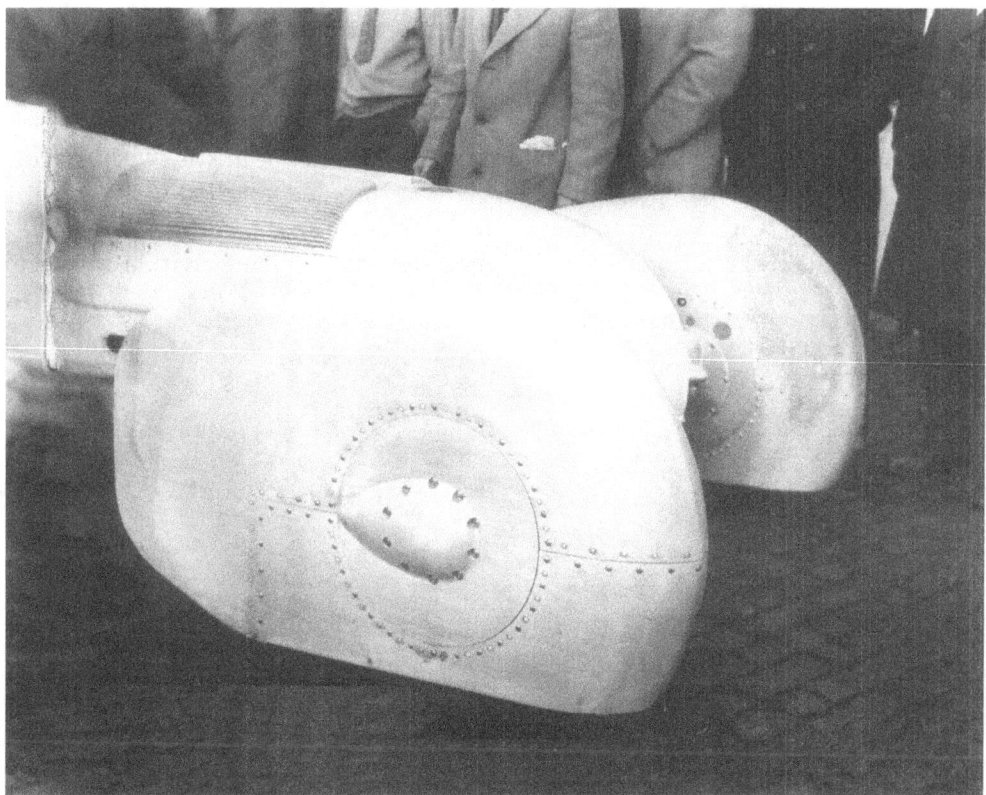

A close-up of the front of the Blackhawk, showing the detail of the wheel fairings. Contrasting with Lockhart's obsessive attention to minimizing additional drag created by items protruding from the body (even rivets were flush with the aluminum sheets of the body), normal rivets were used on the fairings. The decision could have been taken either to skimp on the too-difficult soldering of the curved pieces or because of the rush to stay within the deadline. Nevertheless, the streamlined cover over the wheel nut is a real work of art.

justify in such a refined construction. Maybe it was a solution driven by the short time left to complete the car prior to shipping it to Daytona Beach.

Lockhart's inclination towards complex machining and difficult and sophisticated solutions won over practicality. There is always a danger in over-engineering, as happened with some other top automotive designers: a striking and well-known example is Professor Ferdinand Porsche with his Mercedes and Auto Union grand prix cars and the T-80 Mercedes land speed record car.

Zenas Weisel, chief designer charged with detailing the basic project, decided the width of the body following Harry Miller's method, also used many years later by Colin Chapman when he stipulated the monocoque cross-section of the Lotus 25 single-seater for Jim Clark: he measured the width of the driver's shoulders. Zenas Weisel decided on 24 inches; i.e., Lockhart's shoulder width plus some room to move his arms.

The total lift of the body was measured at 54 pounds, an exceptionally low

Appendix 1: The Aerodynamics of the 1928 Vehicles

value that allowed the reduction in the ground clearance to five inches, with zero rake; i.e., zero negative incidence.

They discarded the fully enclosed body due to the excessive amount of power required to overcome drag, even though the power output of the engine was estimated by slide rule to be 385 HP @ 7,000 rpm: it was too optimistic (wrong, actually), an estimate which in publicity material was rounded up to 400 HP.[21]

The Weisels were forced to adhere to Lockhart's obsession with the smallest achievable cross sections: they designed the wheel fairings with a wide gap

The top view of the Blackhawk during the January 12, 1928 shakedown at the Indianapolis Speedway. Despite the long shadows on a Midwest winter's day, the slim shape of the car can be appreciated. The wheel fairings were 12 inches outside the central body. The front ones were stationary and allowed for the computed one-inch increase in the diameter of the tire at maximum speed. They also included the maximum possible steering angle: 0°6'. Such a limited turning circle forced the movement back and forth of the vehicle when it had to be turned around at the end of the course.

Appendix 1: The Aerodynamics of the 1928 Vehicles

from the body. The inner tolerance for the centrifugal expansion of the tires was only one inch when the wheel was spinning at the maximum rate of 3,000 rpm, as determined by the tests on the dynamometer at the Stutz factory.

Zenas Weisel drafted a front extension that he thought was enough to position the center of pressure ahead of the wheel axle. He was nevertheless forced to draw a longer rear extension to streamline the fairings correctly.

It was a mistake that increased the sensitivity to crosswinds, always blowing on the ocean rim. The front wheel fairings, longer than the rear ones, moved the whole vehicle's center of pressure dangerously forwards. The position of the center of pressure ahead of the center of gravity was further worsened by the heavy 40-gallon fuel tank in the tail. It was too large for the short runs on the beach, and it became clear (today only, alas) that it was another deadly design mistake, quite hard to understand from men as expert as Lockhart and the Weisel brothers. The only possible explanation for such a decision could be the intention to load the rear axle to improve grip and road-holding.

To further stress the point of the mistakes, it could be noted that the 1933 Blue Bird had a 23-gallon fuel tank for a Rolls-Royce engine of a capacity 12 times larger than Blackhawk's. Reid Railton computed the consumption for each cycle—warm-up and two runs—at 20 gallons.[22]

The center of pressure of the "fuselage," i.e., the main body, was determined in wind tunnel tests. That done, it became possible to work out the sensitivity to crosswinds: one-inch deviation in a 10 mph wind and two inches in 15 mph. It was determined an acceptable flaw given the skill and fast reactions of the driver, assisted by a steering ratio of 18.5:1 with a lock-to-lock span of only 0°6' in the steering.

No one knew the real force of the wind that always blew on the Daytona Beach sand strip. Nobody forecast or measured the lateral component. Furthermore, the limited knowledge of the period made it impossible to tell the effect of the wheel fairings apart from testing the body in a wind tunnel. In the runs the fairings acted as sails and generated directional instability.

On his February 22, 1928 runs Lockhart had to correct the direction of the car, which was heading towards the dunes. He called on his sensitivity and skill built up over years of driving neutral cars at lower speed on racetracks. Yet as soon as the angle of the car's travel deviated from the intended direction of the run, the inherent instability exacerbated the angle of deviation, forcing the driver to make a correction that, due to the instability, immediately became excessive and sent the car heading towards the water.

In short, the limited knowledge of vehicle dynamics led to the design and construction of an unstable car, despite every possible theoretical computation or forecast. The final product was a car that no driver could tame, even one as skilled as Frank Lockhart.

The long streamlined tail covering the fuel tank was effective in lowering the drag, yet it did not contribute to the stability of the car without a tailfin. The tailfin could have been used to make the vehicle more stable, moving the center of pressure behind the center of gravity.[23]

Malcolm Campbell, too (as already noted), had doubts about the effect of the tailfin. It was Captain Irving who later re-thought the issue correctly in 1929: he designed the Golden Arrow land speed record car with a long tailfin that was an extension of the cockpit fairing beyond the screen of the rear wheels. Yet another top designer, Reid Railton, remained skeptical of the tailfin, using it mainly for aesthetics on the Blue Birds (1931–1935) and avoiding it on the Railton (1937–1947).

For people fond of the "ifs" of history, it is pretty certain that Lockhart, despite the Blackhawk's instability, would have lived after setting the new record if he had made the runs on a flat, open, and windless surface like the Bonneville Salt Flats. Yet in 1928 the site was still unknown to land speed record seekers. In any case, the tire blowout would have killed him anywhere.

During the runs in Daytona Beach it would have been quite difficult to change the wheels/tires within the half-hour allowed, especially as the too-small team had to take off and replace the four fairings. It seems that the mechanics with Lockhart in Florida had trained to complete the operation within the allowed time, but during the runs they never managed it.

Such tight fairings presented the additional risk of wet sand encrustations building up inside them. They could have unbalanced the wheels and stopped them running smoothly. There is a single image, shot on April 24, in which the Blackhawk appears without its front wheel fairings; whether because of the impossibility of refitting them within the half-hour or doubts about the car's stability is unclear.

The larger side surface of the front fairings appears clearly in the photograph, which also highlights the absence of a tailfin. The result was an intrinsically unstable vehicle due to the center of pressure ahead of the center of gravity and the wheel fairings acting as sails in a crosswind.

Appendix 1: The Aerodynamics of the 1928 Vehicles

Another problem due to the shape of the body was the lack of air entering the carburetors. The inlets were on top of the engine cover, just behind the finned radiators for the intercoolers: they generated a strong turbulence that didn't allow enough air to enter the inlets and the ram pipes. Some adjustments were made to the ram pipes during the trial spins, which solved the problem.

Furthermore, the engine did not "breathe" regularly due to the short exhausts that did a poor job of extracting the fumes and, due to the too-tight streamlining of the body, generated some counter-pressure.

The ice tank (75 pounds) worked perfectly and contributed to the longitudinal balance of the car. It was made of steel and made up the front section of the body. The ice for cooling was an innovation, adopted 10 years later by the Germans and English on their record cars.[24]

This photograph could have been taken in April, or in February judging by the sweater worn by Lockhart. It is one of the best images of the complete vehicle. It could have provided an understanding of the shape of the carburetor air intakes on top of the body just behind the intercooler fins, but unfortunately the intakes were covered by a shroud to protect them from sand blown by the wind. We'll never know if there was some sort of scoop on them.

Appendix 2
Campbell's 1928 Blue Bird

Technical Characteristics, Dimensions, Main Suppliers

Malcolm Campbell's garage is a main component of the tale he built with utmost pain and was amplified by many articles and books lavishing him with praise. An example is the text by R.S. Lyons,[1] more enthusiast than expert author, who interviewed Campbell in 1938 at his Headley Grove, Surrey, home when the land speed record season was definitively over.

He narrated the feeling he felt when entering the garage: "The first impression one gets is that here is a motorist's paradise. Steering wheels of all sizes seem to meet one everywhere. There are drawers full of spanners, wrenches, hammers, drills and other impedimenta. There are jacks—small, large and medium—and acetylene welding plant. It was in this garage—though in another house—that the earlier Blue Bird was built and prepared, and this will give some idea of the completeness of his equipment."

Brushing aside the myth, the true facts tell another story.

Malcolm Campbell did the simpler operations of preparing and fine-tuning in the garage, thanks to the broad and deep know-how and expertise of Leo Villa and his helpers, mainly on racing cars. On the land speed record vehicles he had to contract outsiders to do jobs as needed because of the size, weight, and complexity of these vehicles and to fulfill his never-ending quest for the best, always and everywhere.[2]

Campbell possessed a keen expertise in selecting the best suppliers, and he was a master at involving them in his projects deeply.

Sponsorship had yet to take off in 1927–1928, yet the new Blue Bird was the product of contributions by the main suppliers and the British Air Ministry: the latter gave him, on free-of-charge loan, two Napier Lion Series VIIB "Sprint" engines, still on the ministry's secret list.

The small size of many suppliers' operations made the production of special purpose items easier, even in single units. Nevertheless, the involvement of workers right up to top management was fundamental to meet the usually tight schedules and the complexity of the jobs.

Appendix 2: Campbell's 1928 Blue Bird

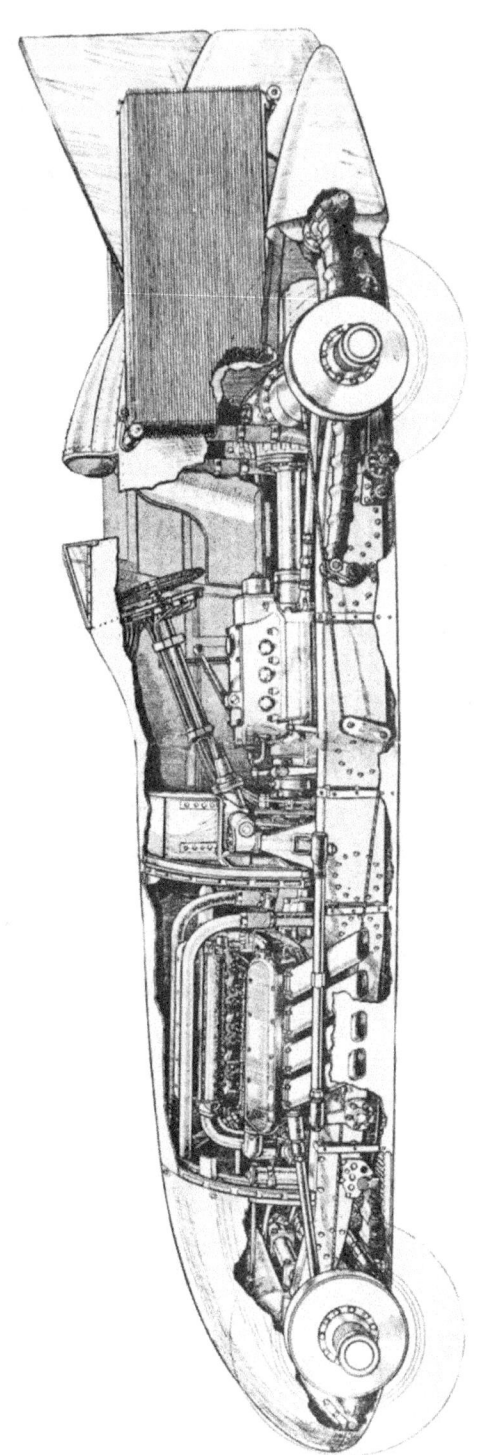

A beautiful cutaway of the 1928 Blue Bird, drawn for *The Autocar*, London, January 27, 1928, pp. 162–163. The key elements of the vehicle are clearly and precisely presented. The only significant item missing is the connection between the engine and the surface radiators on the tail. The high and dangerous position of the driver's seat on top of the transmission torque tube can be seen (courtesy Haymarket Media Group Limited, London).

It would have been quite difficult for Malcolm Campbell to fund the full cost of the production of components, parts, accessories, and the whole vehicle, even though he was well off without tight financial constraints, but he perpetuated the myth that he did.

National pride was the explanation for having so many people and companies on board in his endeavors. The land speed record was the feather in the cap of the British motor industry, which was neither an innovator nor a leading manufacturer of mass-produced everyday cars. It was very seldom at the forefront of international racing, with most races at Brooklands being either at local or club level.

The 1928 Blue Bird was the product of the Malcolm Campbell team: Joseph Maina was the designer of the three-speed gearbox and the transmission, and he supervised final assembly and preparation of the vehicle. He took on the jobs left by Charles Amherst Villiers (1900–1991), who designed the basic shape of the vehicle, the suspension and rear axle mounting on the frame.

Period articles don't mention any single person in charge of aerodynamics, which were finalized after extensive wind tunnel tests on scale models. We can assume that they were the result of a working group of Campbell, the designers Maina and earlier Amherst Villiers, Napier, Fairey Aviation, and Barker & Co., builders of the body.[3]

Maina's original design included a massive transmission based on a clutch with 16 discs of 11.25-inch diameter and an epicyclic gearbox with ratios of 0.333 for first gear, 0.666 for second, and 1 for top gear. The size of the gearbox and clutch forced the throttle and brake pedals to be placed on the right of the transmission case with the clutch on the left of it. The gear lever was in the center of the cockpit, underneath and behind the steering wheel.

A short transmission shaft within a sturdy aluminum case linked the clutch to the rear axle where the worm drive had a 1.5:1 ratio. The Napier aero engine was quite low-revving, as was normal practice at the time: 3,300 rpm when producing true and reliable 875–900 HP peak power.

The live rear axle was suspended on two semi-elliptical springs 37 inches long and was bolted to the gearbox by two reaction arms. The whole assembly of rear axle transmission shaft and gear casing was a single suspended block, swaying beneath the driver's feet and bottom under rear axle movements.

The front axle, two sections rigidly joined in the center, was linked to the front cross members of the frame through two friction dampers acting in unison with two semi-elliptical springs 50.5 inches long. The steering system was of the Marles double type.

The brakes on the four wheels were 18-inch × 1⅝-inch drums turned from aluminum. Cooling fins were on the external face. A Dewandre vacuum brake servo assisted braking action.

The unsprung mass was significant, yet it was regarded as irrelevant in a vehicle due to travel in a straight line on a reasonably smooth surface.

Total weight, fully loaded, was quoted by a source (American) as 2.5 long tons, or 5,600 pounds.[4]

The bulky transmission and relatively short wheelbase (145.5 inches) due to the compact size of the W12 engine forced the placement of the driver's seat much higher than the frame rails. A "hump" was needed to shield the driver, a solution that increased the cross section and made the profile of the car quite ugly, further worsened by the side radiators on the tail.

The high seating and lack of safety belts (nobody used them in those days) were the causes of the dangerous mishaps that befell Campbell on the February 16 and 19 runs on the sands of Daytona Beach.[5]

The frame, originally built for and used in the 1927 Blue Bird, and some components of the 1928 vehicle were later merged in the Blue Birds built from 1929 to 1935, even though the use of the new, longer R-Type Rolls-Royce V12 engine in 1933 and 1935 forced the lengthening of the frame.

The following list of the main suppliers of the 1928 Blue Bird was published by British magazines.[6]

Engine: Napier (Series VIIB "Sprint" Lion: broad angle W12, total capacity 1,360 cubic inches, bore × stroke 5.5 inches × 5.125 inches, compression ratio 10:1, estimated effective power output 875/900 HP @ 3,300 rpm).
Frame: Vickers-Armstrong and Napier
Body: Barker & Co. Coachbuilders
Radiators: Fairey Aviation Co. Ltd.
Spark plugs: K.L.G.
Magneto: B.T.H.
Carburetors: Claudel-Hobson
Steering: Marles
Wheels: Rudge-Whitworth
Tires: Dunlop
Shock absorbers: Hartford
Shock absorber springs: Woodhead
Front axle: Alford and Alder
Brake linings: Ferodo
Vacuum brake servo: Dewandre
Roller bearings: Hoffman
Fuel tank: Ewarts
Windscreen: Triplex
Instruments: Smiths
Rev-counter: Elliott
Oil: Castrol

Appendix 3
Stutz Blackhawk Special

Technical and Design Characteristics and Dimensions

Technical and constructional characteristics of the Stutz Blackhawk Special were detailed in some period articles and later sourced in a couple of good pieces published in *Speed Age* in 1949 and 1952. They were also included by Griffith Borgeson in his 1966 book.[1]

What follows is the outcome of crosschecking many different published sources and the description of the car mailed to the author by Jim Weisel, son of John (one of the two credited designers of the car). In cases of conflicting items priority was given to the period (1928) sources.

The design of the Blackhawk was highly refined, sketched and managed by Frank Lockhart and developed into constructional detail by Zenas and John Weisel. Stutz engineers, foremen, and specialists may also have contributed to the car's final design, but their names haven't been recorded for posterity.

The best U.S. suppliers of parts and components received contracts from Lockhart, who knew them well thanks to the common focus on racing cars. Milling, turning, lapping, and every mechanical job required was done in the Stutz factory, one of the leading car manufacturers in Indianapolis, at that time the racing car capital of the United States.

The small team of highly specialized workmen assembled by Lockhart took charge of shaping the body, mounting the parts, and carrying out the final assembly and tuning: Myron Stevens, master body-builder; Jean Marcenac, a mechanic of unrivalled genius; Floyd Dreyer; Ray Splinder; Jimmy Lee; and Bud Miller.

The Blackhawk pioneered the use of aluminum in racing cars, from the engine to the transmission, the brake drums, the body, and the wheel fairings. An advertisement of the Aluminum Company of America, the aluminum supplier, headquartered in Pittsburgh, Pennsylvania, listed 46 parts and components of the car made from the metal.

In a signed letter Frank Lockhart praised aluminum and summed it up by saying, "There is only one reason why any particular material was used in the car: because it was the best possible obtainable."[2]

Appendix 3: Stutz Blackhawk Special

Body: Shaped by Myron Stevens in aluminum, with the sole exception of the front, which was made from a foil of steel to act as a tank for the cooling ice. Length: 186 inches. Width: 24 inches. Height: 31 inches. Ground clearance: 5 inches. Maximum height from the ground to the top of the driver's head: 43.5 inches. Cross section: 10 square feet. Gap between body and wheel fairings: 12 inches.

Some British sources of the period and later stated erroneously that the body was covered by fabric.

Engine: Two parallel eight-cylinder Miller 91 banks (to be more precise, four four-cylinder blocks), purchased from the builder. Angle between the rows: 30 degrees. Purpose-built crankcase in aluminum to host the lower transmission crankshaft, connected to each row's crankshaft by a widely spaced spur gear with 1:1 ratio.

Bore and stroke: 2.188 inches × 3 inches. Tubular rods of chromium-nickel steel, length 6 inches. Piston pin diameter: 0.625 inches. Lynite (aluminum) pistons with three rings, surface area 61 square inches, weight per unit: 5 ounces: very lightweight for the period, allowing the high longitudinal velocity (3,750 feet/second) needed to reach the maximum 7,000 rpm.

Total capacity: 181 cubic inches.

The main elements of the engine displayed on a clean tabletop in the Stutz workshop. The two superchargers, one per bank, stand as the larger component: impeller diameter 8 inches, casing precisely finned. The impeller was connected to the crankshaft through a 5.35:1 reduction gear; thus when the engine was at full power (7,000 rpm) the supercharger rotated at 37,450 rpm, emitting the whine that so impressed onlookers in Daytona Beach (original by Jim Weisel; from Tom Kinney collection).

Appendix 3: Stutz Blackhawk Special

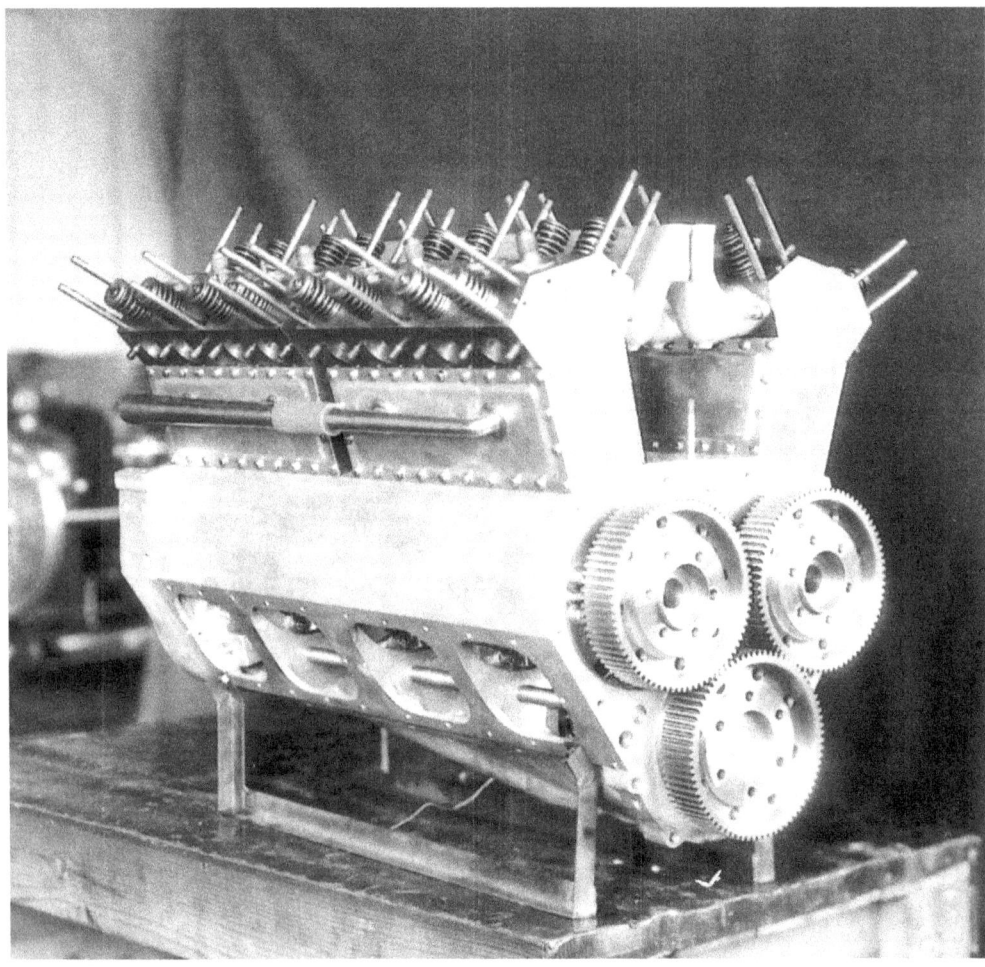

The Blackhawk's engine without the cam covers. The purpose-built crankcase carried the two crankshafts, one per block, the lower one connecting them at 1:1 ratio. The equal diameter of the three gears is clearly visible. The cylinder banks were angled 30 degrees (original by Jim Weisel; from Tom Kinney collection).

Compression ratio: 5.7:1 with supercharging pressure 28 psi. Firing order by a Delco distributor (one per row of cylinders): 1, 5, 3, 7, 4, 8, 2, 6.

Distribution: DOHC on each row, two valves per cylinder at 30-degree angle, same diameter for inlet and exhaust valves 1.187 inches. Valve timing as used on the Miller engines.

Inlet circuit: Two Zenith-Lockhart special downdraft-type carburetors, each one connected to the corresponding centrifugal supercharger. Impeller diameter 8 inches. Impeller connected to the crankshaft through a 5.35:1 reduction (i.e., the impeller rotated at 37,450 rpm at 7,000 engine revs per minute). After passing through the blower, the fuel mixture was directed to the intercooler, a finned aluminum casting in the upper part of the body. After traversing the finned portion of the intercooler the mixture reached the inlet valve through another flat tube. Tubes and intercooler were said to carry a $3,400 price tag.

Power output: It should be one of the best known and talked about figures for any engine, yet not for this one, even though it outlived Lockhart and the Blackhawk and powered an Indianapolis racer from 1939 to 1946: it is still preserved in the Speedway Museum.

In the years 1927–1928 Stutz did not have a test bench capable of withstanding the anticipated power output. For the understandable reason of privacy the team decided not to use any test rig outside of the factory. As a consequence every power figure released and published was the theoretical extrapolation by slide rule of data taken in the wind tunnel tests on the Muroc 91 Miller and the Blackhawk.

Today we know that the 91 model could have been wrong in size, forcing the error in the Blackhawk data extrapolation. The team figured out 385 HP @ 7,000 rpm; a figure rounded up to 400 HP is found in the press releases by Bill Sturm.

Only one source, Jim Weisel, wrote about 406 HP @ 7,000 rpm and, exaggerating, 566 HP @ 8,300 rpm. The latter figure is simply the result of graphical extrapolation on the theoretical (and incorrect) power curve versus rpm. In the real world the engine could not have reached such a high rpm without self-destructing.[3]

Engine cooling: Open circuit without radiator through an ice pack in a 75-pound tank shaped into the car's front. The ice allowed 10 minutes at full throttle before the water would reach the 180°F critical temperature. The ice cooling system was used for the very first time in a racing or record car. British and German record cars used the system 10 years later. The tank in front had the additional advantage of being cooled by the airstream.

Clutch: Designed by Lockhart, it had four driving and four driven discs, all 5.875 inches in diameter. When the pedal was released the friction clutch picked up the load first, which was then, during the last part of the release motion, transferred to the positive drive "lock-in" device, i.e., the internal-external toothed discs.

Gearshift and transmission: Designed by Lockhart. Three forward: first 2.762:1, second 1.355:1, third 1:1, one RM. The forged steel transmission shaft, 2.25 inches in diameter, was connected to the clutch by a universal joint and ended with worm gears of 2.83:1 reduction ratio, i.e., six leads on the worm and 17 on the wheel. Wheels of 16 and 18 leads, equal to 2.66:1 and 3.00:1 ratios, were also machined, yet no one knows anything about their actual use.

Gears: Purpose-built by Timken. That fact makes highly improbable the theory that the seizure of the worm drive was the cause of the fatal accident on April 25, 1928. Unbelievable rumors about it added that the worm drive was a regular Stutz-made one, sourced from a stock car, and thus of course not designed for the stresses of very high speed.

Since worm speed of 7,000 rpm had not previously been encountered, it was necessary for the builders of the gears to carry out considerable experimental work to solve the early problem of seizure after only three minutes at top speed. The right solution was found and tested for many hours of work without ever going beyond the safe temperature of 180°F, the upper limit to avoid any risk of seizure. An oil pump provided cooling for the gears.

Rear shaft: Steel, diameter 2.75 inches.

Wheels: Steel disc, size 29 × 4.5: tire rims bolted by 18 hi-tensile steel bolts and nuts.

Brakes: Lockheed hydraulics. Aluminum 16-inch diameter drums, 3 inches wide, machined from solid and finned with 0.75-inch-deep fins. Each brake element consisted of two light alloy shoes with asbestos lining.

The front wheel brakes worked by hand-operated lever and the rear ones by a conventional pedal. Each brake assembly weighed 57 pounds. The unsprung mass (wheels and brakes) was quite high due to the design decision to give precedence to rigidity and heat resistance rather than lightness, knowing that the car had to move in a straight line on a smooth and easy surface.

The brakes were oversized, without a rational explanation but maybe due to Lockhart's know-how from track racing. On the Daytona Beach sand strip, with four miles to slow down, such a heavy braking fixture appears excessive today. Furthermore the presumed strength of braking of the rear wheels at the end of the second—northbound—run is blamed as the cause of the April 25 disaster.

Frame: Two U-shaped rails made from nickel steel, arched over the rear axle and joined together at the rear by a forged fitting. The fitting held the supports for the large fuel tank. Four nickel steel cross-members, outside diameter 1.689

The front axle was the most unconventional and complex part of the Blackhawk. Springs and dampers were placed inside the narrow body to obtain a clean and smooth external surface. The axle was split into three sections, to which the upper mount of the dampers was connected. The whole suspension system allowed maximum deflection of 0.75 inches each way, which proved insufficient when the sand was rough and bumpy (original by Floyd Dreyer, Jr., and Mike Dreyer; from Tom Kinney collection).

inches, linked the side rails. The front and rear cross-members held the upper suspension attachments.

Dampers and springs: The most unconventional and complex part of the car, the result of a highly refined design. To avoid additional aerodynamic resistance the springs were placed inside the body. To fit within the very restricted space the springs were machined from a solid billet, milling each upper and lower section (10 inches long) with a 3/16 cutter. The leaves were attached to the frame rigidly at the lower end and to the axles at the upper end. The system had very high resistance to lateral forces and allowed a 1.5-inch maximum deflection. Today it seems unnecessary to have such a complex piece of machinery just to have a 0.75-inch maximum higher deflection, to absorb the roughness of the sand. The proof may come out from the frames of the film-clip of the accident: the frames show that the damping effect of the suspension was very low, almost ineffective. Despite Campbell's worries about lightness, the car was heavy at 3,000 pounds.[4] In comparison, the density (weight/side surface ratio) was rather close to that of Segrave's 1927 1000 HP Sunbeam, whose length was 283 inches, i.e., 52 percent longer, and weighed dry 8,500 pounds.

Steering: Ross-type mechanism with two drag links and steering arms, one per side. No transverse link between the front wheels, joined together by a three-piece rigid axle. The central section of the axle, inside the body, carried the upper attachments of the springs. The extreme care in design and construction is evident in the aerodynamic shape of the steering rods: no effect on drag reduction yet a beautiful piece to look at.

The Main Suppliers[5]

Plain bearings: Federal Mogul, Detroit MI
Carburetors: Zenith, Detroit MI

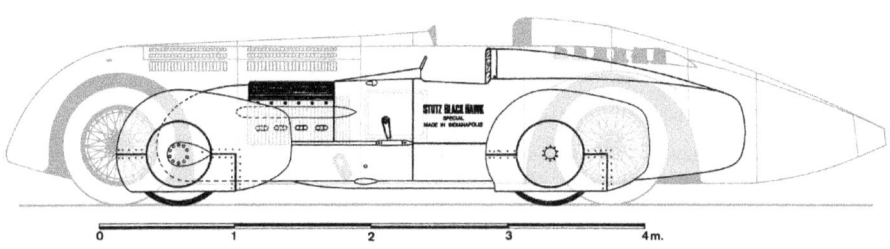

Comparison of the side profiles of the Blackhawk and the 1927 Sunbeam 1000 HP, the record holder. Despite the huge difference in dimensions, the cars were comparable in terms of density, i.e., weight/side surface ratio. The Blackhawk was stated to weigh 3,000 pounds (we don't know if that was the dry or fully-loaded figure, yet it appears too heavy for either). The Sunbeam's dry weight was reported to be about 8,500 pounds (author's drawing).

Appendix 3: Stutz Blackhawk Special

The Ross-type steering was activated by two arms and links, one per side, without any cross element. Lockhart's attention to detail and streamlining is clear in the shape of the front fairing covering the junction of arm and link. Note the two small protruding volumes on the front to cover the dampers. Bill Sturm, in cap and checkered socks, waits together with two members of the team.

Ball bearings: New Departure, Bristol CT
Spark plugs: Champion, Toledo OH
Ignition: Delco, Grand Blanc MI
Battery: Prest-O-Lite, Indianapolis IN
Camshafts: L.O. Gordon, Muskegon MI
Valves: J.A. Drake & Sons, Beedley, Chicago IL
Valve springs: Givson, Chicago IL
Pistons: Aluminum Company of America, Pittsburgh PA
Piston rings: Simplex, Cleveland OH[6]
Steering gear: Ross Gear Co., Lafayette IN
Universal joints: Mechanics Machine Co., Rockford IL
Transmission: Detroit Gear and Machine Co., Detroit MI
Axles and gears: Timken Axle Co., Detroit MI
Frame: A.O. Smith Co., Milwaukee WI
Instruments: Moto-Meter Co., New York NY; Consolidated Instruments Co., New York NY
Brakes: Lockheed, Burbank CA
Oil: Mobil–Socony, New York NY
Fuel: Ethyl Corp., Richmond VA

Appendix 4

The Engines

1. The Napier Lion

The 1917 Napier Lion aero engine was a very good design and full of foresight. During the 12 years of development until 1929 the power output grew from the original 480 to 1,450 HP without substantial changes in layout or structure. This affirms the strength of the design of the most innovative and powerful engine of the period, when aeronautics and engines had hardly grown out of their early infancy.

In 1916 Napier decided to design the aero engines that it would produce in-house. Arthur Rowledge was appointed as head of the design team that completed the drawings in a few months around mid–1917.

Basic features of the new engine were lightness, low frontal area, high power, and water-cooling. The team selected the broad arrow (W-type) architecture, i.e., three parallel rows of four cylinders each.[1] Each row had double overhead camshafts operating four valves per cylinder.

The very first four-cylinder DOHC racing engine was designed by Ernest Henry in 1912 (only four years earlier) for Peugeot in France. Nothing similar had been seen in aviation before Napier, nor in a mass-produced unit. And using four valves per cylinder.

The prototypes were built from a milled aluminum block, but milling and cooling problems soon forced a reversion to traditional steel cylinders screwed by unit to the crankcase.

The team opted for bore and stroke of 5.5 inches × 5.1215 inches: the over-square architecture was a clever solution to reduce the floating of the side pushrods in a three-row engine where the three pushrods are in the same section of the crankshaft, the two side pushrods eccentric to the central one.

Total capacity was 1,461.6 cubic inches. Total dry weight 960 pounds. Compression ratio 5.8:1. Claimed power output 480 HP @ 2,200 rpm, the highest power output of the period for an aero engine, higher than the 420 HP of the Liberty L-12 U.S.-built engine.

Further development raised the output to 950 HP in the Series VIIB "Sprint"

The Napier Lion Series VIIB "Sprint" aero engine loaned to Malcolm Campbell by the British Air Ministry to be fitted to his 1928 Blue Bird. Developed for the seaplanes that won the 1927 Schneider Cup in Venice, Italy, the engine was still on the Air Ministry's secret list. Two units were loaned and sent sealed to Campbell to avoid any disclosure of the inner workings. To protect secrecy, the fitment of the engine into the car took place at the Napier plant at Acton Vale, north London (courtesy of the National Automotive History Collection, Detroit Public Library).

version, which powered the Supermarine S.5, winner of the 1927 Schneider Trophy in Venice, Italy, flying at 281.6 mph and beating the Italian competition. The "Sprint" version was loaned to Malcolm Campbell for his 1928 Blue Bird.[2]

In the inter-war years the Napier Lion powered 150 different types of aircrafts for military, commercial, and racing purposes.

The addition of a supercharger in 1929 raised the output further to 1,450 HP, making the Lion everyone's preferred choice in the quest for air, land, and water speed records.

Two unlimited racing cars at Brooklands utilized the engine: the best known is the Napier-Railton driven by John Cobb (and others) to many endurance records and the overall Brooklands lap record of 143.44 mph in 1937, a record that will stand for eternity.[3] The car still exists and, lovingly cared by the dedicated staff of the Beaulieu Motor Museum, England, is occasionally fired up and driven in exhibition runs.

Henry Segrave used the "Sprint" Lion in his 1929 Golden Arrow record-breaker: 231.362 mph on March 11 in Daytona Beach. John Cobb and Reid Railton opted for lightness and minimum frontal area of two Lion engines for the 1937 car,[4] which won three outright speed records by 1947. The final figure—394.20 mph—stood unbeaten until 1960, sensational proof of the quality of an engine designed 30 years earlier.

To celebrate Malcolm Campbell's record, *The Motor* couldn't avoid the self-laudatory elegy of British engineering: they reprinted the comment from the 1927 Schneider Trophy victory of a British Supermarine S.5 powered by the Napier "Sprint" Lion:

> It is of particular interest to remember that the British engineering concern that built the engine which made the record achievement possible was one of the first in the country to manufacture internal combustion engines for motor cars in the early years of the XX century. The progress represented by the engine, when compared with competition, is such that no relative combination of scientific and engineering advancement in a like period in connection with locomotion can be found to compare with it.[5]

2. The L-12 Liberty Engine

There were 13,500 L-12 Liberty engines manufactured by the end of the Great War. Manufacturing continued until the end of 1919 to use up the full stock of available components, parts, and tooling. The final count exceeded 20,000 units.

The Liberty engine was the key element of the U.S. government's aeronautical program during the Great War. Jointly designed by a group of experts in both aero and car design and manufacturing, it was expected to provide a standard unit for mass-production in four modular versions: 4, 6, 8, and 12 cylinders. The latter was the only one ever actually mass-produced: 13,500 units built by 1918 and 20,000 plus by December 1919 when all available components had been used up. Three units, sourced on the second-hand market, were used by Jim White on the Triplex record car (courtesy of the National Automotive History Collection, Detroit Public Library).

Appendix 4: The Engines

A mass-production facility of the Liberty L-12 engine. It had an initial power output of 420 HP @ 1,800 rpm: it was the second most powerful aero engine of the Entente Powers behind the Napier Lion. It suffered many teething problems and forced the administration to issue some 1,400 changes to the specification, increasing manufacturing costs and delaying mass-production by automobile companies Ford, Lincoln, Packard, Marmon, Cadillac, and Buick (courtesy of the National Automotive History Collection, Detroit Public Library).

What to do with them?

The U.S. government had invested about $640 million in the aeronautical program, the mainstay of which was the Liberty engine.[6]

The Liberty engine was a first in the aeronautical industry, then in the very early stages of technology, design, and mass manufacturing. It was envisaged to do for aircraft what the Model T Ford had done for automobiles: a standard, one-size-fits-all, mass-produced engine in four modular versions (four, six, eight, and 12 cylinders). Even though by the end of the Great War the production of lower-capacity engines was marginal, every airframe would have had the right version of the 12-cylinder engine: fighter (then called "pursuit"), reconnaissance, trainer, and multi-engine bomber.

Standardization for ease of mass production was the most innovative feature of the engine, a sort of revolution given that France, the world leader in aviation, produced 47 different aircraft engines, with the UK making 37 different types.

By the end of the war the U.S. had neither debts nor war reparations to repay, and the government decided to get rid of the L-12 Liberty engines. Some were donated to the Air Mail Service; many others were sold at pennies on the dollar to vocational schools and barnstormers.

The preferred airframe was the JN-4 Curtiss, the "Jenny," used for carrying mail across the States and for stunt flying at country fairs. Both uses built up the myth of the aviation in the "Roaring Twenties." Some good books were written on that: e.g., the mail flights have been described by Charles Lindbergh in his 1927 work *Of Flight and Life*. On the world of barnstorming the masterpiece is *Pylon*, a 1935 novel by William Faulkner.

A widespread, yet illegal, use of surplus L-12 Liberty engines was their conversion into marine engines to propel the smugglers' high-speed boats on the Great Lakes and in the Caribbean Sea during the years of Prohibition in the United States. No Coast Guard cutter could match the speed of those boats.

When the government refused to sell Jim White surplus L-12 Liberty engines, he bought three marine units on the secondary market from unknown sources in the Great Lakes region, to be installed in the Triplex record car. Jim White himself refused to speculate on the identity of the sellers and what the engines had been used for.

The L-12 Liberty was a 45° V water-cooled engine, total capacity 1,649.3 cubic inches, bore and stroke 5 inches × 7 inches, two valves per cylinder, compression ratio 5.4:1, takeoff power output 420 HP @ 1,800 rpm.[7] The steel cylinders were single-screwed to the block, which was split into two elements at the center plane of the crankshaft. The propeller was mounted directly on to the extension of the crankshaft without a reduction gear.

The choice of the 45-degree angle between the rows of cylinders and the unusual ignition sequence were the origin of torsional vibrations of the crankshaft that were not adequately damped and caused many failures on the 50-hour acceptance test. Rumors went around that the early engines needed a complete overhaul after only 50 hours of service. Such a disappointing figure was later improved to 75 hours between overhauls, and later models reached 300 hours. Reliable statistics are not available because military mechanics opted for a complete change of engine when it was either close to failure or had already failed.

The Liberty engine was hurriedly designed by a group of aero and auto designers and engineers. It suffered from having been designed by a committee and not by a single chief designer who would have been in charge of development and fine-tuning.

In the first nine months after the assignment of the manufacturing contracts, the government issued some 1,400 changes to the specification, forcing the contractors to rework partially assembled engines and to order new tooling. As a consequence, standardization went astray, delivery schedules were destroyed, and quality control became loose.

Manufacturing was contracted to automobile companies: Lincoln, Packard, Marmon, General Motors' Cadillac and Buick Divisions, and Ford, then the leader in mass-production. Scandals and schedule disruptions affected the whole program. It was said that many top managers emerged from it much richer than when they had started.

Final Word
The Lockhart Saga—A Review

At the end of April 1928, everything was already set for building up the legend of a hero killed by fate at 25: Frank Lockhart was a true American boy, at the top of car racing, the first winner of the Indy 500 as a rookie, killed while driving at an unheard-of speed to conquer the World Land Speed Record for America.

It all began with an article by Bill Sturm, written on the spot by the top journalist who as the PR manager was closely linked to Frank Lockhart.

The article was published in the April 26, 1928, edition of the *Indianapolis News* daily. The headline set the mood of the story: Frank Lockhart was called "Little Boy" who "was trying to get along." No fanfare, no glorification of a hero, no superior aim to get something unique while racing into the unknown.

The opener:

> Frank Lockhart was more than a great racing driver. He was one of the finest characters I have ever known. He had a straightforward way of doing business that made many think him brusk, even conceited. But he was not.
>
> There were no halfway measures with anything in which he was concerned. In everything from his clothes to his racing cars, he took infinite pains. He always believed that the best was the thing to be striven for.

Following the low-key opener, the sentences built to a symphonic crescendo: "Lockhart was exceptional in a profession that is made of exceptional men. He was the cleverest racing driver in America, not only in preparing the car, but in designing it and driving it. He was fearless, and the demonstration of it no doubt cost him his life."

The final words sound like a farewell tune: "Lockhart, the little gentleman, the straight-from-the-shoulder boy, has gone. But he will be remembered a long time for his wonderful driving and for his courage."[1]

Let's try to check Bill Sturm's words against what we know today about period racing and record-breaking, what we learned about the short life of Frank Lockhart and the detailed description of the Blackhawk and its intrinsic design faults.

Fred Moskovics, still deeply upset having been so close to the tragedy, spoke at a meeting of the Society of Automotive Engineers in Chicago on May 15, 1928.[2] He praised Lockhart "both as a man and an engineering wizard, and the greatest driver [he had] ever seen." Moskovics added: "He had an uncanny mechanical knack even though he never took an engineering course."

Lockhart's biography confirms that his formal education was very limited due to the depth of his involvement in mechanics and racing cars. His reluctance to speak and appear in front of any audience might be due to his lack of schooling, as proven by his basic handwriting in the very few signed texts we know of, mostly telegraphic dedications on photos.

Maybe excessive in praising Lockhart, even more than Sturm, was the unknown writer of the Central Press syndicate who wrote the story published in *The Indianapolis Star*: "Lockhart died as one of the greatest race drivers of all time. Lockhart's canny skill and his utter lack of fear made him an invaluable man to the business of testing automobiles to which he lent himself. He seemed to be unconscious of danger in all the fearful uproar of the speedways, with his car rocketing along at a frightful speed over tracks drenched in oil."[3]

Pete de Paolo, a top driver of the same period and also one of Lockhart's fiercest competitors in the 1926 and 1927 AAA Championship rounds, didn't show the superiority complex of a celebrated champion when dealing with a newcomer.

On Lockhart he wrote in his first-class book *Wall Smacker—The Saga of the Speedway*:

> He was a natural mechanic, an artist with mechanical tools, so he converted an old Ford into a racing car and joined the "outlaws" and soon proved a consistent winner. Just a few second-hand parts and an old Ford engine, but Lockhart put them together and made speed that was hard to beat. He even gave Uncle [Ralph DePalma,[4] his mother's brother hence de Paolo's uncle] in his Miller some real competition. ... He improved with every race and the followers of the sport had to admit that he was one of the greatest dirt track drivers of all time.[5]

The whole set of quotes and the story bylined by Sturm show what today appears as an irredeemable contradiction: genius with ferocious attention to detail and perfection and fearless driver with no inner sense of limitations. To be fearless is today rated as a negative characteristic in a race driver because they are supposed to know the limits, both their own and of the track. In those years, a driver had to be fearless to race on those tracks, first and foremost board tracks. The technology of handling, brakes, tires, and the whole vehicle dynamic were far behind the speeds the racers achieved. The long list of drivers killed on board tracks and speedways is quite frightening. Despite that, people and media glorified the courage of fearless drivers, and most of all serial winners such as Lockhart.

Every U.S. racing driver's career started then on the dirt tracks; it was a racing mode that refined driving sensitivity and enhanced fast reactions to the surprises of speed.

Driving a car on a dirt track was different from driving on speedways or board tracks: the dirt surface provided plenty of adhesion and absorbed each action, even excessive, to correct a mistake before it could get out of control.

De Paolo wrote about the first appearance of Lockhart in a Miller at the Culver City 1.25-mile board track, shortly after it opened on December 14, 1924. As a rookie he had to do a solo pre-qualifying run.

He stormed the boards and, entering the first banked turn, "he got the surprise of his life. He did the usual thing that [a] novice will do on a turn when going at a terrific pace. He oversteered for just a fraction of a second. His car shot upward, hit the top rail and then waltzed down the track in a series of glides and slides, finally coming to a stop with the tail flattened against the inner concrete wall.

That ended Lockhart's interest in the coming race. He went back to the dirt tracks and continued to star there."[6]

Lockhart had a troublesome debut on the board tracks, yet he climbed to the top fast: in two years—1926 and 1927—he entered 22 races, won eight, and was on the podium four more times. His cumulative purse on board tracks amounted to $40,900.[7]

In 1926 he was a rookie at Indianapolis, where he arrived without a guaranteed drive. He began to build his legend there: he won, the first rookie ever to do so, two laps ahead of Harry Hartz (Miller).

The *Motor Age* chronicle of the race closed with a recap of the Lockhart story: "He came here practically unknown, except on dirt tracks, to become famous overnight. All of which goes to show that pre-race predictions do not always mean so much. The prophets failed to include Lockhart in their ticket."[8]

Lockhart's life and the description of the 1928 record runs prove that more than pre-race forecasts can be wrong. Even the best scientifically designed and painstakingly built car could miss its goal.

Furthermore, as Malcolm Campbell wrote and said many times, a driver had to be perfectly fit, arms and hands first, to achieve the record. On the day of his fateful run, Lockhart was not.[9]

Chapter Notes

Chapter 2

1. The story about the palm reading is published on p. 80 of Wilbur Shaw's autobiography, *Gentlemen, Start Your Engines*. The palm-reading skill of Mrs. Means is mentioned again on p. 117, where Shaw wrote that she managed to foresee Segrave's untimely death.

2. Leo Villa and Kevin Desmond, *Life with the Speed King* (London: Marshall, Harris & Baldwin, Ltd., 1979), 111. Leopoldo Alfonso "Leo" Villa (London, November 30, 1899–London, January 18, 1979) was born into a family of Swiss immigrants from Lugano in the Italian-speaking region of Switzerland. Following his early employment as assistant waiter in a London restaurant owned by Italians, he took his preferred job as a mechanic for Giulio Foresti (1888–1965). Foresti was one of the leading drivers at Brooklands and the Itala importer for the UK. He served as a mechanical specialist in the Royal Flying Corps (later to become the Royal Air Force, or RAF) during the Great War. After the war he returned to Foresti and with him, as riding mechanic, entered many races including the 1921 Targa Florio on May 29 in the Itala 51 Sport, where he finished first in class and fifth overall. In 1923 he joined Malcolm Campbell thanks to better financial terms and the promise of a house for his family. He was chief mechanic, yet he soon became Malcolm Campbell's right arm on track and on every record run in cars and boats. He stayed with Donald Campbell until he met his death on Coniston Water on January 4, 1967. In June 1979 his grandson Phil married Gina Campbell, Donald's daughter, continuing the link with the Campbell family for the third generation in a row.

3. Dorothy Lady Campbell, *Malcolm Campbell—The Man as I Knew Him* (London: Hutchinson & Co. Publishers Ltd., 1951), 18.

4. Ibid., 9.

5. David "Dunlop Mac" McDonald and Adrian Ball, *Fifty Years with the Speed Kings* (London: Paul Stanley, 1951), 132.

6. "Malcolm Campbell on the Surprises of Speed; What 200 m.p.h. Really Means—Two Rounds of a Fight with 'Blue Bird,'" *The Motor*, May 15, 1928, 688. According to the British habit of using a more significant title than just "Mr.," Malcolm Campbell was always called "Captain" by the media, the rank he reached when serving in the Royal Flying Corps during the Great War. Further to his 1928 land speed record in Daytona Beach, proof of his growing popularity was the common omission of his former military rank. Leo Villa and the team members referred to him as the "Skipper" until he was knighted by King George V after his 1931 record (245.736 mph). After that everyone referred to him as "Sir Malcolm."

7. Campbell, *Malcolm Campbell—The Man as I Knew Him*, 10.

8. Gina Campbell and Michael Meech, Michael, *Bluebirds—The Story of the Campbell Dynasty* (London: Sidwick & Jackson, 1988), 33.

9. Ibid., 59.

10. In early 2022 value the sum would be $646,049.

11. In early 2022 value the sum would be $562,331.

12. "Frank Lockhart and His Speed Car Reach City; William F. Sturm and Mrs. Lockhart Accompany Driver Here," *The Daytona Beach News-Journal*, February 14, 1928, 1. Most of the headlines mentioned here have a single column width, typed all in capital letters. To respect U.S. period procedures, they have been written here with capital initial letters. The Daytona Beach local daily also used capital letters for adverbs and conjunctions while Indianapolis dailies nearly always preferred lowercase initial letters for them. Sub-headings were usually typed using capital initial letters: the originals have been respected even though blatantly incorrect. A similar approach has been adopted for British media, always respecting the original spelling, even though clearly mistaken.

13. George Eyston, *Fastest on Earth* (Los Angeles: Floyd Clymer Publishing, 1946), 14. (This is the first U.S. edition of the book published in 1939 in the UK.)

14. Two obituaries of William Sturm—"William F. Sturm, Auto Race Authority and Writer, Is Dead" and "Sturm's Death Recalls Early Race Exploits to Automotive Veterans"—were

published in *The Indianapolis News* on August 26, 1937 on pp. 1–5 and 4/II.

15. "High Power Not Vital for Top Speed, Says Lockhart," *The Daytona Beach News-Journal*, February 16, 1928, 1–2.

16. "White and Huge Triplex Speed Car Reach City; Builder Says His Car Is Made as Sporting Proposition," *The Daytona Beach News-Journal*, February 13, 1928, 1.

17. "How Segrave Attained the World's Speed Record of 231 M.P.H.; Probable Causes of Fatal Incident to American Rival. Trenchant Criticism of the Construction of the Ill-fated 'Triplex' Which American Drivers Refused to Pilot," *The Motor*, March 19, 1929, 342.

18. "Some Inside Stuff on High Speed Racing; The Builder of the Triplex Passes a Few Interesting Facts That Were Taught Him by Experience," *Motor Age*, July 5, 1928, 22.

19. The AAA rules for identifying the cars/drivers entered in the National Championship rounds stated that the racing number should be the position in which the driver finished the previous year. Keech finished second in 1928, like Lockhart did in 1927.

20. At early 2022 value the sum would be $522,388.

21. Data and historical background on the city of Daytona Beach have been taken from *Polk's Daytona Beach City Directory 1926* (Jacksonville, FL: R.I. Polk & Co., Publishers, 1926), kindly supplied by Mrs. Kim E. Dolce, Genealogy/Reference Librarian, Port Orange Regional Library, Volusia County, Florida in 2018.

22. Paul Ellis, "Speed Trials History Goes Back 28 Years," *The Daytona Beach News-Journal*, February 14, 1932 (first published on February 5, 1931).

23. History and results of the beach races in the early years of the twentieth century were published with accurate detail in Dick Punnett, *Racing on the Rim: A History of the Annual Automobile Racing Tournaments Held on the Sands of the Ormond-Daytona Beach, Florida 1903–1910* (Ormond Beach, FL: Tomoka Press, 1997).

24. *Ibid.*

25. The evolution of record runs and races on the beach until the early stock car races and, later, the NASCAR races on the mainland Trioval were published in Tom Tucker and Jim Tiller, *Daytona: The Quest for Speed* (Daytona Beach: *The Daytona Beach News-Journal*, 1994).

26. "Campbell and Lockhart Cars Ready to Speed; Triplex Reverse Is Being Installed; Whippet Is on Beach," *The Daytona Beach News-Journal*, February 21, 1928, 1.

27. "Shaw Drives Into Water in Flames; Four Cylinder Car's Driver Is Unhurt by Fire," *The Daytona Beach News-Journal*, February 23, 1928, 1.

28. Wilbur Shaw, *Gentlemen, Start Your Engines* (New York: Coward-McCann, 1955), 79.

29. "Whippet Four Goes 139 Miles Hour on Beach; Official Average Close to World's Record; Try Again Today," *The Daytona Beach News-Journal*, April 30, 1928, 1.

30. "Whippet Leaves Beach Today on 134 M.P.H. Mark; High Wind Hampers Last Day Attempts for World Record," *The Daytona Beach News-Journal*, April 30, 1928, 1.

31. Shaw, *Gentlemen, Start Your Engines*, 83.

32. At early 2022 value the sum would be $55,943.

33. The Shaw autobiography, *Gentlemen, Start Your Engines*, was published again in 2018 by the Boyle Racing Headquarters, Indianapolis adding a final chapter by Bob Gates on the life and races of Wilbur Jr. "Bob," Wilbur's son.

34. The story of Michael Joseph "Mike" Boyle has been told in Brock Yates, *Umbrella Mike: The True Story of the Chicago Gangster Behind the Indy 500* (New York: Thunder's Mouth Press, 2006).

35. Leo Villa and Tony Gray, *The Record Breakers: Sir Malcolm and Donald Campbell, Land and Water Speed Kings of the 20th Century* (London: The Hamlyn Publishing Group, 1969), 45.

36. Villa and Desmond, *Life with the Speed King*, 85.

37. *Ibid.*

38. "British Driver Expected Here About Feb. 12," *The Daytona Beach News-Journal* February 6, 1928, 1.

39. "Capt. Campbell Honored Guest of Kiwanis Club; Express Appreciation For Kindness Extended," *The Daytona Beach News-Journal*, February 15, 1928, 1.

40. "England Has U.S. All Wrong, Says Campbell; No Nation So Misunderstood, Racer Tells Audience," *The Daytona Beach News-Journal*, January 6, 1932. The story is based on an article published in the *Surrey Herald* in the UK.

41. "Protest Rule Governing Race," *The Indianapolis News*, February 4, 1928, 15. The same article was published on the front page of *The Daytona Beach News-Journal* on February 6, 1928, under the headline "Sturm Charges English Prize Rule Is Unfair; Thinks Cash Offer Should Be for Highest Speed Not First High."

42. Villa and Desmond, *Life with the Speed King*, 85.

43. Villa and Gray, *The Record Breakers*, 48.

44. Malcolm Campbell, *My Thirty Years of Speed* (London: Hutchinson & Co. Publishers, 1935), 160.

45. *Ibid.*, 163.

46. McDonald and Ball, *Fifty Years with the Speed Kings*, 69.

47. "Campbell Hits High Speed in Risky Attempt; Drives 180 Miles an Hour; Car Damaged Under Beach Conditions," *The Daytona Beach News-Journal*, February 16, 1928, 1.

48. "White and A.A.A. Agree on Device, Triplex to Race; Reverse Mechanism to Be Attached After Early Trials," *The Daytona Beach News-Journal*, February 16, 1928, 1.

49. The word "disqualified" is found in British articles written many years after the event. British media wrote libelously about the Triplex, or ignored it. As an example, *The Motor* (February 28, 1928, p. 151) mentioned Frank Lockhart as the only "serious contender" to Campbell. *Motor Sport* (March 1928, p. 223) described the Triplex as a "monstrous nightmare of a machine."
50. "White's Car Ruled Out; Philadelphian's 36-Cylinder Machine Found Ineligible by A.A.A.," *The Indianapolis Star*, February 23, 1928, 10.
51. No reliable and detailed biographical information on John and Zenas Weisel has been found in period sources or online. Some notes came to the author from Jim Weisel, son of John, thanks to Tom Kinney. John Levi Weisel was born on August 27, 1904, in Rudolph, Ohio, and grew up in Santa Barbara and Los Angeles. He graduated from Caltech, in Pasadena, in June 1927; his thesis was titled "Portable dynamometer for testing racing car superchargers." After graduation, he worked for Frank Lockhart together with his brother Zenas. In 1929 he was hired by Menasco Motors in Burbank, California, where he designed air-cooled engines for light airplanes. In 1938 he started working for Douglas Aircraft in Santa Monica, California. He retired after 29 years as senior executive advisor, Powerplant/Thermomechanical Section from the Long Beach plant. He was among the chief designers of the DC6 and DC9 civil aircrafts. He died in 1994. Zenas Weisel graduated from University of California, Berkeley, with a B.S. degree in mechanical engineering. He joined his brother John in 1927 to work on Lockhart's beach car. During World War II he was experimenting with fiber optics for a sniper scope, then he focussed his work and research on transmission. This culminated in a court case against his employer that ended with the two brothers on opposite sides. He rode motorbikes and suffered three accidents. Without wearing a helmet he sustained a head injury partially incapacitating him. According to Jim Weisel, Uncle Zenas was very creative but did not have much business sense.
52. "Lockhart to Try on World Speed Record in Indianapolis-made Car; Will Drive on Daytona Beach (Fla.) Mile Straightaway," *The Indianapolis News*, December 28, 1927, 13.
53. William Sturm, "World's Record Lockhart's Goal; Test February 15 to 23. Race Driver Building Car to Compete for Crown at Daytona Beach. Indianapolis Machine to Be Known as Stutz Black Hawk Special," *The Indianapolis News*, February 28, 1928, 12.
54. *Ibid.*
55. Cyril Posthumus, *Sir Henry Segrave* (London: B.T. Batsford Ltd., 1961), 165.
56. Paul Ellis, "Speed Trials History Goes Back 28 Years; Campbell First Shattered World Record in 1928 but His Mark Fell Before Ray Keech's Bid and Segrave Then Boosted the Speed Still Higher," *The Daytona Beach News-Journal*, February 5, 1931 and February 15, 1932.
57. Major H.O.D. (Henry O'Neal De Hane) Segrave, *The Lure of Speed* (London: Hutchinson & Co. Publishers Ltd., 1928), 243.
58. Ellis, "Speed Trials History."
59. "Races 50 Cents Today," *The Daytona Beach News-Journal*, February 19, 1928, 1.
60. "Son of English Lord Pulls for Campbell to Win," *The Daytona Beach News-Journal*, February 16, 1928, 1.
61. "Segrave and Campbell on Phone Today," *The Daytona Beach News-Journal*, February 17, 1928, 1.
62. Campbell, *My Thirty Years of Speed*, 162.
63. Ellis, "Speed Trials History."
64. Campbell, *My Thirty Years of Speed*.
65. "Three in Race Today for Record; Lockhart Runs First Trial on Sand Saturday; Anderson Wins Unofficial Contest Between Stutz Cars," *The Daytona Beach News-Journal*, February 19, 1928, 1. Under the leading headline a large photo of the beach was published with the caption: "Automobile Speed History May Be Written Here Today."
66. Campbell, *My Thirty Years of Speed*, 163.
67. "(Campbell) Hurls Car Over Florida Course at 206.956 M.P.H.; Lockhart Ends His Stutz Blackhawk Speeding Along Same Route at 181 M.P.H. in Trial Spin," *The Indianapolis Star*, February 20, 1928, 1.
68. "Malcolm Campbell on the Surprises of Speed," *The Motor*, May 15, 1928, 498. The same words are in Malcolm Campbell, *My Thirty Years of Speed* (London: Hutchinson & Co. Publishers, 1935), 161.
69. *Ibid.*
70. Campbell, *My Thirty Years of Speed*.
71. McDonald and Ball, *Fifty Years with the Speed Kings*, 68.
72. Ellis, "Speed Trials History."
73. Campbell, *My Thirty Years of Speed*.
74. Ellis, "Speed Trials History."
75. Campbell, *My Thirty Years of Speed*.
76. "Campbell Back Again; Famous Record Breaker Interviewed. His Exciting Experience at Daytona Beach," *The Autocar*, March 16, 1928, 498.
77. McDonald and Ball, *Fifty Years with the Speed Kings*.
78. Campbell, *Malcolm Campbell—The Man as I Knew Him*, 112.
79. "Mrs. Campbell Watches," *The Daytona Beach News-Journal*, February 20, 1928, 1.
80. "Campbell Sets New World Record Mark," *The Indianapolis Star*, February 20, 1928, 1.
81. McDonald and Ball, *Fifty Years with the Speed Kings*, 70.
82. Campbell, *My Thirty Years of Speed*, 165.
83. *Ibid.*
84. McDonald and Ball, *Fifty Years with the Speed Kings*.
85. Villa and Desmond, *Life with the Speed King*, 49.
86. Campbell, *My Thirty Years of Speed*.
87. Ellis, "Speed Trials History."

88. "English Speed Driver Takes Segrave Crown; Easily Adds Three Miles Per Hour to Record Before Huge Crowd," *The Daytona Beach News-Journal*, February 20, 1928, 1. Campbell's record was validated over the flying mile only, the "classical" length used in the Anglo-Saxon world. The official record over the flying kilometer remained in the hands of Henry Segrave, who won it on March 29, 1927 in Daytona Beach: 202.54 mph. A five-kilometer course was also measured in 1927: Segrave achieved the new record over the distance at 203.61 mph. The flying kilometer record was later improved on by Segrave himself on March 11, 1929 in Daytona Beach: 231.57 mph. The five-kilometer record fell to Malcolm Campbell on April 24, 1929 at Verneuk Pan, South Africa: 216.03 mph.

89. "Britain Shows the World; All-British Triumphs on Land and in the Air," *The Motor*, February 28, 1928, 151.

90. "Bravo Campbell," *The Autocar*, February 24, 1928, 341.

91. "Rumblings and Exhaust Notes," *Motor Sport*, March 1928, 223.

92. Headline of the Dunlop full-page ad showing a profile photo of Blue Bird: "Captain Malcolm Campbell in his wireless telephone message to 'The Evening News' on Feb. 20th said:" (*Motor Sport*, April 1928, 249). Interesting the mention of the wireless transatlantic call, at that time a very rare option instead of using established contacts via undersea cables.

93. "(Segrave) Builds Car for Beach in Case England Loses; Will Race Motor in Daytona Beach and Boat in Miami in 1929," *The Daytona Beach News-Journal*, February 22, 1928, 1.

94. *Ibid.*

95. "Triplex Driver Scalded by Steam; White Entry Is Still in Running Order Despite Mishap; Stutz and Auburn Car Record; Lockhart Loafs," *The Daytona Beach News-Journal*, February 20, 1928, 1.

96. "White Declares Triplex Speed Was 253 M.P.H.; Is Adding Reverse Gear For A.A.A. Sanction and New Attempt," *The Daytona Beach News-Journal*, February 21, 1928, 1.

97. *Ibid.*

98. "Frank Lockhart Makes Trial Speed of 200.22 Miles an Hour; Adjustments of Carburetors Made—Black Hawk Runs 'Under Wraps' Attaining Only 6,000 Revolutions Per Minute—Hopes to Try for Record Either Tuesday or Wednesday—Wade Morton, Driving Auburn, Shows Best Speed in Stock Car Event," *The Indianapolis News*, February 21, 1928, 21.

99. McDonald and Ball, *Fifty Years with the Speed Kings*, 70.

100. Ellis, "Speed Trials History."

101. *Ibid.*

102. "Lockhart Tells How He Felt As Speedster Dived; A.A.U. [sic] Head Here Blames Attempt to Turn at 225 for Crash," *The Daytona Beach News-Journal*, February 23, 1928, 1.

103. "Lockhart Injured as Racer Hits Sea; Leaves Course While Speeding at Record Clip; Pilot Suffers Lacerations and Shock When Stutz Special Somersaults Going 225 M.P.H.," *The Indianapolis Star*, February 23, 1928, 1.

104. Ellis, "Speed Trials History."

105. "Shaw Drives Into Water in Flames."

106. "Lockhart's Car to be Rebuilt for New Trial; Moskovics Will Apply for New A.A.A. Sanction in Short Time," *The Daytona Beach News-Journal*, February 23, 1928, 1.

107. Campbell, *My Thirty Years of Speed*, 167. Campbell was wrong. On the Blackhawk the reduction ratio from the steering wheel to the steering arm gears was 18.5:1. With that ratio and the 0°6' maximum steering angle the highest hand movement possible at the crown of the steering wheel (diameter 14 inches) was 2.756 inches. Such a position makes an over-correction lock-to-lock by the driver at the steering wheel rather improbable. Furthermore, the maximum value of the steering angle of the front wheels was computed, assuming the adherence coefficient of the sand equalled 5, to avoid the risk of an uncontrolled skid and also to limit the width of the fairings. The February 22 accident was due to the flawed aerodynamics of the vehicle, the instability of which amplified the minimal corrections by the driver causing it to hit a soft sand spot.

108. "Lockhart Tells How He Felt As Speedster Dived; A.A.U. [sic] Head Here Blames Attempt to Turn at 225 for Crash," *The Daytona Beach News-Journal*, February 23, 1928, 1.

109. "Lockhart's Car to Be Rebuilt for New Trial; Moskovics Will Apply for New A.A.A. Sanction in Short Time," *The Daytona Beach News-Journal*, February 23, 1928, 1.

110. Campbell, *My Thirty Years of Speed*, 166.

111. "Car Smashed, Lockhart Talks in Ambulance of Another Trial; Pilot, Braving Fog and Rain to Satisfy Crowd and Officials, Plunged Into Sea at 230 Miles an Hour; Fastest Auto Speed Ever Made—Youth Shocked, Bruised," *The Indianapolis News*, February 23, 1928, 1.

112. "Lockhart's Luck and Pluck; America's Champion Fortunately Only Slightly Hurt After Terrible Experience when Essaying Record in Unsuitable Weather," *The Autocar*, March 2, 1928, 408.

113. John Bentley, *Great American Automobiles: A Dramatic Account of Their Achievements in Competition* (Englewood Cliffs, NJ: Prentice-Hall Inc., 1957), 352.

114. "Shaw Drives Into Water in Flames."

115. "White's Triplex 203.86 M.P.H. in Unofficial Run," *The Daytona Beach News-Journal*, February 24, 1928, 1.

116. "Whippet Driven Afire Into Surf; Race Meet Ends; Indianapolis-Made Machines Speed Over Florida Sands at 106.52463 and 105.54089 M.P.H.; Lockhart Seeks Another Chance," *The Indianapolis Star*, February 24, 1928, 1. The mention of Campbell's exhibition run is confined to a

few lines reporting also that it took place late in the afternoon when the incoming tide had already reached the ocean-side picket line of the course.

117. "Campbell Pays Fine Tribute to Daytona Beach; Dinner for Racing Starts Marks Close of Speed Classic," *The Daytona Beach News-Journal*, February 24, 1928, 1.

118. Campbell, *My Thirty Years of Speed*, 220.

119. Malcolm Campbell returned to Daytona Beach four times to win four more land speed records driving rebuilt Blue Birds, designed and set up by Reid Railton. For the final two record runs (1933 and 1935) the car used the new R-Type Rolls-Royce aero engine, the power output of which reached 2,500 HP, much higher than the 1,450 HP of the latest version of the Napier Lion used in 1931 and 1932. The flying mile records are: February 5, 1931, 245.736 mph; February 24, 1932, 253.968 mph; February 22, 1933, 272.116 mph; and March 7, 1935, 276.816 mph. Disappointed by that last speed when his target had been 300 mph, he blamed the sand as the cause of excessive wheel-spin. He then went to the Bonneville Salt Flats (Utah, USA), where, on September 3, 1935, he reached his target: 301.129 mph, i.e., over five miles a minute. Having achieved his lifelong target and turning 50 years of age, he put an end to his land speed record runs.

120. Villa and Desmond, *Life with the Speed King*, 49.

121. "Campbell Tells Nation How He Broke Record; Broadcast Fame of Beach Sunday from Station WJZ," *The Daytona Beach News-Journal*, February 27, 1928, 1. The broadcast from New York was aired just before the Campbell party boarded the transatlantic liner *Berengaria* bound for Southampton. WJZ radio station was one of the most powerful at the time. The initial 'W' of the name was assigned to the U.S. by a 1927 international agreement to identify all radio stations east of the Mississippi river. The stations west of the river were designated by initial letter 'K.' The WJZ station still exists under a different name.

122. "Captain Campbell is Made Member of Police Force," *The Daytona Beach News-Journal*, February 26, 1928, 1.

Chapter 3

1. "Lockhart Party Leaving Today; Repeats Determination to Return Here," *The Daytona Beach News-Journal*, February 28, 1928, 1.

2. "Campbell Back Again; Famous Record Breaker Interviewed. His Exciting Experiences at Daytona Beach," *The Autocar*, March 16, 1928, 488.

3. *Ibid.*

4. Campbell, *My Thirty Years of Speed*, 232.

5. Richard Hough, *BP Book of the Racing Campbells* (London: Stanley Paul, 1960), 78.

6. "Lockhart, Bandaged, Undaunted, Welcomed Home And Stutz Factory Presents A Medal," *The Indianapolis News*, February 29, 1928, 1.

7. "Lockhart Home After Crash Thinks Stutz Can Hit 240 Clip; Injured Race Driver Feels Sure "Black Hawk" Will Set Speed Mark," *The Indianapolis Times*, February 29, 1928, 1.

8. Jim White, "Some Inside Stuff on High Speed Racing; The Builder of the Triplex Passes a Few Interesting Facts That Were Taught Him by Experience," *Motor Age*, July 5, 1928, 22.

9. "Triplex Awaits Smooth Beach for New Trials; White May Postpone The Race 30 Days If No Change in 2 Weeks," *The Daytona Beach News-Journal*, April 4, 1928, 1.

10. "Triplex Waits Reverse Gear Installation; No Further Word Today from Lockhart and Wilbur Shaw," *The Daytona Beach News-Journal*, April 2, 1928, 1.

11. Major H.O.D. Segrave, "Segrave's Own Story; An Exclusive Description to 'The Autocar' of the Preliminary Trials, the Record Itself, and Impressions," *The Autocar*, April 22, 1927, 679.

12. Segrave, *The Lure of Speed*, 253.

13. Campbell, *My Thirty Years of Speed*, 163.

14. "Capt. Malcolm Campbell on the Future of Speed and Motor Racing," *Motor Sport*, May-June 1928, 267.

15. Campbell, *My Thirty Years of Speed*, 165.

16. "Moskovics Phone Hopeful; Stutz President Says Lockhart Was Not Badly Hurt," *The Indianapolis Star*, February 23, 1928, 10.

17. "Lockhart Will Return Here to Try for Record; Hoosier Driver Tells Radio Audience of His Speed Trial Plans," *The Daytona Beach News-Journal*, March 7, 1928, 1.

18. "Lockhart Wrist Seen Improving; Indiana Doctor Consults Physician Here," *The Daytona Beach News-Journal*, March 11, 1928, 1.

19. Scoops over the air intakes to the carburetors do not show up in any of the many known February photos. A cutaway drawing of the Blackhawk, whose author and date are unspecified, shows ram pipes, topped by a filter, inside the engine bay flush with the body. Ram pipes were a well-known improvement in widespread use on Miller engines. The few photos taken in April show no detail of the intakes. In the best-known one, shot during a photo op on the beach, the intakes are shrouded by a piece of fabric. Some images of the wreck depict one of the intakes with no scoop. We'll never know if they were torn away in the crash. The best guess is that the outer ends of the ram pipes were modified, inside and underneath the body lines.

20. "Sturm Arrives in City Today; Lockhart Will Reach Here Tomorrow," *The Daytona Beach News-Journal*, April 17, 1928, 1.

Chapter 4

1. "Motor Trouble Slows Triplex in Record Try—Keech Makes 155 Miles Per Hour in

Dawn Trial On Beach," *The Daytona Beach News-Journal*, April 12, 1928, 1.

2. "Triplex Trial Called Off for Several Days—Beach Prevents Speed Today Higher Than 117," *The Daytona Beach News-Journal*, April 13, 1928, 1.

3. The 50-cent entry ticket was charged for the Sunday, February 19 runs, as published in *The Daytona Beach News-Journal*. Nothing was published about entry tickets to the dunes for the April runs.

4. "Triplex Goes 204 Miles Hour One Way," *The Daytona Beach News-Journal*, April 20, 1928, 1.

5. The precise indications of speeds and times come from the report by Arthur Means, assistant secretary of the Contest Board and head of the AAA officials in Daytona Beach, addressed to the AAA Contest Board on May 1, 1928: five typed pages dealing with Lockhart's April runs and accident. The report tells that between April 22 and 25 Lockhart did 13 two-way runs covering 117 miles. The final run covered less than four miles. As a comparison, Ray Keech ran 450 miles on the beach in February and April, and Campbell only 36 miles in February.

6. "Lockhart, Shaw, Keech to Make New Try Today—Lockhart Drives 200 m.p.h. on Beach Saturday; Keech 202.07," *The Daytona Beach News-Journal*, April 22, 1928, 1.

7. "Keech Is Holder of New Record for High Speed," *The Daytona Beach News-Journal*, April 23, 1928, 1–2.

8. *Ibid.*

9. Jim White, "Some Inside Stuff in High Speed Racing," *Motor Age*, July 5, 1928, 22.

10. The chronicle doesn't quote any exchange of words between Keech and the AAA officials. The story of Keech's angry words is mentioned by Wilbur Shaw in his autobiography, *Gentlemen Start Your Engines* (see page 82).

11. "Keech Is Holder of New Record for High Speed," *The Daytona Beach News-Journal*, April 23, 1928, 1–2.

12. *Ibid.*

13. The AAA agreed to adopt the AIACR rules on the land speed record after the Great War. The American record-holders prior to 1918 usually listed in the histories of the record were not officially acknowledged by the AIACR: they were U.S. national records only. Keech was therefore the first American driver to hold the official *world* land speed record.

14. "Keech's Auto Record Stirs British Rivals; Campbell and Segrave Plan to Try to Reach 300 Miles Per Hour and Regain Honor," *The New York Times*, April 24, 1928, 28.

15. The tale of the cable sent by Frank Lockhart to his mother is published on page 256 of Griffith Borgeson, *The Golden Age of the American Racing Car* (New York: W.W. Norton & Co., 1966). Borgeson re-launched it in his long essay, "Tragic Superhero of American Racing," in *Road Trips, Head Trips, and Other Car-Crazed Writings*, ed. Jean L. Jennings (New York: Atlantic Motor Press, 1966), 74–85. Due to the credibility of the author the tale has been reprinted many times by other writers.

16. "Overcast Skies Halt Trials on Beach at 3 p.m.; No Agreement to Stop," *The Daytona Beach News-Journal*, April 23, 1928, 1.

17. "The Weather," *The Daytona Beach News-Journal*, April 26, 1928, 4.

18. The name of the lady in the car along with Ella Lockhart is mentioned by Fred Booth in his long story "Golden Age of Racing in Daytona Beach" published in 1953 by Florida dailies.

19. "Nation Hears Story of Crash on A.P. Wires—Second Accident at High Speed Recounted by Correspondent," *The Daytona Beach News-Journal*, April 25, 1928, 1. As a sort of excuse for not having dispatched a reporter to the beach who would have witnessed the accident, the daily published a long foreword to the AP dispatch. The foreword was bylined "Ed.," i.e., the editorial staff: "Hardly had Frank Lockhart's inert body being [sic] thrown to the sand that Associated Press operators throughout the breadth of the United States started ticking the message to their newspapers, and extra editions appeared on the streets of the major cities. T. H. Gill, the special Associated Press correspondent detailed to the racing event wrote a running story which is appearing as follows on the front pages of the leading newspapers of the country today." To tell the truth, like in *The Indianapolis News* (see note 18), the story was published elsewhere in a more complete version, as was customary in a running story. The whole background shows how news had a very quick and widespread circulation even decades before the web, Wi-Fi, and real-time instruments that are always connected. Period dailies, then the more powerful medium (the radio was still in its pioneer years of broadcasting), had flexible and always at-ready editorial staff. The production process enabled extra editions around the clock.

20. "Stutz Car Turns Over at 200 Miles an Hour—Widow Sees Fatal Trial; Lockhart Speeds to Death on Florida Sands," *The Indianapolis News*, April 25, 1928, 1. The long article tells that the car hit a spot of soft sand (false) and that the beach was in worse condition than the previous week (almost correct).

21. "Lockhart Hurtles to Death Speeding 200 Miles an Hour; Auto Racer Is Killed Trying to Set a New Record at Daytona Beach—Machine Leaps 1,000 Feet—Goes Into Air as It Hits Ridge in Sand, Then Bounces, Throwing Driver Out—Disaster Is Laid to Tires—Car Grazes Group in Plunge, Injuring Photographer—Mrs. Lockhart Sees Husband Crash," *The New York Times*, April 29, 1928, 1. The very long and detailed headline contains the whole news. Note the difference from *The Indianapolis News* (see note 18) when mentioning "Mrs. Lockhart" instead of "Widow."

22. "Bad Tire Cause, Says Cupernall," *The Daytona Beach News-Journal*, April 25, 1928, 3.
23. *Ibid.*
24. Griffith Borgeson, *The Golden Age of the American Racing Car* (New York: W.W. Norton & Co., 1966), 258. See also Gordon Eliot White, *The Marvelous Mechanical Designs of Harry A. Miller* (Hudson, WI: Iconografix, 2004), 75.
25. A summary of the S.A.E. report was mailed to the author by Jim Weisel, John's son, thanks to Tom Kinney, in 2003.
26. The film clip can be seen on many websites.
27. "301.129 mph. Sir Malcolm Campbell's Own Story," *The Motor*, October 29, 1935, 637. The article continues in the November 5, 1935 issue on page 684. It is a detailed description, bylined by Campbell himself, of the September 3, 1935, new record on the Bonneville Salt Flats. Campbell re-caps the former records on the sands of Daytona Beach. He criticizes the difficulties encountered on the beach and the problems he had to solve. Campbell appears to be rather harsh about a site whose organizers had invited, hosted, and financed him five times (in 1928, 1931, 1932, 1933, and 1935). Daytona Beach was a site he had openly praised and until 1935 was the only suitable and known one in the entire world, as proved by the failure of his 1929 expedition to Verneuk Pan, South Africa.
28. "Features of Lockhart's Car to Seek World's Speed Record," *The Indianapolis News*, February 18, 1928, 15.
29. The Firestone Tire & Rubber Company: report by Mr C. D. Smith, Development Department in Akron, Ohio, to Mr E. Waldo Stein c/o Firestone, 500 N. Capitol Ave., Indianapolis, dated January 23, 1928 re: "Lockhart Straight-Away Car."
30. Firestone supplied tires to Jim White's Triplex record car. Period news made no mention of any tire change between the many trial runs and the ones for the record on April 22. The Triplex ran on the beach for 450 miles, mileage never equalled by any other record challenger.
31. Griffith Borgeson is the best-known writer among them. See page 254 of his book *The Golden Age of the American Racing Car* (New York: W.W. Norton & Co., 1966).
32. Sarah Morgan-Wu and James O'Keefe, *Frank Lockhart: American Speed King* (Boston: Racemaker Press, 2012).
33. Many U.S. and British monthlies usually had the cover date of the next month following the on-sale date: it means the end of validity of the issue. They are sometimes on sale during the first days of the month before the cover date. It is possible that the ad page by Dickinson was finalized and forwarded to the magazine before April 25.
34. Arthur Means report (see note 5).
35. "Moskovics, Meyers Term Lockhart Motor Genius," *The Indianapolis News*, April 25, 1928, 3.
36. "British Grieve for Racer; Campbell and Segrave Pay Tributes to Lockhart as a Man," *New York Times*, April 26, 1928, 28.
37. Arthur Means report (see note 5).
38. Among the books on the land speed record, the following ones could be mentioned, with no intention of compiling a classification:
- Cyril Posthumus and David Tremayne, *Land Speed Record: A Complete History of the Record-Breaking Cars from 39.24 to 600+ m.p.h.* (London: Osprey Publishing Limited, 1985), 251.
- William Huon, *Records de vitesse auto: Un siècle de défis* (Boulogne-Billancourt: E.T.A.I., 2006), 68.

39. "Was Sacrificed to Auto World," *The Daytona Beach News-Journal*, April 25, 1928, 1.
40. "Ray Keech Sad Over Accident," *The Daytona Beach News-Journal*, April 25, 1928, 1.
41. "Campbell Greatly Grieved by News of Racer's Death," *The Daytona Beach News-Journal*, April 26, 1928, 1. "Campbell Grieved at News," *The Indianapolis News*, April 25, 1928, 3.
42. *Ibid.*
43. *The Daytona Beach News-Journal*, April 26, 1928. Another statement by Henry Segrave is reported by David McDonald on page 71 of his book *Fifty Years with the Speed Kings*. According to McDonald, Segrave said, "You can take it from me. Lockhart will either exceed 200 mph or be dead within a fortnight."
44. "British Grieve for Racer; Campbell and Segrave Pay Tributes to Lockhart as a Man," *The New York Times*, April 28, 1928, 18.
45. "Another Hero Has Gone West—Says Automobile Official," *The Daytona Beach News-Journal*, April 25, 1928, 3. Wilbur Shaw's words are in the article with the emotional headline reporting the sympathy message by Odis Porter, head of the AAA officials in Daytona Beach, on behalf of the Association.
46. "Souders Lauds Dead Rival—1927 Speedway Winner Terms Lockhart 'Greatest Driver,'" *The Indianapolis News*, April 25, 1928, 3.
47. "Lockhart Burial at Los Angeles—Body of Speed Pilot, Killed in Florida Smashup, Lies in State," *The Indianapolis Star*, April 26, 1928, 7.
48. "Public Mourning Period Declared for Lockhart," *The Daytona Beach News-Journal*, April 25, 1928, 1. The uppercase words are in the original.

Chapter 5

1. "Daytona Beach Mourns Death of Speed Ace; Lockhart's Mother Begged Him to Stop Trying for Records," *The Daytona Beach News-Journal*, April 26, 1928, 3.
2. Harry Arminius Miller (Menomine, Wisconsin, December 8, 1875–Detroit, May 3, 1943) was a master at designing racing cars, the example that inspired many protagonists of the development of the automobile, including Ettore

Bugatti. At the end of the year 1922 Miller started the design of the new two-litre (122-cubic-inch) in-line eight engine. He began using a supercharger in 1924 and further improved it in 1929, notwithstanding the fact that he was one of the leading experts and among the top manufacturers of carburetors. The use of the centrifugal supercharger and leaded fuel pushed the output of the Type-122 engine to 236 HP @ 5,800 rpm: proof of the quality of design and the advantages of a flexible and robust engine. The same basic design concepts and overall dimensions were later used in the 91 car/engine: it soon became the winning proposition on U.S. tracks and supplied some key components in the Blackhawk's 16-cylinder engine. He continued along a constant line of innovation and painstaking quality during the whole span of the thirties, yet without reaching the performances and results of the previous decade. In the early World War II years he designed engines for tanks and aeroplanes. Harry Miller's temperament was well known as egocentric and quite difficult to cope with. Like Enzo Ferrari some decades later, he had the untarnished credo that his racing cars were the embodiment of absolute perfection: any change on them was considered sacrilege.

3. "Mother Pleaded," *The Daytona Beach News-Journal*, May 15, 1928, 1.

4. Griffith Borgeson, *The Golden Age of the American Racing Car* (New York: W.W. Norton & Co., 1966), 256.

5. John G. Printz, "Frank S. Lockhart. Boy Wonder of the American Speedways," Programme for the inaugural Michigan 500, Michigan International Speedway, Brooklyn, Michigan, July 19, 1981, 54. Thanks to Tom Kinney, Indianapolis.

6. Tom Tucker and Jim Tiller, *Daytona: The Quest for Speed* (Daytona Beach: *The Daytona Beach News-Journal*, 1994), 13. It seems quite unbelievable that such fake news could have been written by a Daytona Beach journalist, who was for many years the sports editor of the local daily, and by a photographer of the same daily. The book focuses on the history of races on the Trioval, NASCAR first, and shows a portfolio of the most spectacular images of the races. Obviously, the authors did not check the 1928 facts in the period issues of their paper.

7. "Flower Heaped Body of Frank Lockhart Is Borne Northward," *The Daytona Beach News-Journal*, April 28, 1928, 1–2.

8. *Ibid.*

9. "Mother Delays Racer's Rites; Lockhart Funeral Postponed Until Tuesday by Relatives," *The Indianapolis Star*, April 29, 1928, 8.

10. "Lockhart Rites Held in North; Editor Asked to Represent City at Funeral," *The Daytona Beach News-Journal*, May 1, 1928, 1.

11. "Racing Capital Pays Tribute to Frank Lockhart; Sturm and Keech May Try for Record Here in Fall," *The Daytona Beach News-Journal*, May 2, 1928, 1–2.

12. *Ibid.*

13. "Lockhart's Car May Be Rebuilt; Wrecked Stutz Being Returned to Factory—Keech Promises to Pilot It," *The Indianapolis Star*, May 1, 1928, 13.

14. "Ray Keech Expected to Drive in 500-Mile Speedway Race," *The Indianapolis Star*, May 4, 1928, 13.

15. "Flower Heaped Body of Frank Lockhart Is Borne Northward," *The Daytona Beach News-Journal*, April 28, 1928, 2.

16. Data and facts related to Frank Lockhart's estate have been published in Sarah Morgan-Wu and James O'Keefe, *Frank Lockhart: American Speed King* (Boston: Racemaker Press, 2012), 21.

17. *Ibid.*, 22.

18. "Sturm Denies Story Lockhart Died Penniless; Manager Pays Tribute to Friends and Wife of Speed Driver," *The Daytona Beach News-Journal*, May 15, 1928, 1.

19. William Sturm's story carried the headline "Little Boy Trying to Get Along. Lockhart's Own View of Self" and was published in *The Indianapolis News* on April 26, 1928, on page 19. It was reprinted with the headline "Sturm Found Lockhart A Boy, Intense, Fearless" on the front page of *The Daytona Beach News-Journal* on April 27, 1928.

20. Grids and results of the Indianapolis 500-Mile Races have been published in Rick Popely and L. Spencer Riggs, *Indianapolis 500 Chronicle* (Lincolnwood, IL: Publications International Ltd., 1998).

21. It took 50 years for a car to exceed Mach 1: Thrust SSC, an all-British vehicle, designed and built by a team headed by Richard Noble, powered by two Rolls-Royce Spey jet engines, reached 763.035 mph (Mach 1.02) on October 15, 1997, at Black Rock Desert, USA, driven by Andy Green. The thrust of the two jets with afterburners was said to be 100,000 HP. Weight was reported as being 14,000 pounds.

22. The Bonneville Salt Flats, Utah, are named after a French explorer, Benjamin Louis Eulalie Bonneville (1796–1878), who saw them in 1833 when mapping the wild west of North America. In 1904 the transcontinental railway line crossed them by way of the so-called Lucin Cutoff, built by the Southern Pacific Company, making the site easier to reach and initiating the construction of the village of Wendover. The first unofficial record car was taken on the salt in the summer of 1914 by Teddy Tezlaff, driving a Blitzen Benz at the unlikely speed of 141.73 mph over the flying mile. The next record car on the salt was a special Pierce Arrow, prepared and driven by Ab Jenkins, a prominent resident of Salt Lake City, Utah's capital, in 1932: he established the 24-hour record, covering 2,710 miles, not officially recognized by the AAA and AIACR. After that run he promoted the 10- by 15-mile site to the British record seekers Campbell and Cobb. Eyston followed soon after and, from September 1935 until the 1990s,

the Salt Flats were the site of choice for any land speed record attempt.

23. The proposal of negative lift "wings" found practical use on the Opel Rak-2 experimental rocket car, designed and constructed by Fritz von Opel (who was also the driver), Friedrich Wilhelm Sanders and Max Valier in 1928, and on Porsche's Mercedes T-80 record car in 1939.

24. A fatal accident occurred to the Triplex on a record run on the Daytona Beach sands on March 13, 1929, killing the rather inexperienced driver Lee Bible and a cameraman on the scene, Charles Traub. The car was a total wreck. Sir Henry Segrave was killed on his boat while chasing the water speed record on June 13, 1930, at Lake Windermere, England.

25. "The Next Great Record; 203.79 m.p.h. in 1927, 206.95 m.p.h. in 1928; ? m.p.h in 1929," *The Autocar*, April 20, 1928, 798.

Chapter 6

1. Henry O'Neal de Hane Segrave (Baltimore, Maryland September 22, 1896–Lake Windermere, UK June 13, 1930), born into a wealthy family and educated at Eton, joined the Royal Flying Corps as a pilot in the Great War. Discharged with the rank of major, he started car racing in Brooklands in 1920. He soon climbed to the top in the STD (Sunbeam-Talbot-Darracq) racing team to be the surprise winner of the 1923 Grand Prix de l'ACF in Tours, France—the first ever grand prix won by a British driver on a British car. He won the 1924 Spanish Grand Prix in Lasarte and then focused on the land speed record. His name appears three times in the list: the first record was achieved on March 16, 1926 on the Southport (UK) sands driving a Sunbeam at 152.336 mph. The second one was on March 29, 1927 in Daytona Beach, 203.792 mph, first time over 200 mph. Rated as the chief adversary of Malcolm Campbell (whom he surpassed in driving skill), he left the chase of the land speed record in 1929, after raising the limit to 231.362 mph in Daytona Beach driving the Golden Arrow. He received the knighthood in 1929 and switched to the water speed record, which he won twice: September 1929 in Venice (Italy) at 93.52 mph (unofficial single-engine boat record) and June 13, 1930 at 98.76 mph at the helm of the single-step hydroplane Miss England II on Lake Windermere (official world water speed record). Alas, the last one was clinched on the day of his death.

2. Press kit by Daytona Beach organizers.

3. John Samuel Irving (Manchester March 29, 1880–Acocks Green, Birmingham March 28, 1953) joined Daimler Co. in 1903 following a technical apprenticeship. In 1910 he moved to the Balloon Factory, later renamed the Royal Aircraft Establishment in Farnborough, where he focused on the development of airships and aero engines. In the Great War he joined the Royal Flying Corps, reaching the rank of captain, which he continued to use as was customary in the UK then. After the war he joined Sunbeam, where he was closely connected with the design and preparation of the racing cars and was responsible for the tuning of the V12 4-litre car driven by Henry Segrave to a new world land speed record over the flying kilometer: 152.336 mph at Southport, UK on March 16, 1926. Together with Louis Coatalen, chief designer at Sunbeam, he worked on the Sunbeam 1000 HP record car, the first land vehicle to travel faster than 200 mph, at Daytona Beach on March 29, 1927. He left Sunbeam in 1928 when he was appointed chief engineer at Humphrey Sandberg, an automobile components company, manufacturer of free-wheel devices and gearboxes. The company granted him permission to work on the Golden Arrow, whose design he completed in a couple of months, aided by eight draughtsmen. Following a short spell at Hillman-Humber, where he was part of the design team for the new Minx saloon car, he joined Bendix in 1931. Appointed a member of The Institution of Automobile Engineers, he served as president in 1936–1937. These biographical notes are based on an interview published in *Motor Sport* (May 1929, page 33) and on the Wikipedia page.

4. "Bravo, Segrave!" *The Autocar*, March 15, 1929, 531. The article reports the names of the six mechanics: Baguley, Calvert, Irvin, Lavender, Peach, and David McDonald (a.k.a. Dunlop Mac).

5. "The Irving Napier Special Leaves for America," *The Motor*, January 29, 1929, 122. The list of companies providing components and accessories for the Golden Arrow is quite long: they are about the same as those enlisted by Malcolm Campbell for his 1928 Blue Bird. The basic concept when designing the Golden Arrow, a.k.a. Irving Napier Special, was that everything should be British-made. The body was shaped by Thrupp and Maberly, the frame rails came from John Thompson Motor Pressings, the front and rear axles from Vickers, and the whole assembly was completed at the Robin Hood Engineering Works. The main sponsors, i.e., the men providing funds without either labor or components, were mentioned as Mr. Henry S. Horne, Mr. Oliver Piper, and Sir Charles Wakefield, who also provided the lubricants free of charge. The cost of the car from early drawing to completion was reported by J.S. Irving (see note 7) as amounting to £10,059 15s 4d, and the estimated value of parts supplied free of charge—including three (only three!) sets of Dunlop wheels and tires—was reported to be £1,500. Packing, transport, and expenses in Daytona Beach were mentioned in the range of £2,000. We don't know the amount of money received from the organizers. In the year 1929 the exchange rate between the British Pound Sterling and the U.S. Dollar was £1 = $4.87. The total cost of the Golden Arrow in 1929 dollars roughly equalled $66,037, close to the unofficial, yet widely communicated, cost of the 1928 Lockhart Stutz Blackhawk Special.

6. "The Irving Napier Special Leaves for America," *The Motor*, January 29, 1929, 122.

7. J.S. Irving, "The Golden Arrow and the World's Speed Record" (speech, London, March 7, 1930), *The Institution of Automobile Engineers Proceedings Vol. XXIV, 1929–1930*.

8. *Ibid.*

9. "Celebrating British Success," *The Motor*, April 30, 1929, 605.

10. William F. Sturm, "Speed," *The Saturday Evening Post*, August 16, 1930, 23. Sturm was appointed by Segrave as his manager while in Daytona Beach in 1929. The appointment was confirmed in 1930 for the fateful boat record run on June 13 at Lake Windermere, UK.

11. The attendance figure was widely reported as proof of the positive answer of the crowd to the organizers' invitation to the White Triplex to stage the America versus Britain battle of the previous year once more. In 1929 Jim White's Triplex was the record holder and the defender in the Speed Trials in Daytona Beach. The car had been checked and overhauled during the months since April 1928, and a reverse motion mechanism was fitted according to the AAA and AIACR rules. The car was a sturdy one, having covered 450 miles on the beach in 1928, and was still undamaged to run again. The 1929 Triplex driver was a newcomer, Lee Bible, a mechanic from Tennessee with a minor career as a racing driver on local dirt tracks and sound experience of car manufacturing and repairing. He was not licensed by the AAA and had to pass a sort of rookie test on the beach to show officials that he could manage Jim White's beast. No other driver was available: Ray Keech refused to sit in that hot seat again; Harry Hartz and other top league drivers contacted by Jim White followed Keech's advice and declined the offer. Lee Bible and the Triplex were ready to go for the record runs on March 13, 1929, two days after Segrave's new record had been set. The beach was in perfect condition and the wind was quite light. Following the usual and necessary runs to warm up the engines, he started northbound to attack the record. The Triplex entered the mile "thundering and vibrating from the tip of its chisel nose to its blunt stern" (words by Paul Ellis in his long story: "Speed Trials History Goes Back 28 Years," published in *The Daytona Beach News-Journal* on February 5, 1931 and reprinted on February 14, 1932.) Just short of the exit from the measured mile, witnesses noticed exhaust smoke shooting out of an engine in single puffs, maybe either a sign of bad ignition (it happened many times in 1928) or the sticking of a piston in one of the 11-year-old quite worn-out engines. By the end of the mile, the car swerved suddenly, out of control, towards the soft sand of the dunes, somersaulting and killing the photographer Charles Traub and the driver. The car was intrinsically unstable due to the center of gravity close to the rear end and the erratic center of pressure somewhere in the front where the chisel nose offered some lateral surface to the side wind. The cause of the skid was never fully explained: seized piston or sudden lack of pressure on the throttle, maybe caused by an unexpected jump on a ridge that made Bible's right foot involuntarily slide off the pedal? A too-fast throttle release when the engine is running at full power is a sure way to induce a massive skid that for Lee Bible and the Triplex ended in the fatal outcome. Jim White, by a strange decision of fate, was not on the beach on the fateful day that saw the final end of his record attempts. The car was a total wreck: nothing of it survived apart from the cap of one of the magnetos seen by the author some 30 years ago in Daytona Beach.

12. Sturm, "Speed."

13. "Celebrating British Success," *The Motor*, April 30, 1929, 605.

14. Cyril Posthumus, *Sir Henry Segrave* (London: B.T. Batsford Ltd., 1961), 180.

15. "The Prince and Major Segrave," *The Motor*, April 23, 1929, 554.

16. "Celebrating British Success," *The Motor*, April 30, 1929, 605.

17. Organizers' press kit dated Daytona Beach, February 10, 1930.

18. "The Next Great Record, 203.79 m.p.h. in 1927. 206.95 m.p.h. in 1928. ? m.p.h. in 1929," *The Autocar*, April 20, 1929, 798. The headline and the text ignored the Keech/Triplex record.

19. Norman Leslie "Wizard" Smith (Enfield-Richmond, Sydney, New South Wales, Australia, July 13, 1890–Kogarah, Sydney, October 1, 1958) was the youngest in a family of nine children. His parents were farmers. After the Great War he joined as a salesman Dalgety & Co., agents for the Hudson and Essex marques in Sydney and drove their cars on many transcontinental raids, on local tracks, and in hill-climbs. Further to his maiden win in a hill-climb at the State National Park in 1919, he won so many races that he became known as "Wizard." He established new records across the continent and, in 1926, asked Donald Harkness to design and a build a record car, the "Anzac" (the name of the Australia & New Zealand Army Corps in the Great War), using a Rolls-Royce engine on a Cadillac frame. In January 1930 he set a new Australasian 10-mile record of 148 mph on the Ninety Mile Beach (Oneroha-a-Toe in the Maori language) on the north tip of New Zealand's north island. The record was not acknowledged because the timing system was rated inadequate by the AIACR. In the meantime, he became motoring editor of the *Sunday Times* newspaper group in Sydney. He was refused the right to use the name "Anzac" any longer so he had to christen his next record car with the name of his main sponsor: Fred H. Stewart, a businessman. The goal for the new car was more ambitious than that for the Anzac: the mile record, then held by Henry Segrave. At the same time, rumors about the car being a probable contender in the Speed Trials reached Daytona

Beach. The car, again designed by Donald Harkness, used the supercharged Napier Lion VIID broad-arrow engine and had the same general lines of the Golden Arrow. The side surface radiators of the latter were discarded in favor of ice tanks and radiating surfaces on the front wheel fairings, which proved to be ineffective and forced the addition of an enormous, ugly, and heavy radiator at the front, destroying the aerodynamic finesse of the whole car. He went to Ninety Mile Beach in January 1932 and on the 26th, on a wet and bumpy surface, he set the official world record of 164.084 mph over 10 miles. He was then forced to call a halt due to the very poor condition of the beach, a decision that raised a lot of adverse publicity: he was called "Windy" instead of "Wizard." His mile record challenge failed once and for all on May 1, 1932, when, on the approach to the mile, the engine misfired and cut off due to a fire caused by the magnetos which, flooded with water, burnt wires and rubber hoses. He was able to jump out of the burning car and called it a day both for the car and for himself. Subject to harsh criticism and with the burden of very low standing with the public, he retired to Sydney. In 1938 he joined the Sydney motor dealers Stack & Co., where he stayed until his retirement in 1957. A biography of Norman Smith can be read in Steve Simpson, *The Real Story of Wizard Smith* (Sydney: Murray Book Distributors Pty Ltd., 1977).

20. "1928 Champion Plans Machine to Beat Arrow; He Will Eliminate Windscreen and Steer with Periscope," *The Daytona Beach News-Journal*, June 2, 1929.

21. Kaye Ernest Donsky, better known as Kaye Don (Dublin, Ireland April 10, 1891–Chobham, Surrey, UK August 29, 1981), started racing on motorcycles in his native country in the 1910s. He serviced in the Royal Flying Corps during the Great War and reached the rank of captain before his discharge, a rank that, strangely enough, was never used before his name (unlike Henry Segrave, J. S. Irving, and Malcolm Campbell). After the war he switched to cars, spending most of his career at Brooklands: his first race there was recorded by William Boddy on October 13, 1921 in a 1.4-litre AC, later driven to a new Light Car Class record for Brooklands over 100 kilometers at 94 mph. It was just the beginning of a long list of track and distance records Driving one of his three V12 former Grand Prix Sunbeams, named "Cub," "Tiger," and "Tigress," he held the Outer Circuit record on three occasions: 131.76 mph on September 22, 1928; 134.26 mph on August 5, 1929; and 137.58 mph on June 9, 1930. On the Brooklands track he also set an impressive series of Class distance records up to 200 miles. He never ventured to the Continent to widen his racing résumé and was selected as driver of the Sunbeam Silver Bullet land speed record car in 1930. He later took up motorboat racing, taking the helm of the fateful *Miss England II* in which Sir Henry Segrave was killed on Lake Windermere on June 13, 1930. He managed to steer the boat to a new water speed record of 110.22 mph. At the helm of the new, revised single-step hydroplane *Miss England III* he bettered the performance to 119.81 mph on July 18, 1932, at Loch Lomond, Scotland. In May 1934 he was involved in an accident on the public roads of the Isle of Man during testing of an MG Magnette, which caused the death of his riding mechanic. He was found guilty of manslaughter by the local court and sentenced to four months in prison, where he was sent in September 1934 amidst strong protests from his fellow racing drivers. He then gave up racing and in the 1940s established and developed the Ambassador Motorcycle company, where he stayed until his retirement in 1962. The Brooklands career of Kaye Don can be found in William "Bill" Boddy, *The History of Brooklands Motor Course 1906–1940* (London: Greenville Publishing Company Ltd., 1979).

22. Louis Coatalen (Concarneau, France, September 11, 1879–Paris, May 23, 1962) was already semi-retired when he designed the Silver Bullet. He was living on the sunny Italian island of Capri, strongly reducing his presence at the British and French factories of the company he had joined as technical director in 1914 to a bare minimum.

23. "Don May Stay Around as Long as He Wishes; British Driver Has Hard Luck with Daytona Beach Race Attempt," *The Daytona Beach News-Journal*, April 5, 1930, 1.

24. "Engine, Beach, Water, and Delay Prevent Record," *The Daytona Beach News-Journal*, April 10, 1930, 1.

25. Paul Ellis, "Racer Cancels Run Today. Says Beach Won't Do; Evades Question About Prospects; Decision Expected Soon. Has Cabin Booked," *The Daytona Beach News-Journal*, April 11, 1930, 1.

26. "Don, Sailing, Says He'll Be Back Next Year; Blames Beach Conditions for Failure This Year—25 Rainy Days," *The Daytona Beach News-Journal*, April 16, 1930, 1.

27. "Mr Kaye Don's New Plans; May Go to S. Africa for Speed Attempt," *The Daily Mail*, May 3, 1930.

28. "301.129 M.P.H. Sir Malcolm Campbell's Own Story," *The Motor*, October 29, 1935, 637. The long article, even though written later than the events to be dealt with in these pages, recaps the rationale of choosing the Bonneville Salt Flats, leaving behind the sands of Daytona Beach as the site for record attempts.

29. "Race Cost Less Than $4,000; Balance of Allowance Goes to Campbell," *The Daytona Beach News-Journal*, February 6, 1931, 1. No mention of the sums received in Daytona Beach has ever been reported in Campbell's autobiography or in articles about Campbell by the British media.

30. Reid Anthony Railton (Chorley, Cheshire, UK, June 24, 1885–Berkeley, California, September 1, 1977). On completion of his university studies in engineering he joined Leyland Motors in

1917, working under Parry Thomas. He left the company to establish the Arab Motor Company in 1922, aiming to produce high-performance sports cars in Letchworth Garden City, north of London. The venture lasted until 1927, when he joined Thomson & Taylor in Brooklands as chief engineer, adding daily contact with the racing and record-seeking community to his already well-proven capabilities in car design. In 1933 he started his long relationship with John Cobb, designing and developing two superlative record cars for him: the 1933 long-distance Napier Railton and the 1937–1947 land speed record vehicle Railton Mobil, whose performance in 1947 remained unbeaten until 1965. In the meantime (1933–1937) he was heavily involved in the design and manufacturing of the ERA voiturettes and profoundly modified and designed the three final models of Malcom Campbell's Blue Birds, driven to the mile record from 1931 to 1935. He was also involved in the road-going sports cars of Invicta and Hudson. In 1934 the first of the sports tourers carrying his own name appeared on the market. By 1947, when his company was legally liquidated, 1,492 had been manufactured. In 1939 he left England for California to join Hall-Scott Motor Co. He kept his links with John Cobb and was the designer of the fateful "Crusader" jet boat in which the British record-seeker met his death on Loch Ness on September 29, 1952, aged 52. He continued with consultancies in the automotive industry, including Hudson in the U.S., until his death at home. His final words provided an understated recap of his exceptional life: "I didn't make much money at my peculiar jobs, but I had a good deal of fun." The most complete, best researched, and detailed biography of Reid Railton can be found in Karl Ludvigsen, *Reid Railton: Man of Speed* (Sherborne, UK: Evro Publishing, 2018): two hardbound tomes of 848 pages in total, in a slipcase.

31. Betty Carstairs's contribution is mentioned by Leo Villa on page 91 of his book *Life with the Speed King* (see note 41). Betty Carstairs (1900–1993) was described by Malcolm Campbell as "the best sportsman I know." Openly lesbian, she lived an eccentric life focussing on motorboat racing, a costly endeavor she could afford, having inherited a fortune from her American mother and grandmother, made from Standard Oil. She was a regular presence at Brooklands, always wearing a black beret. She not only contributed to the 1931 Blue Bird but also presented John Cobb with the two engines from her Estelle V boat, to use on his 1937–1947 record car, designed by Reid Railton.

32. "Fund reaches $1,604," *The Daytona Beach News-Journal*, January 27, 1932. Another side text in the main story tells about the promotion launched by the organizers: road posters to be erected on the city limits, special advertising at the Volusia County Fair and the South Florida Fair in Tampa, ads in the Florida and Washington newspapers, radio spots aired by local stations, leaflets to be given out in the county: a good example of pioneering total communications.

33. "Speed Regatta Promise for 1932 Trials; Prospects of Three British Supercars and One American," *The Daytona Beach News-Journal*, February 15, 1931, 1. Note the presence of the term "supercar"—maybe a first.

34. Campbell, *My Thirty Years of Speed*, 226.

35. "Sturm Will Decide Speed Trial Program Next Week; Manager of Last Year's Record Runs Visits New York Before Coming South for Conference," *The Daytona Beach News-Journal*, January 8, 1932. One can observe here the power acquired by William Sturm, who, as manager of Malcolm Campbell, the only record-seeker expected to be in Daytona Beach, could command the date and program of the event.

36. It was a sort of unwritten agreement among land speed record-seekers to go faster than the existing limit by only a small margin. That was to ensure the option to defend the title (and the related money awarded by Sir Charles Wakefield) should another contender beat the newly established record. The issue didn't surface in the years when Malcolm Campbell was the sole contender. The situation re-presented itself in the 1960s when the battle between the two leading American tire manufacturers, Firestone and Goodyear, sponsoring the main rivals Craig Breedlove and Art Arfons, pushed the records to over 600 mph. Yet by that time the Wakefield Trophy and the money awarded by Sir Wakefield were history.

37. "267 M.P.H. Campbell's Own Story: Record Breaking Dash at Daytona; Sir Malcolm Talks by Atlantic Phone to the 'Herald,'" *Daily Herald*, February 25, 1932. Other headlines on the page: "Rush by Crowd of 10,000. Daytona Fetes the Man Who Saved the Town"; "I Am Going a Lot Faster."

38. "Armstrong Invites Wizard and Strapp," *The Daytona Beach News-Journal*, January 26, 1933. Norman Smith, the Aussie driver, was referred to only by his nickname. The Frenchman's name was misspelt.

39. André Stapp and his funny-looking vehicle have the distinction of finding a place in the history of the Land Speed Record despite the fact that information about them is scant: a few photographs taken on the roads outside Paris and a smidgen of news about the demise of the car, burnt on a run on the beach at La Baule in Brittany, France, on June 26, 1932. Nothing is known about Stapp's engineering background or automotive skills. The photos show a huge, 33-foot vehicle shaped like a cylinder over a box, fitted with truck-sized wheels. Being driven on public roads, it had a spare wheel perched on the left-hand side and French license plate: 8104-RF 3. The driver looks ahead, standing in a hole in the middle of the left-hand side. A similar porthole is said to be on the right-hand side for the riding mechanic. (There are no known photos of the right-hand side). The cylindrical body has a rounded front and a cone-shaped tail with 18 holes, maybe for

the exhaust from the engines, claimed to be two (some sources say three) 800 HP radial Bristol Jupiter aero engines converted to "turbines," whatever that meant. Behind the cone a fabric-covered stabilizer tailfin looks like a makeshift trick to further improve the imposing image of the vehicle. Total weight was said to be 5,000 pounds. An additional engine was said to be in the car, which was built on a Voisin saloon frame. This engine was probably the only one able to move the vehicle when it was shown at La Baule, where it caught fire and forced Stapp and the mechanic to jump out. The former suffered bruises and a broken kneecap. The car was destroyed, and Stapp claimed that he would build a second model to go to Daytona Beach to increase the mile record to 375 mph, the self-proclaimed target speed of the vehicle.

40. Harry Arminius Miller was the designer providing credibility to the project of a monster car, longer than 34 feet, powered by a purpose-built broad arrow W24 engine claiming to deliver 2,400 HP, with semi-enclosed wheels, an aircraft-type closed canopy, dry weight of over 4,000 pounds and integral traction. Money to build it never materialized, and after a few months Miller was declared bankrupt. Barney Oldfield (1878–1946) was one of the greatest pioneer drivers of early American races in the first decades of the twentieth century. Exuberant and rebellious, he was nevertheless a media star even after retiring from racing.

41. Campbell, *My Thirty Years of Speed*, 242.

42. Campbell, *My Thirty Years of Speed*, 266.

43. The same problem hampered Frank Lockhart on the beach car in 1928. He fixed it by modifying the air intakes, whilst the British team was unable to find the solution in Florida.

44. Sir Malcolm Campbell, "301.129 M.P.H.—Sir Malcolm Campbell's Own Story; Behind the Scenes at Utah—The Full Facts of 'Blue Bird' Historic World Record Revealed for the First Time. Trials and Difficulties Which Led to the Final Triumph," *The Motor*, October 29, 1935, 637.

45. Villa and Desmond, *Life with the Speed King*, 109.

46. Sir Malcolm Campbell, "301.129 M.P.H.—Sir Malcolm Campbell's Own Story; The Record Achieved—The Sensations at Five Miles a Minute—Moments When the Driver Was Gassed by Fumes—Behind the Scenes at Utah," *The Motor*, November 5, 1935, 684.

Appendix 1

1. *The Sunday News-Journal* (Sunday edition of *The Daytona Beach News-Journal*), March 20, 1932.

2. The frame of the 1927 Blue Bird was built by Vickers in 1926, and the car was completed at the Robin Hood Engineering Works at Kingston Vale, London. The engine was a Napier Lion Series VIIA.

3. "Campbell's Forthcoming Record Attempt; 'Blue Bird' on the Way to Participate in Thrilling Speed Contest," *The Motor*, February 7, 1928, 7.

4. "Capt. Malcolm Campbell on the Future of Speed and Motor Racing," *Motor Sport*, May-June 1928, 267.

5. "Malcolm Campbell on the Surprises of Speed; What 200 m.p.h. Really Means—Two Rounds of a Fight with "Blue Bird," *The Motor*, May 15, 1928, 688.

6. "Capt. Malcolm Campbell on the Future of Speed and Motor Racing," *Motor Sport*, May–June 1928, 267.

7. "Malcolm Campbell on the Surprises of Speed"

8. Reid Railton, "'Blue Bird,' 1930–1933," *Proceedings of the Institution of Automobile Engineers* 28, no. 1 (1933): 102–146. The words by Capt. Irving he is referring to were published in the same proceedings: John Samuel Irving, "The Golden Arrow and the World's Speed Record," *Proceedings of the Institution of Automobile Engineers* 24, no. 2 (1930): 684–734.

9. *Ibid.*

10. "Campbell Back Again," *The Autocar*, March 16, 1928, 489. The story is a good recap of the record's highlights.

11. Jim White, "Some Inside Stuff on High Speed Racing; The Builder of the Triplex Passes a Few Interesting Facts That Were Taught Him by Experience," *Motor Age*, July 5, 1928, 22.

12. John Samuel Irving, "The Golden Arrow and the World's Speed Record," *Proceedings of the Institution of Automobile Engineers* 24, no. 2 (1930): 715.

13. "White and Huge Triplex Speed Car Reach City; Builder Says His Car Made As Sporting Proposition," *The Daytona Beach News-Journal*, February 19, 1928, 1.

14. "Three Special Cars Differ Considerably in Design," *The Daytona Beach News-Journal*, February 19, 1928, 1.

15. Leo Villa and Tony Gray, *The Record Breakers: Sir Malcolm and Donald Campbell, Land and Water Speed Kings of the 20th Century* (London: The Hamlyn Publishing Group, 1969), 47.

16. Campbell, *My Thirty Years of Speed*, 162.

17. *Ibid.*

18. In the assessment of the Lockhart estate a $689.49 invoice from the Curtiss Aeroplane Co. appeared for wind tunnel tests.

19. Personal talks with the author, 1975.

20. Statement reported by Paul Ellis in his story "Speed Trials History Goes Back 28 Years—Lockhart Tries Again," published in *The Daytona Beach News-Journal* on February 5, 1931. Blackhawk's weight was 3,000 pounds (we don't know if dry or fully loaded). It could be checked against the 2,200 pounds of the W25R Mercedes record car that, driven by Rudi Caracciola, recorded the Class B flying mile record at 268.656 mph on January 28, 1938, on a German Autobahn.

21. "Hurls Car over Florida Course at 206.956 M.P.H. in Trial Spin," *Associated Press* despatch originated at Daytona Beach published in *The Indianapolis Star*, February 20, 1928, 1.

22. Reid A. Railton, "Blue Bird; Difficulties in Design of Daytona Cars. Some Notes on Sir Malcolm Campbell's Record-Breaker," *The Autocar*, January 6, 1933.

23. Everything written about the position of the center of pressure versus center of gravity refers only to rear-wheel driven vehicles moving in a straight line.

24. All technical data and aerodynamics comments are based on the detailed description of the Blackhawk written by Paul Dumas in the February 25, 1928, issue of *Automotive Industries* Versailles, Kentucky, page 332.

Appendix 2

1. R.S. Lyons, *Sir Malcolm Campbell's Book of Famous Motorists* (Los Angeles: Floyd Clymer Publishing, 1944), 99. First U.S. edition of the book published by Blackie & Sons Limited, Glasgow 1937.

2. In 1927–1928 the garage was on Malcolm Campbell's estate in Povey Cross, Surrey, south of London. The last Blue Bird to be prepared in Povey Cross was the former Sunbeam 350 HP driven by Campbell to the 150.76 mph record on July 21, 1925, on Pendine Sands. Subsequent Blue Birds were built in third-party facilities. Campbell's garage was used for final preparation only. The 1935 Blue Bird was prepared in the Campbell shed at Brooklands, closer to Thomson & Taylor, builders of the vehicle to Reid Railton's design.

3. "Campbell's Forthcoming Record Attempt; Blue Bird on the Way to Participate in Thrilling Speed Contest," *The Motor*, February 7, 1928, 7.

4. M. W. Bourdon, "Details of Campbell's Engine—British Admiralty Secret; Same as used in seaplane which won Schneider Cup race last year. Has 12 cylinders and 10 to 1 compression," *Automotive Industries*, February 25, 1928, 337. Other sources report dry weight of 5,200 pounds.

5. See pages 40 and 54 of the book.

6. The list recaps what was published in *The Motor* on February 28, 1928, page 160 and in the March 1928 issue of *The Autocar*.

Appendix 3

1. **1928 sources**: "Features of Lockhart's Car to Seek World's Speed Record," *The Indianapolis News*, February 18, 1928, 15.
   - Letter by C.D. Smith, Development Dept., Firestone Tire & Rubber Company, to E. Waldo Stein, January 23, 1928.
   - Paul Dumas, "Lockhart Crashes While Traveling at 225 M.P.H.; Accident Costs Him Opportunity to Break Campbell's Record," *Automotive Industries*, February 18, 1928, 332.

   Later sources: Roger Huntington, "Blackhawk—Lockhart and Daytona; Frank Lockhart, the 'Comet that came out of the West,' reached the peak of his fame in a short two-years span—a brilliant automotive engineer," *Speed Age*, November 1949, 16.
   - Peter S. deBeaumont, "Was America 11 Years Ahead in Grand Prix Cars?; Pete deBeaumont, one of America's outstanding authorities, here comes up with some revelations that America had 1939 Grand Prix car as early as 1928, a car that would still command respect, even by today's standards," *Speed Age*, March 1952, 46.
   - Griffith Borgeson, *The Golden Age of the American Racing Car* (New York: W.W. Norton & Co., 1966), 248–258.
   - Gordon Eliot White, *The Marvelous Mechanical Designs of Harry A. Miller* (Hudson, WI: Iconografix, 2004), 69–76.

2. "Aluminium and the Stutz-Blackhawk Special," *The Daytona Beach News-Journal*, February 20, 1928, 3.

3. Figure quoted by Jim Weisel in his paper mailed to the author through Tom Kinney.

4. No fully reliable source has been found about the actual weight of the car. We do not know by sure if 3,000 pounds was the dry or the fully loaded weight.

5. "Features of Lockhart's Car to Seek World's Speed Record," *The Indianapolis News*, February 18, 1928, 15.

6. Simplex was the main sponsor whose name was on the 91 Miller racer driven by Frank Lockhart in his winning debut at Indianapolis 1926, on May 30. The wording "Simplex Piston Ring Special" was again on the second Miller-Lockhart entered by the Yagles for Ray Keech in Indianapolis 1928 (fourth) and 1929 (winner).

Appendix 4

1. It is interesting to note that in 1990 Franco Rocchi, former draughtsman and co-designer of many Ferrari racing engines, designed a W-12 three-liter F1 engine after leaving Maranello. It was named "Life" by its owner Pasquale Vita ("Vita" in Italian means "Life"), who financed the project. It was installed in a former Copersucar monocoque abandoned by the Italian driver Lamberto Leoni, who had hoped to race it under the name "First." The entire Life enterprise was under-financed. Unresolved problems with the engine meant it never qualified for any F1 race in which it was entered. The car was to have been driven either by Gary Brabham, son of Sir Jack, or by Bernd Schneider. Both drivers withdrew, and the car was driven unsuccessfully by Franco Scapini and Bruno Giacomelli. The car and its engine were later rescued by an Italian collector, Lorenzo

Prandina, who entered it in the 2009 Goodwood Festival of Speed. Driven by Arturo Merzario, the Life managed to reach the top of the hill successfully, earning well-deserved applause.

2. Malcolm Campbell used the Napier Lion Series VIIA in his 1927 Blue Bird for the 174.883 mph record at Pendine Sands, UK, February 4.

3. The lap record will stand forever because the Brooklands circuit was almost completely obliterated during the World War II years to create more space for the Vickers aircraft factory.

4. The design constraints of the vehicle's size forced the use of the obsolete Napier Lion engines despite the availability of the more powerful but larger and heavier Rolls-Royce R-Type, designed for speed and records. It also helped that Miss Betty Carstairs offered the two engines free of charge.

5. "Britain Shows the World; All British Triumphs on Land and in the Air," *The Motor*, February 28, 1928, 151.

6. The value in early 2022 dollars would be $15.1 billion. The Programme was a national priority, like the Manhattan Project in World War II. By 1918 the Programme promised to produce 6,000 fighters, 3,000 reconnaissance planes, and 2,000 bombers. The actual outcome consigned these figures to the dream world, and U.S. pilots on the European front flew European-made aircraft: French Spad and Nieuport fighters, British de Havilland for reconnaissance, and Italian Caproni for bombing.

7. The 1,800 rpm maximum speed is the figure for early units. Later, improved models reached a higher speed. Jim White wrote about 2,500 rpm for the L-12 Liberty engines installed in the Triplex.

Final Word

1. "Little Boy Trying to Get Along—Lockhart's Own View of Self; Infinite Pains with Race Cars and Genius of Young Driver on Track Related by Friend—Earnestness Sometimes Mistaken for Conceit," *The Indianapolis News*, April 26, 1928, 19. The article was re-published in *The Daytona Beach News-Journal* on April 27, 1928, on page 2 under the headline "Strum [sic] Found Lockhart A Boy, Intense, Fearless; Racer's Manager Pays Tribute To Memory."

2. "Engineer Lauds Lockhart's Work; Tribute Paid to His Memory—Moskovics Cites Contributions to Auto Industry," *The Indianapolis Star*, May 16, 1928, 10.

3. "Frank Lockhart Ends Career Seeking 14th Record," *The Indianapolis Star*, May 6, 1928, 28.

4. Ralph (Raffaele) DePalma (Biccari, Italy, December 19, 1882–South Pasadena, California, March 31, 1956) was one of the top U.S. drivers in the first three decades of the twentieth century. He came to the U.S. as a child when his family, de Palma in Italian, emigrated. He joined the motor racing fraternity in 1909. He rose to fame when, whilst in the lead of the 1912 Indianapolis 500, his Mercedes suffered engine failure on the back straight three laps from the chequered flag. He pushed the massive vehicle to the finishing line and was classified eleventh, two laps behind the winner. He won the 1914 Vanderbilt Cup in Santa Monica, California, in a Mercedes, and the 1915 Indianapolis 500. In the same year he achieved his first title of National Champion. On January 12, 1919 he drove a special Packard at Daytona Beach to a new 150.563 mph land speed record over a flying kilometer, not recognized in Europe. He drove a Ballot in the 1920 Indianapolis 500, starting from pole and finishing fifth, slowed down by ignition problems when he was in the lead. He came second behind Jimmy Murphy (Duesenberg) in the 1921 GP de l'ACF driving a Ballot. He became a U.S. citizen in 1920 and gradually reduced his number of races, the final one being in 1936. Despite the unbelievable figures of 2,889 starts and 2,257 wins (88.5 percent), printed and reprinted too many times, his true résumé lists 439 starts and 221 wins (50.3 percent).

5. Peter De Paolo, *Wall Smacker: The Saga of the Speedway* (Cleveland: Thompson Product Inc., 1935), 196. To assess the dangers in period races the author wrote a dedication in the frontispiece: "To all those daring heroes of the roaming road who gave their lives in the cause of industry, science and automotive transportation is this book dedicated." Peter "Pete" de Paolo (Roseland, New Jersey, April 6, 1898–Vineland, California, November 26, 1980) was born the son of Maria Giovina (Mary) de Palma and Tommaso di Paola, who changed the family name to de Paolo when he landed at Ellis Island after emigrating from Italy. He was the nephew of Ralph DePalma, his mother's younger brother. He started his racing career as riding mechanic with Uncle Ralph, with whom he entered many races in the U.S. and Europe. He drove a Frontenac in the 1922 Indianapolis 500, finishing 20th out of 27 starters whilst Uncle Ralph was fourth. He won the 1925 Indianapolis 500, his third start, recording the first average speed to exceed 100 mph, a performance unbeaten until 1932. He was national champion in 1925 and 1927. In the years 1922–1927 he started 48 races on the board tracks, winning 26 and netting a total purse worth $103,766. He called it a day racing cars in 1934 as a consequence of a serious crash in practice for the Penya Rhin race in Spain, in a privately entered Maserati. He remained part of the motor racing world as a team manager and authoritative racing journalist.

6. Ibid., 198.

7. In early 2022 value the sum would be $668,722.

8. *The Motor Age* pages have been reprinted in *Floyd Clymer's Indianapolis 500 Mile Race History* (Los Angeles: Floyd Clymer, 1946). The book

covers the years 1909–1941 and publishes the full list of winners: out of the 25 1911–1941 winners, nine were already dead, killed either in races or in record-breaking attempts.

9. Credit for the headline "The Lockhart Saga" is due to Griffith Borgeson, who deserves praise for having revived the short life and racing career of Frank Lockhart in two chapters with the above headline in his book *The Golden Age of the American Racing Car* (New York: W.W. Norton & Company, 1966), 239–258.

Bibliography

Bentley, John. *Great American Automobiles: A Dramatic Account of Their Achievements in Competition.* Englewood Cliffs, NJ: Prentice-Hall Inc., 1957.

Boddy, William. *The History of Brooklands Motor Course 1906–1940.* London: Grenville Publishing Company Ltd., 1979.

Boddy, William. *The World's Land Speed Record.* London: Phoenix House Ltd., 1964.

Borgeson, Griffith. *The Golden Age of the American Racing Car.* New York: W.W. Norton & Co., 1966.

Borgeson, Griffith. "Tragic Superhero of American Racing." In *Road Trips, Head Trips, and Other Car-Crazed Writings*, edited by Jean Lindamood. New York: Atlantic Motor Press, 1996.

Calley, Roy. *The World Water Speed Record: The Fast and the Forgotten.* Stroud, UK: Amberley Publishing, 2014.

Campbell, Donald, and Alan W. Mitchell. *Into the Water Barrier.* London: Odams Press Limited, 1955.

Campbell, Lady Dorothy. *Malcolm Campbell—The Man as I Knew Him.* London: Hutchinson & Co. Publishers Ltd., 1951.

Campbell, Gina, and Michael Meech. *Bluebirds—The Story of the Campbell Dynasty.* London: Sidgwick & Jackson, 1988.

Campbell, Malcolm. *My Thirty Years of Speed.* London: Hutchinson & Co. Publishers Ltd., 1935.

Davis, Sammy C. H. *The John Cobb Story.* London: G. T. Foulis & Co. Ltd., 1954.

Drackett, Phil. *Like Father Like Son: The Story of Malcolm and Donald Campbell.* Brighton, UK: Clifton Books, 1969.

Eyston, George. *Fastest on Earth.* Los Angeles: Floyd Clymer Publishing, 1946.

Eyston, George, and W.F. Bradley. *Speed on Salt: A History of the Bonneville Salt Flats, Utah, U.S.A.* Los Angeles: Floyd Clymer Publishing, 1947.

Hinton, Ed. *Daytona: From the Birth of Speed to the Death of the Man in Black.* New York: Warner Bros Inc., 2001.

Holthusen, Peter J.R. *The Fastest Men on Earth: 100 Years of the Land Speed Record.* Stroud, UK: Sutton Publishing, 1999.

Hough, Richard. *BP Book of the Racing Campbells.* London: Stanley Paul & Co. Ltd., 1960.

Houlgate, Deke. *The Fastest Men in the World—On Wheels.* New York: World Publishing Company, 1971.

Huon, William. *Records de vitesse auto: Un siècle de défis.* Boulogne-Billancourt: E.T.A.I., 2006.

Irving, John Samuel. "The Golden Arrow and the World's Speed Record." *Proceedings of the Institution of Automobile Engineers* 24, no. 2 (1930): 684–734.

Jenkins, Ab, and Wendell J. Ashton. *The Salt of the Earth.* Los Angeles: Clymer Motors, 1945.

Käsmann, Ferdinand C. W. *Weltrekordfahrzeuge: Die schnellesten Wagen 1898 bis heute.* Stuttgart: Verlag Kohlhammer GmbH, 1984.

Ludvigsen, Karl. *Reid Railton: Man of Speed.* Sherborne, UK: Evro Publishing, 2018.

Lyons, R.S. *Sir Malcolm Campbell's Book of Famous Motorists.* Los Angeles: Floyd Clymer Publishing, 1944.

McDonald, David, and Adrian Ball. *Fifty Years with the Speed Kings.* London: Paul Stanley, 1951.

Morgan-Wu, Sarah, and James O'Keefe. *Frank Lockhart: American Speed King.* Boston: Racemaker Press, 2012.

Popely, Rick, and L. Spencer Riggs. *Indianapolis 500 Chronicle.* Lincolnwood, IL: Publications International Ltd., 1998.

Posthumus, Cyril. *Sir Henry Segrave.* London: B. T. Batsford Ltd., 1961.

Posthumus, Cyril, and David Tremayne. *Land Speed Record: A Complete History of the Record-Breaking Cars from 39.24 to 600+ M.P.H.* London: Osprey Publishing Limited, 1985.

Punnett, Dick. *Racing on the Rim: A History of the Annual Automobile Racing Tournaments Held on the Sands of the Ormond-Daytona Beach, Florida 1903–1910.* Ormond Beach, FL: Tomoka Press, 1997.

Railton, Reid. "'Blue Bird,' 1930–1933." *Proceedings of the Institution of Automobile Engineers* 28, no. 1 (1933): 102–146.

Segrave, Major H. O. D. *The Lure of Speed.*

London: Hutchinson & Co. Publishers Ltd., 1928.

Shaw, Wilbur. *Gentlemen, Start Your Engines: An Informal Autobiography of an Immortal Racing Driver, Sportsman and Gentleman.* New York: Coward-McCann, 1955.

Simpson, Steve. *The Real Story of Wizard Smith.* Sydney: Murray Book Distributors Pty Ltd., 1977.

Tours, Hugh. *Parry Thomas: Designer-Driver.* London: B. T. Batsford Ltd., 1959.

Tucker, Tom, and Jim Tiller. *Daytona: The Quest for Speed.* Daytona Beach: The Daytona Beach News Journal, 1994.

Villa, Leo, and Kevin Desmond. *Life with the Speed King.* London: Marshall, Harris & Baldwin Ltd., 1979.

Villa, Leo, and Tony Gray. *The Record Breakers: Sir Malcolm and David Campbell, Land and Water Speed Kings of the 20th Century.* London: The Hamlyn Publishing Group, 1969.

Wallen, Dick. *Board Track: Guts, Gold & Glory.* Glendale, AZ: Dick Wallen Productions, 1990.

White, Gordon Eliot. *The Marvelous Mechanical Designs of Harry A. Miller.* Hudson, WI: Iconografix, 2004.

Yates, Brock. *Umbrella Mike: The True Story of the Chicago Gangster Behind the Indy 500.* New York: Thunder's Mouth Press, 2006.

Index

Numbers in ***bold italics*** indicate pages with illustrations

Adams, officer 103
Allen, Joseph L. 105
Amherst Villiers, Charles 131, ***148***, 148, 162
Anderson, Gil 63, 68, ***69***, 73, 74, 76, 117
Armstrong, Edward H. 34, 49, 55, 58, 84, 114, 117, 118
Arnold, Billy 138

Baker, Erwin George "Cannonball" 22
Baker, Warren L. 105
Benoist, Robert 15
Bible, Lee 122, ***129***, 129, 134
Bohannon, Dr. C.C. 111
Borgeson, Griffith 93, 105, 116
Boyer, Joe 29
Boyle, Mike 35
Brady, Tom 81
Brett, Riley ***102***
Brown, the Rev. Dr. Lewis 117, 118
Buehrig, Gordon 106
Burgamy, John 19, 121
Burgamy, Julia 117
Burman, Bob 7, 24, ***33***, 34
Busch, Lee 81
Bush, Judge Malon E. 119

Campbell, Donald 10, 11, 15, 80
Campbell, Lady Dorothy Evelyn (née Whittal) 10, ***11***, 12, 14, 35, 55, 79
Campbell, Gina 12
Campbell, Jane 11, 15
Campbell, William 12
Caracciola, Rudolf 15
Carstairs, Betty 135
Cash, George 103
Chapman, Colin 155
Chevrolet, Louis 119
Clark, Dr. Edmund D. 84
Clark, Jim 155
Clemons, Fred 34

Coatalen, Louis ***50***, 131, 132, 133, 149
Cobb, John 123, 124, 130, 150, 172
Coe, Joe 35, 40, 135
Cooper, Earl 18, 117
Corum, Lora L. 117
Cupernall, Sgt. Ernest 77, 103, 104, 106

Dana, Lilian B. 138
Dawson, Joe 43
De Grineau, Bryan 73
DePalma, Ralph 17, 177
De Paolo, Pete 17, 117, 177
Dolce, Kim 1
Dreyer, Floyd ***20***, ***22***, 45, 164
Dreyer, Floyd, Jr. ***168***
Dreyer, Mike ***168***
Don, Kaye (Donsky, Kaye Ernest) 23, 123, 124, 131, ***132***, ***133***, 133, 134, 135, 138
Douglas Hawkes, William ***18***
Duff, John ***18***
Duray, Leon 17, 122

Eldridge, Ernest 14, ***18***
Ellis, Paul 49, 52, 54, 58, 64, 65
Eyston, George 19, 123, 124, 130

Farrell, Gil ***67***, ***68***, 68, ***69***, 72, 74, 79, 81
Faulkner, William 175
Finke, Herman 131
Foster Welch, Lucia 80
France, William Henry Getty "Bill" 31, 32

Gill, Ted R. 111
Gorrell, Colonel 81
Guinness, Kenelm Lee 14
Gulotta, Tony 79, 117, 119, 121, 122
Guyot, Albert ***18***

Hager, Sgt. Sandy 103
Hall, E.R. 79
Hammond, Girard 36, 37, 77
Hanks, Sam 121
Hartz, Harry 19, 131, 138, 178
Hawkes, Norman 1
Henry, Ernest 171
Hepburn, Ralph 35
Hicks, William Johnson 80
Hill, Bennet "Benny" 17
Hulman, Tony 35
Hurd, Guy 39, 77, 79

Irving, Capt. John Samuel 125, ***126***, 126, 149, 150, 158

Jaray, Paul 147
Jenkins, Ab 145
Joynson-Hicks, Sir William 130

Keech, Raymond "Ray" 4, 5, ***8***, 9, 27, ***28***, 28, ***29***, 52, 53, 60, 61, 74, 75, 78, 80, 82, 87, 88, 89, 90, 91, ***92***, 92, 93, 99, 113, 118, 122, ***129***, 129, 131, 134
King Edward VIII 130
King George V 140
Kinney, Tom 1, ***20***, ***22***, 106, 108, ***109***, ***154***, ***166***, ***168***
Klock, Dr. Guy 61, 78, 79, 84, 111, 116
Knott, Marjorie Dagmar 14
Kreis, Peter 17, 18

Lee, Jimmy ***21***, 45, ***46***, 47, 79, 164
Leech, Harry 76, 135
Lewis, Dave 19
Lewis, Edward 51
Lewis, Ernest 51
Lindbergh, Col. Charles 114, 175
Lindley, aviator 117
Litz, Deacon 120
Liversey, Rita 133

Locke, Sgt. 77
Lockhart, Carrie (*née* Burgamy) 19, 115, 117, 119
Lockhart, Caspar 115
Lockhart, Ella (*née* Corsen) 16, 19, 68, **69**, 72, 77, 78, 79, 81, 86, *100*, 100, 103, 111, 112, 113, 114, 116, 117, 118, 119, 120
Lockhart, Robert 115, 117
Lord Howe 15
Lyons, R.S. 160

Maina, Joseph 55, 135, 148, **149**, 149, 162
Marcenac, Jean **21**, **22**, 45, 47, 79, **85**, 117, 164
Martin, John 64
McDonald, David "Dunlop Mac" 10, 35, 40, 52, 54, 55, 56, 57, 135
Means, Arthur 41, 42, 95, 100, 101, 104, 106, 111, 112, 113, 116
Means, Mrs. Arthur 6, 9, 94
Merz, Charles 119
Meyers, Theodore E. "Pop" 114, 117
Miller, Bud **22**, 45, 164
Miller, George 35
Miller, Harry 17, 18, 115, 121, 141, 147
Miller, Steve 35
Milton, Tommy **8**, 17
Morgan-Wu, Sarah 110
Morton, Wade 63, 76
Moskovics, Fred 42, **45**, 69, 71, 81, 84, 93, 112, 113, 116, 117, 118, 119, 120, 176
Murphy, Jimmy **8**, 44

Nelson, James T. 50
Nicory, Betty 15

O'Keefe, James 110
Oldfield, Barney 141
Olson, Ernie 44
Orte, Hans 103

Patterson, officer 77
Pearson, N.H. 34, 84
Pearson, Reginald 148, 149
Porsche, Prof. Ferdinand 155
Porter, Odis 88, 90, 101, 111, 117
Posthumus, Cyril 48
Pringle, Jeannie 100
Pulliam, Eugene 44, 77, 112, 118

Railton, Reid 15, 132, 135, **136**, 139, 140, 142, **143**, 150, 157, 158, 172
Robertson, Bob 29
Rooney, Tom 52, 63
Rowledge, Arthur 171

Schroeder, Gordon **121**, 121
Segrave, Doris (*née* Stocker) 125, **128**
Segrave O'Neal de Hane, Henry 4, 9, 14, 23, 26, 37, 38, 48, 48, **50**, 51, 59, 60, 64, 80, 83, 92, 93, 96, 114, 123, 125, **126**, 126, **127**, 127, **128**, 128, 129, 130, 131, **133**, 134, 135, 147, 151, 169, 172
Shaw, Wilbur 6, 7, 32, **33**, 33, 34, 63, 66, 74, 78, 82, 84, 89, 95, 114, 120
Sholtz, David 76, 77
Simms, R.O. 100, 111
Slack, Lemuel Ertus 117
Smith, C.D. 108
Smith, Floyd 32, **33**, 114
Smith, Norman Leslie "Wizard" 131, 132, **138**, 139, 141
Sockwell, Jimmy 131
Souders, George 114
Splinder, Ray **22**, **44**, 45, 47, **62**, 67, 72, 74, 79, 81, 164
Stapp, André 141
Stevens, Myron **20**, **21**, **22**, 45, 84, **94**, **102**, 110, 120, 153, 164, 165
Strohl, Daniel 106

Sturm, Teressa (*née* Hess) 19, 23, 47, 79
Sturm, William "Bill" **13**, 19, **20**, **21**, **22**, 22, 23, 24, 38, **44**, 44, 45, **46**, 47, 68, 71, 72, 76, 78, 79, 81, 84, **85**, 96, 111, 117, 118, 120, **127**, 134, **170**, 176, 177
Swanson, Bob 102, 120

Taylor, Ken P.T. **137**
Thomas, Parry 15
Towner, Ethelyn 113
Traub, Charles 122
Tuttle, William 32

Vanderbilt, William Kissim II "Willie K" **31**, 31
Van Deusen, George 52
Villa, Leo 10, **13**, 14, 15, 35, 36, 38, 40, 53, **57**, 57, 77, 135, 141, 148, 152
Voisin, Gabriel 147

Wakefield, Sir (later Lord) Charles 37, **59**, 80, 130
Waldo Stein, E. 108
Webster, Sidney 58
Weisel, Jim **20**, **22**, 106, **109**, **154**, **166**, 167
Weisel, John 17, 44, 61, 93, 106, 108, 156, 164
Weisel, Zenas 44, 61, 93, 106, 107, 108, 155, 156, 164
Wharton, Ira A. 111
White, Jim **8**, 24, 27, 28, **28**, 33, 41, 42, 43, 60, 61, 74, **75**, 77, 78, 81, 82, 84, 87, 88, 89, 90, 125, **129**, 131, 150, 151, **173**, 175
Wilcox, Howdy 27
Wilson Cain, H. 106, 107
Wingate, Cassie 135
Wood, Gar 96

Yagle, Edward 28, **29**, 122
Yagle, Maude 28, **29**, 122

www.ingramcontent.com/pod-product-compliance
Lightning Source LLC
Chambersburg PA
CBHW060344010526
44117CB00017B/2956